THE
SPORTING
SCENE

THE ART OF SEWING

THE SPORTING SCENE

BY THE EDITORS OF TIME-LIFE BOOKS

TIME-LIFE BOOKS, NEW YORK

THE ART OF SEWING
EDITORIAL STAFF FOR
THE SPORTING SCENE
Editor: Fred R. Smith
Assistant Editor: David L. Harrison
Designer: Virginia Gianakos
Text Editor: Gerry Schremp
Picture Editor: Kaye Neil
Chief Researchers: Wendy A. Rieder,
Gabrielle Smith (planning)
Staff Writers: Sondra R. Albert, Dick Friedman,
Marian Gordon Goldman, Angela D. Goodman,
David Johnson, Marilyn Kendig, James Randall,
Sandra Streepey, Reiko Uyeshima,
Timberlake Wertenbaker
Research Staff: Sally French, Laura James,
Ginger Seippel, Cinda Siler, Vivian Stephens,
Jean Stratton
Art Staff: Anne B. Landry (art manager),
Angela Alleyne, Penny Burnham,
Patricia Byrne, Catherine Caufield, Jean Held,
Jill Losson

EDITORIAL PRODUCTION
Production Editor: Douglas B. Graham
Assistant Production Editors:
Gennaro C. Esposito, Feliciano Madrid
Quality Director: Robert L. Young
Assistant Quality Director: James J. Cox
Copy Staff: Eleanore W. Karsten (chief),
Kathleen Beakley, Ricki Tarlow,
Florence Keith, Pearl Sverdlin
Picture Department: Dolores A. Littles,
Susan Hearn
Traffic: Carmen McLellan

THE CONSULTANTS:
Gretel Courtney taught for several years at the French Fashion Academy in New York City. She has studied patternmaking and design at the Fashion Institute of Technology in New York and haute couture at the French Fashion Academy.

Annette Feldman is a knitting and crocheting designer, both for clothing and interior decoration. She is the author of several books, including *Knit, Purl and Design; Crochet and Creative Design;* and *Beginner's Needlecraft.*

Tracy Kendall has for many years designed sets and costumes for commercial films and advertising. She is currently a fashion stylist.

Julian Tomchin is a textile designer who has been awarded the Vogue Fabric Award and a Coty Award of the American Fashion Critics. A graduate of Syracuse University's Fine Arts College, he has been chairman of the Textile Design Department at the Shenkar College of Fashion and Textile Technology in Tel Aviv and now teaches at the Parsons School of Design in New York.

Valuable assistance was provided by these departments and individuals of Time Inc.: Editorial Production, Norman Airey; Library, Benjamin Lightman; Picture Collection, Doris O'Neil; Photographic Laboratory, George Karas; TIME-LIFE News Service, Murray J. Gart; Correspondents Margot Hapgood, Dorothy Bacon and Jerene Jones (London), Ann Natanson (Rome), Elisabeth Kraemer (Bonn), Maria Vincenza Aloisi (Paris).

CONTENTS

1
FREEWHEELING FASHIONS

Although fads may have a powerful effect on current styles, over the long term it is action that shapes attire. Throughout history, work, war and sport—pretty much in that order—have been the major forces that have determined the form that clothes would take. For example, in the 1600s when French coachmen extended their short doublets into long redingotes to keep their legs warm, they created the ba-

LIVELY FORMS THAT FOLLOW FUNCTION

sic design of the ubiquitous overcoat that has been used for street wear by men and women ever since. The doublet itself had developed from the so-called cotehardie that medieval soldiers wore under their armor for padding; its basic form is echoed today in the common waistcoat or vest.

Today golfers, skiers and a host of other outdoor people outnumber soldiers, and sport is where the action is. And it is sport that does most of the shaping. In New York,

Paris, London and Tokyo, men and women now go to the office or a cocktail party in apparel that may have come directly from the links or ski slope. But often the wearer is not an athlete at all, or has only the vaguest interest in sports. Nevertheless, he chooses some aspect of that sports outfit for its comfort and its chic, trendy look.

Even highly specialized sportswear has evolved into other uses. The acrobat's skintight leotard, for example, became the stylish body suit. The zip-on, zip-off warm-up pants of the ski racer double as foul-weather gear for football watchers and snow shovelers.

The role of sport in fashion is astonishingly recent. During the latter half of the 19th Century, most gentlemen sportsmen wore shaggy adaptations of their everyday wear. And the small band of daring pioneer women bold enough to take up such games as golf and tennis did so in floppy flowered hats, corsets and ground-sweeping dresses that were nearly identical to gowns they wore to tea parties.

Many of the fashions of sport started on the playing fields of England or America, then moved around the world. The sports jacket, for example, made its first appearance in mid-century, under the name of lounge jacket, at British seaside resorts, country manors and cricket pitches. The cricketers were particularly fond of its comfortable cut. So were members of the posh Lady Margaret Boat Club at Cambridge University, who had the jacket made in blazing red and renamed it the blazer.

Other sportsmen soon took up the jacket style. And by the time bicycling and tennis came into vogue in the 1860s and 1870s and golf began to grow to a significant pastime, the sports jacket—in much the shape that it appears today—was the accepted costume for virtually every weekend athlete.

To go with it, outdoorsy gentlemen needed something more functional and less elegant than the widely cut floor-length trousers of the day. The Victorian solution was knickers, loose and baggy for comfort, and sensibly cut off and gathered just below the knee. Reminiscent of earlier knee breeches, the pants were named for descendants of the Dutch settlers of New York, who had been called Knickerbockers and had worn similarly baggy-looking pants.

About the same time that the masculine sports jacket was emerging, women took their first tentative step in the general direction of dress reform for active wear. Their leader was the American feminist Amelia Jenks Bloomer, who proclaimed to her hoop-skirted and corseted sisters, "What you find a burthen in belief or apparel, cast off." Amelia herself cast off both hoops and corsets, and replaced them with ankle-length harem-style pantaloons topped by knee-length dresses.

But Amelia, alas, was just about the only one. Most other women found bloomers offensively mannish and might never have taken them up at all had it not been for the invention in 1885 of the safety bicycle.

The safety, forerunner of the modern two-wheeler, displaced the contemporary monster with its seat perch atop a five-foot front wheel, and put the rider between a pair of average-sized wheels. Women loved it, and flocked to ride the contraption in the one garment that seemed perfectly designed for it—Mrs. Bloomer's bloomers.

From bicycling, bloomers quickly spread until a few daring young ladies even wore them to dances. In 1895, Miss Gyda Stephenson, a Chicago schoolteacher, went so far as to wear bloomers not only while cycling to school but in the classroom too. The brouhaha that resulted was resolved only when the school board decided it could not find anything immoral about her costume.

Women golfers, however, continued to languish in the prison of their Victorian clothes. As Mabel Stringer, a British golfer of the early 1900s, recalls it: "We still had the high, stiff linen collar, and the higher and stiffer the collar, the smarter was the wearer considered!" Skirts were worse, hovering only slightly above the ground and encumbered with a heavy strip of leather around the hem to keep the fabric clean.

All of that changed after World War I, when sportswomen, caught up in the postwar wave of emancipation, finally discarded the last of their corsets, ground-brushing skirts, Gibson Girl hats and puffy-sleeved shirtwaists. They now appeared for golf in slim skirts ending at mid-calf and in open-necked blouses. Meanwhile tennis players (pages 86-87) and other women athletes were keeping pace.

Functional as the ladies' new garb was, its adherence to dull colors or pure white made it look drab beside the flashy sports ensembles that American golf hero Walter Hagen was pioneering for men. Hagen dazzled his onlookers with color. When he won his first U.S. Open in 1914, he wore—in-stead of the traditional dun—a white silk shirt with rainbow stripes, a red bandana knotted at his neck, white flannel trousers and a loud tartan cap.

A flamboyant athlete who eventually won two U.S. and four British Opens and more Professional Golf Association championships (five) than anyone else in history, Hagen sometimes seemed to be more concerned with his style victories than his golfing. At his first British Open in 1920, although he placed 53rd in a field of 54, he proudly reported later, "Golfers and gallery alike made a special detour around me to take in my sartorial splendor."

As with Amelia Bloomer in her time, however, Hagen turned out to be a lonely innovator. Most other athletes stuck stubbornly to conservative colorations. It was not until the 1950s, when golfers like Jimmy Demaret flashed combinations of such hues as chartreuse and orange, that the men's pro golf tour—and the public links too—finally turned into the colorful fashion parade Hagen had envisaged. And the madras plaids, bold stripes and bright knits that golfers wore marched straight on to street wear.

Again women were surprisingly slow in catching up—until the 1970s when a pair of pretty youngsters, Wimbledon champion Chris Evert (page 87) and Laura Baugh of the Ladies' Professional Golf Association, joined the colorful revolution the men had begun. Wearing giddy-colored rib-knit pullovers, short shorts and shorter skirts, Miss Baugh (page 82) turned heads on the course. Miss Evert did the same on the courts with her delicate pastel outfits. More important in a television generation, they both caught the camera's eye to set leisure-wear styles for millions of women who couldn't swing a club or racquet.

What hunting, cycling, golf and tennis did for everyday warm-weather wear, skiing did for cold-weather gear. German designer Maria Bogner and her husband, Willy, produced the first stretch pants in 1952. Three years later the somber military hues traditional to ski clothes gave way to colors like persimmon and lavender. And finally, quilted parkas arrived in 1958. Together, the slim pants, puffy parkas and bright colors sent the skier on his downhill run looking far more sleek and colorful than many a city-bound sophisticate. In fact, the new ski wear turned out so bright and sleek, warm and comfortable that parka-like car coats and stretch-style slacks began to show up miles from the nearest mountains.

Today there is no season in everyday wear—and scarcely a part of the body—that has not benefited from sportswear design. The yachtsman's nonskid sneaker has moved onto rain-drenched sidewalks. The Everest climber's thermal sock warms the toes of snowbound suburbanites. And even tiny infants have received a lift from sports design as the wilderness hiker's pack frame turns into the papoose-style device in which young parents carry babies when going to the supermarket.

Victorian sports costumes for ladies were geared more to propriety than to the action, as these 1890s fashions published in *Harper's Bazar* clearly show. Only the racket and club distinguish the tennis dress *(left)* and golf outfit from prim street wear. The swimmer is barely buoyant in her caped, calf-length costume. The only innovator is the bicyclist *(right)*, who flouts convention in bloomers—a naughtily mannish style in those days.

Sportswear style for all seasons

The supple weaves, bright styles, lightweight insulation and ingenious fastenings on today's sports clothes make them so versatile that they can be worn with comfort and dash, not only for their appointed sport in the traditional season but year round. For example, featherweight ski jackets like those on page 18 have become favorites for casual wear anywhere for all but the hottest days. Through the mastery of special techniques, a home craftsman can produce any of the items shown on these pages, achieving the double satisfaction of creating a unique garment while saving as much as two thirds of standard prices.

SPRING sports call for clothes that are both warm and airy. From left to right, the male golfer's cotton knit shirt and cotton-backed polyester checked trousers are topped by a cotton jacket. His partner's Orlon sweater adds warmth to a cotton knit shirt and short corduroy golf skirt. The two warm-up suits at right are of stretchable and absorbent knit—ready to give with any move the wearers may make.

SUMMER sportswear is cool and easy to care for. The tennis dress and the man's shorts and pullover of crisp cotton and polyester dry quickly from perspiration, and stay in shape after many washings. A competition-model bathing suit of almost weightless nylon is another quick-drying item that holds its shape —as is the jacket worn over white cotton-and-polyester pants and a cotton turtleneck.

16

AUTUMN sport clothes are designed for changeable weather. A synthetic rubber suit keeps out rain; a down-filled nylon vest, worn over corduroy knickers and a flannel shirt, protects against cold; the combination of rubberized English riding coat, wool gabardine slacks and a wool sweater keeps the wearer both warm and dry; and the snug corduroy safari suit is cool with the jacket unbuttoned.

WINTER outdoor wear must be warm yet light in weight. Ski outfits *(far left)* of coated nylon are insulated with a featherweight layer of acrylic fibers that is comfortable when the temperature is zero. A belted, A-line skating dress is of warm wool jersey; and the wool twill knickers and poplin jacket of a cross-country skiing outfit are treated for water resistance.

2
SUITED UP
TO MAKE
A SPLASH

Flipping over with the sleek grace of a dolphin, the young swimmer on the preceding pages whisks away from a turn in a gossamer-thin tank suit designed to shave precious milliseconds off her time. Made of a blend of nylon and Lycra spandex fibers, the suit is skin-tight, slippery and strong, yet it weighs less than an ounce. That's right; less than an ounce. Wearing it feels so much like skinny-dipping that one member of the U.S. swim-

BIG WINNERS
IN THE WIDE-OPEN
FABRIC FIELD

ming team exclaimed, after making a turn: "I wanted to reach down and see if I still had my suit on."

The suit was still there, of course—and it looked perfectly smashing, as does most of today's ultrafunctional, ultraslick sporting wear. Thanks to fabric makers such as those who devised the nylon-spandex combination, not only swim suits but sport clothes of all kinds are working better—and looking better, too. Modern skiers can maneuver more adroitly in lightweight nylon jackets and pants than could their fathers in the bulky outfits of 20 or 30 years ago. Tennis players now appear as fresh as they feel in crisp polyester blended with cotton to absorb perspiration. Golfers can play right through a light drizzle in clothes coated with water-repellent plastic.

So far, no one fabric has been produced that is versatile enough to fit every possible kind of sports use. But in their efforts to meet the requirements of various sports, chemists have devised fabrics and finishes that give sportsmen—and home seamstresses —options undreamed of a generation ago.

There are synthetic stretch filaments, more durable and stronger than rubber itself, that produce the flexible kinds of cloth needed for a spinning arabesque on the ice. There are polyesters—made of air, water and petroleum—that are chemically transformed into wrinkle-free and resilient fabrics for warm afternoons on the fairways. There are acrylic fibers that are knitted into airy fabric for jogging comfort, and nylons that are light yet sufficiently weatherproofed for the vagaries of sailing.

Moreover, most of these superfibers can be made up in almost endless variations of design, color, construction—and combined with one another or with natural fiber. Nylon alone is made in more than a hundred fiber types of differing strength, shape, shininess and resiliency that can be woven or knitted into at least a hundred specialized fabrics. The ripstop nylon favored for hiking and camping gear, for example, is designed with threads that are paired to-

gether to add strength, then woven in a checkerboard pattern. The result is a fabric that never tears because a puncture in one square of the checkerboard cannot run into another square.

Despite such advantages, even the most modern synthetics must still compete—not always successfully—with traditional fabrics. Wool and cotton, two of the oldest fibers known, remain unbeatable in many ways. Wool has a natural curliness that provides a thickness, softness and resilience no straight-fiber synthetic can match. Cotton, whose fibers are hollow inside, expands upon contact with water, so that the fibers actually become stronger when wet.

Equally important to sports use, both cotton and wool have an innate characteristic technicians call moisture regain. This means that the fibers can absorb body moisture quickly yet release it so gradually that the wearer does not get chilled—even in a strenuous activity like handball. In addition, undyed wools have natural oils and a shingle-like structure so that raindrops tend to bounce off them; and both cotton and dyed wools can now be treated to make them similarly water-resistant outdoors.

While even the finest of natural fibers are being improved by science, the makers of synthetics are trying to impart qualities such as moisture regain to their own wares. For the home seamstress the upshot is a rich spectrum of sporty materials, many of them shown on the following pages. All are stylish, sewable and sturdy for storming the slopes or breasting the waves—or just dressing with the sportman's confident flair.

Versatile natural performers

The natural-fiber wools and cottons in these swatches offer warmth in winter and coolness in summer. In addition, both fibers can be spun, woven, dyed and finished in so many different ways that one or the other can serve for anything from golf shirts to lumber jackets.

CHOOSING AND HANDLING WOOLS AND COTTONS

CHOOSING WOOL FABRICS: Wool fibers are composed of microscopic coils that stretch and spring back naturally to give the fabric the resilience, durability and wrinkle resistance desirable in jackets, shirts and pants. Blanket cloth—a thick, tightly woven, medium-to-heavyweight fabric with a deep, soft surface nap; best used for warm, simple garments such as capes or coats. Blanket cloth comes in large plaids and stripes. Camel's hair—a soft, tightly woven, lightweight fabric produced from the hair of the Asiatic Bactrian camel. Top qualities, used for fine overcoats, pants and skirts, have extremely short, fine naps and are light tan; poor grades have coarser naps and are brownish black. Flannel—a soft, tightly woven fabric with a fine nap, available in light shirt cloth as well as heavyweight coating. Flannels also are made of cotton and of fiber blends; all-wool flannel comes chiefly in solid colors, plaids and stripes. Gabardine—a firm, tightly woven twill fabric characterized by closely set diagonal ribs. Very popular for suitings, gabardine comes in light and medium weights in a wide range of colors, and may also be made of cotton or a fiber blend. Loden—a coarse, heavy-napped fabric with some natural water resistance. Loden usually comes in dull green or gray, and is popular for overcoats. Melton—a smooth, heavyweight fabric with a fine, short nap, usually made up in coats, capes and jackets. Melton comes in a wide array of colors. Tweed—a durable fabric of medium weight that is often twilled, or diagonally ribbed, suitable for sportswear only if it is a tightly woven variety. Tweeds come in many colors and textures, some soft and finely napped like herringbone tweed, others hairy and nubby like Harris tweed. Whipcord—a tough, medium-weight twill weave with high, narrow diagonal ribs, sometimes made of cotton or fiber blends. Whipcord comes primarily in shades of tan, brown and green, and is traditional for riding wear.

PREPARING AND CUTTING WOOLS: All wools suggested for sportswear have a nap, so purchase the amount of fabric recommended for a "with nap" pattern layout, and lay out the pattern on the fabric accordingly. Before starting to cut and sew, preshrink all wools by dry-cleaning or ironing them with a steam iron. If the basic fabric is heavy, use a lightweight fabric for facings, and cut out pattern pieces from a single layer of cloth. Transfer pattern markings with a saw-toothed tracing wheel and dressmaker's carbon paper.

SEWING WOOLS: Using mercerized cotton or polyester thread, baste with a Size 5 to 7 needle, then machine stitch with a Size 14 to 16 needle after setting the machine at 10 to 12 stitches to the inch. With heavy fabrics, cut away the material inside darts to avoid bulk.

CARING FOR WOOLS: Press twill fabrics on the wrong side, setting the iron as indicated on the dial for wool. Press other napped fabrics on the wrong side—or on the right side with a pressing cloth. Follow the cleaning instructions on the hang tag or bolt end of the fabric.

CHOOSING COTTON FABRICS: Because each fiber in a bolt of cotton is made up of 20 to 30 concentric rings of cellulose, cotton fabrics produce strong and wear-resistant shirts, skirts, jackets or pants. Bedford cord—a sturdy, tightly woven medium-weight fabric with slightly raised, closely set lengthwise ribs. Sometimes made of wool, Bedford cord is generally sold only in solid colors and is most commonly used for pants, skirts and jackets. Canvas—a strong, tightly woven plain-weave fabric produced in many weights for a broad range of garments, shelters and carry bags. Canvas, or duck, as it is often called, may be pliable or stiff, solid-colored or patterned. Corduroy—a durable, light-to-medium-weight fabric with rounded, lengthwise wales (or ridges) of various widths. Very good for jackets, skirts and pants, corduroy comes in solid colors or patterns. Denim—a rugged, medium-to-heavy-weight, diagonally ribbed twill fabric that has become a universal material for casual and rough wear. Traditionally an indigo blue cotton, denim is now available in many colors and in fiber blends. Poplin—a lustrous, tightly woven light-to-medium-weight fabric distinguished by slightly thicker crosswise threads. Poplin comes in solid colors and patterns for use in pants, coats and jackets.

PREPARING AND CUTTING COTTONS: For napped cottons, purchase the amount of fabric recommended for a "with nap" pattern layout, and lay out the pattern accordingly. Before starting to cut and sew, preshrink all cottons that are not labeled preshrunk by washing them as directed on the hang tag or bolt-end label. If the fabric is heavy, use a lightweight fabric for facing and cut out the pattern pieces from a single layer of cloth. Transfer pattern markings with a saw-toothed tracing wheel and dressmaker's carbon paper.

SEWING COTTONS: Using mercerized cotton or polyester thread, baste with a Size 7 needle and machine stitch with a Size 14 needle—after setting the machine at 10 to 12 stitches to the inch. With heavy fabrics, cut away the material inside darts to avoid excess bulk.

CARING FOR COTTONS: Press Bedford cord and corduroy on the wrong side, canvas, denim and poplin on the right side. Preset the iron as indicated on the dial for cotton and test it on a swatch. Follow the cleaning instructions on the hang tag or bolt end of the fabric.

The diverse textures attainable from cotton and wool include (clockwise from top left), cotton corduroy, wool melton, cotton canvas, twill-weave wool whipcord and blanket wool.

Stretch to match the action

Sports clothes such as bathing suits and warm-up outfits—which must fit snugly and flex easily—require fabrics with built-in stretchability. The most readily available stretch materials for home sewing such garments are modern knits like the ones displayed in the swatches here.

WORKING WITH STRETCH FABRICS

CHOOSING STRETCH FABRICS: Though knits are the most popular stretch fabrics for home sewing, some woven fabrics also can be made to stretch so that they recover their original shape. However, these stretch weaves—used in ready-made ski pants and swim suits—are usually sold only to clothing manufacturers, and thus are not easily available for home sewing.

Knit fabrics, however, are readily obtainable and the sensible choice for planning most home projects. Knits are made by locking loops of yarn together, rather than by weaving them. As a result, they are more flexible than other materials. The degree of stretchability and recovery of a knit varies with the fiber content and the manner in which the yarn loops interlock. **Stable knits** are so called because of their limited flexibility compared to other knits. Their greatest stretch is in the crosswise direction; and most of them contain synthetic fibers such as nylon or polyester, or blends of natural and synthetic fibers. Structurally, there are two types of stable knits—single and double knits. Single knits, constructed of a single layer of closely looped yarns, are generally used in casual clothes that do not require the stretch of more active sportswear. Double knits are made by interlocking two layers of fabric together and have even less stretch then single knits. But because of the insulation provided by the double fabric layer, these fabrics are particularly good for loose-fitting warm-up suits. Both types of knits come in a wide range of colors and patterns, and in textures as varied as ribs and velours. **Stretch knits** are made of special heat-resistant synthetics, used alone or blended with natural fibers. They have a much higher degree of elasticity and recovery. This extra flexibility makes the fabrics especially good for use in active sportswear such as tennis, biking or bowling. They are available in a wide range of colors and patterns and may have smooth, ribbed, terry or napped surfaces. **Spandex-reinforced stretch knits** provide the most flexibility of any knit fabric. They are commonly made from a blend of nylon and spandex, the generic name for a chemical filament that can stretch more than 500 per cent without breaking and—equally important for clothing—snap right back into shape. Spandex knits come in many colors, patterns and textures, and are especially popular for swim suits or as inserts at stress points on any sportswear.

WARNING: Most knits require patterns specially designed for stretch fabrics. (Stable double knits are an exception; they can be used with ordinary patterns designed for woven material.) These patterns have a stretch gauge printed along the side of the envelope.

Before you buy a knit fabric, compare its stretch with that indicated on your pattern gauge.

PREPARING THE FABRIC: Preshrink knits by following the directions for cleaning or laundering that appear on the hang tag or bolt end of the fabric. If the fabric is not straight after preshrinking, pull it diagonally to restore uniform shape. Before starting to work, you will need very sharp dressmaker's shears or finely serrated knit scissors; a smooth-edged tracing wheel for marking; polyester thread; and ballpoint pins and ballpoint needles, which will not create pulls in the fabric.

LAYING OUT AND CUTTING SUGGESTIONS: Lay out the fabric on a flat surface large enough to accommodate the entire piece. If the surface is too small and a substantial piece of fabric hangs over the edge, it may stretch out of shape while you are working. If the fabric is slippery or bulky, cut out the pattern pieces in a single layer. As you cut, very stretchy knits may spread. To compensate, increase vertical seam allowances to 1 inch. Mark the fabric with dressmaker's carbon paper and a tracing wheel or tailor tacks (Glossary).

SEWING STRETCH KNITS: Baste with a Size 7 ballpoint needle. Machine stitch with a Size 14 ballpoint needle and with the sewing machine set at 10 to 12 stitches to the inch. Use an even-feed or a roller-presser foot attachment. Test the machine tension and stitch length on a double thickness of the fabric. Before you assemble the garment, stitch the seam allowance of all curves and other off-grain edges to prevent stretching. For all other stitching, use a zigzag stitch or stretch the fabric slightly as you sew to build flexibility into the seam. Use seam tape to reinforce shoulder seams of particularly stretchy knits. To avoid a bulky look in heavy knits such as stretch terry cloth and velours, use a bias-tape facing instead of a self-fabric facing at the neck and armholes. Reinforce buttonhole areas with a lightweight facing. Hang the garment for 24 hours before hemming, so that the fabric will assume its final shape. On very stretchy and heavy knits, make a double-stitched hem to ensure that these fabrics will not sag further.

CARING FOR STRETCH FABRICS: To prevent the nap from flattening on stretch terry cloth and velours, press on the wrong side, using a warm iron. For all other knits, set the iron for the fiber content of the fabric; then test a swatch. Use a pressing cloth and press lightly along the lengthwise grain on the visible side of the fabric. Between wearings, *never* store stretch garments on hangers; instead, fold them up and store them flat. To prevent fold lines, place tissue paper between the folds. Follow the directions on the hang tag or bolt end of the fabric for washing or dry-cleaning instructions.

Knits that vary in texture as well as stretchability include (clockwise from left) terry stretch knit, smooth double knit, ribbed stable knit, napped stretch knit and nylon-spandex.

Coated against the weather

A variety of chemical and plastic finishes turns lightweight sportswear fabrics into reliable shields against wind, snow and rain. And new spinning techniques give nonskid (or antiglisse) texture to nylon or polyester ski wear that was once so slick a fallen skier could not stop his slide.

WORKING WITH WEATHER-RESISTANT FABRICS

CHOOSING FABRICS: In sportswear fabric, special coatings and finishes are available to safeguard the wearer against specific weather elements—and to specific degrees. **Chemically coated fabrics** are moisture resistant, but not waterproof. When rain or snow is brief or gentle, raindrops or snowflakes tend to collect on the surface of these coated fabrics and roll off without penetrating them. Most familiarly known by such trade names as Cravenette, Scotchgard or Zepel, the coatings are most effective when applied by fabric producers; but they can be added to any appropriate fabric by a professional dry-cleaner or even put on at home with a spray can. However they are applied, the coatings are invisible and do not affect the texture or appearance of the base fabric; thus they are suitable for any garment for which the untreated fabric would be used. **Urethane-coated fabrics** are topped with a film of urethane plastic that gives the material a variety of distinctive finishes—glossy or dull, smooth or crinkly, depending on how the film itself is treated. They also provide varying degrees of protection. When applied in a thin layer, urethane creates a water-resistant coating. Used more thickly, the coating forms a truly waterproof and windproof shield that keeps the base cotton or synthetic fabric dry in the heaviest storms —but it also makes the fabric hot to wear. Urethane coatings are always flexible and may be clear, colored or patterned. Fabrics that have been thinly coated are suitable for general outdoor garments such as ski jackets and warm-up pants; those with thick coatings are good for heavy-duty foul-weather gear. **Vinyl-coated fabrics** are covered with a film of vinyl, which gives the cloth a smooth and somewhat stiff surface that can be either glossy or dull. These coatings are used to make cotton or synthetic fabrics completely waterproof and windproof; but like the thick-coated urethanes, they are hot to wear. Available in solid colors and patterns, vinyl-coated fabrics are useful for heavy-duty raincoats, capes, hats and pants. **Rubber-bonded fabrics** are made by fusing a thin layer of natural or synthetic rubber between two pieces of some other material. These other fabrics are tightly woven, and themselves have been treated with a chemical coating to make them rain resistant. The rubber makes the finished fabric completely waterproof, windproof—and warm to wear. Available in solid colors, rubber-bonded fabrics are traditional for foul-weather boating and riding clothes. **Antiglisse nylons and polyesters** are woven from threads that have been spun out of short lengths of filament, rather than from the unspun filaments customarily used in nylon or polyester fabric. The spinning process creates a dull-finished, textured thread and a similarly dull and textured cloth that tends to catch on snow or ice, rather than sliding. Antiglisse fabrics come in a wide range of solid colors and patterns for use in ski and skating clothes.

LAYING OUT AND CUTTING FABRICS: Whenever the finished or coated side of the fabric is slippery, lay out the fabric wrong side down so that it will not slide while being cut. Before pinning, test the effect of pins on pieces of scrap; use ballpoint pins for nylon, silk pins for any other coated fabric. If the pins leave visible holes, pin only in the seam allowances. Transfer all pattern markings with a smooth-edged tracing wheel and dressmaker's carbon paper.

SEWING FABRICS: Use mercerized cotton or polyester thread. Baste chemically coated and antiglisse fabrics by hand with a Size 7 needle; because of their heavier weight, baste urethane-coated, vinyl-coated and rubber-bonded fabrics by machine with a Size 14 to 16 ballpoint needle, and set the machine at 6 stitches to the inch. For regular stitching on all coated fabrics, set the machine at 10 to 12 stitches to the inch. Before sewing the garment, test a double-thickness swatch of the fabric to check machine tension and stitch length. If the fabric sticks, use a roller-presser or Teflon-coated foot attachment, or insert tracing paper between the foot and the fabric. To keep nylon fabrics from puckering, be sure to hold the fabric taut as you stitch. To prevent these fabrics from raveling or fraying, use a zigzag stitch along the raw edges of the seam allowance, or bind the edges with bias tape. Chemically coated or urethane-coated fabrics may require topstitching (*Glossary*) to hold the seams and hems flat.

PRESSING FABRICS: Preset the dial on the iron to the temperature indicated for the base fabric. (On rubber-bonded fabrics, set the iron at "warm" and test the iron on a swatch.) Press nylon fabrics on the wrong side with steam, vinyl-coated fabrics on the wrong side with a cool, dry iron. Use a pressing cloth—and light pressure—on the right side of chemically coated fabrics; use a cloth and heavy pressure on the right side of rubber-bonded ones. Do not press urethane-coated fabrics at all. Heat may crack or discolor them.

CLEANING FABRICS: Always follow the cleaning or laundering instructions on the hang tag or bolt end of the fabric. Chemically coated, rubber-bonded and antiglisse fabrics can be safely sent to a dry-cleaner. Urethane-coated fabrics, too, may be dry-cleaned—or washed with a damp sponge and mild detergent. Vinyl-coated fabrics cannot be dry-cleaned; instead wipe them with a damp sponge and warm, soapy water.

Fabrics that foil the elements include (*clockwise from top left*), chemical-coated nylon, antiglisse nylon, plastic-coated synthetic and cotton, antiglisse polyester and chemical-coated poplin.

3
A BIG JUMP
IN SPORTSWEAR
DESIGN

Ski jackets like the one worn by the leaping deep-powder runner on the preceding pages represent the quintessence of sportswear engineering. In fact a jacket such as this one includes more basic elements used in the general construction of outerwear than does any other single garment.

Decades of experiment have gone into refining the ski jacket's construction and styling. The fabrics from which it is made

THE ULTIMATE OUTDOOR JACKET

represent the last word in sturdiness, durability and wind-and-water resistance. Every stout seam serves a critical purpose, and enhances the garment's racy design. Each of the fittings on the jacket is eminently functional. And the insulation is as light and effective as modern technology can make it.

For all that, constructing a ski jacket is within the sewing abilities of any home seamstress. Furthermore, in creating such a jacket the home seamstress not only enjoys the satisfaction of putting together a handsome garment, but she also will use most of the skills needed to create other items in her sports wardrobe.

Making a ski jacket must start—like all other sports sewing projects—with analyzing the functions of the garment and then picking out materials that work efficiently. With the jacket, the choice of a fabric for the outer shell comes first. And its requirements are similar to those of jackets made for fishing, backpacking, climbing and paddle tennis. The ideal ski shell keeps out wind and snow and withstands hard wear, yet at the same time it is lightweight and roomy enough for the skier to move freely inside it. In addition, since skiing is a very sociable and style-conscious sport, the fabrics available for the outer shell come in a spectrum of vibrant colors. The range of fabric materials, mostly polyester or nylon, is almost as rich. They are tightly woven, water repellent and as tough as they are handsome.

Fittings of a ski jacket are items for which the home seamstress will find dozens of other sportswear uses. For example, the ready-made stretch-knit cuffs that snug the skiers' wrists will be just as welcome on tennis jackets and joggers' and cyclists' warm-up suits. A boating jacket requires the same sort of tight pocket seals as does a ski jacket. And the kinds of cinching devices and fasteners *(pages 34-35, 48-61 and 74-81)* skiers prefer —the adjustable belts, Velcro tape closures and nonstick plastic or metal zippers that are easily opened and shut even with gloved or mittened hands—can be a boon to almost any outdoorsman.

Similarly the strategic placement of sturdy seams that allow a ski jacket to withstand all kinds of active use and the foulest kind of weather will work just as dependably on an equestrian's jodhpurs, a woodsman's lumber jacket or a duck hunter's coveralls.

Perhaps the most critical element of all in a ski jacket is its insulation, which means as much to a cold-weather garment as it does to a house. Heat, or thermal energy, is a tangible force that tends to flow toward lower temperatures. Insulation holds the body's heat in (not the cold out) and in so doing keeps a person comfortable while also conserving his energy.

The insulation for today's trim ski jacket is light in weight and far less bulky and constricting than the layers of wool sweaters that skiers piled on in the past. Goose down, popular with professional skiers— and campers and hunters—is perhaps the lightest and most efficient of insulating agents for clothing. But it is expensive, and difficult for the home seamstress to handle. Instead, most jacket makers use such materials as polyester batting *(pages 38-41)*.

Readily available to the home seamstress, the batting weighs only 3.3 ounces to the 46-inch-wide yard, is a mere half an inch thick, yet traps sufficient heat to keep the active wearer warm in temperatures as low as 20° F. Extra batting can be added to jackets meant for even colder climates.

Despite the apparent complexity of the garment, no special sewing machine is required for making a ski jacket. And the requisite sewing techniques are standard for all active wear.

Hardware for fastening and fitting

The hardware that provides closures and other fittings for sports apparel is designed to stand up to the rigors of strenuous use. Zippers and snaps must hold fast against a swiveling skier's turn or a cool-weather golfer's lustiest swing. The shank buttons, hooks and toggles (*below*) keep heavy garments closed. Thin snaps do the same on lightweight jackets; linked shank buttons serve double duty on reversible wear; grommets of all sizes hold drawstrings and ventilate rain gear.

Buckles (*near right*) fit belts of various widths and D rings cinch belts or straps; suspender fasteners allow straps to be adjusted. Velcro tabs (*bottom*) make pockets easy to seal and open, even when hands are sheathed in mittens or gloves.

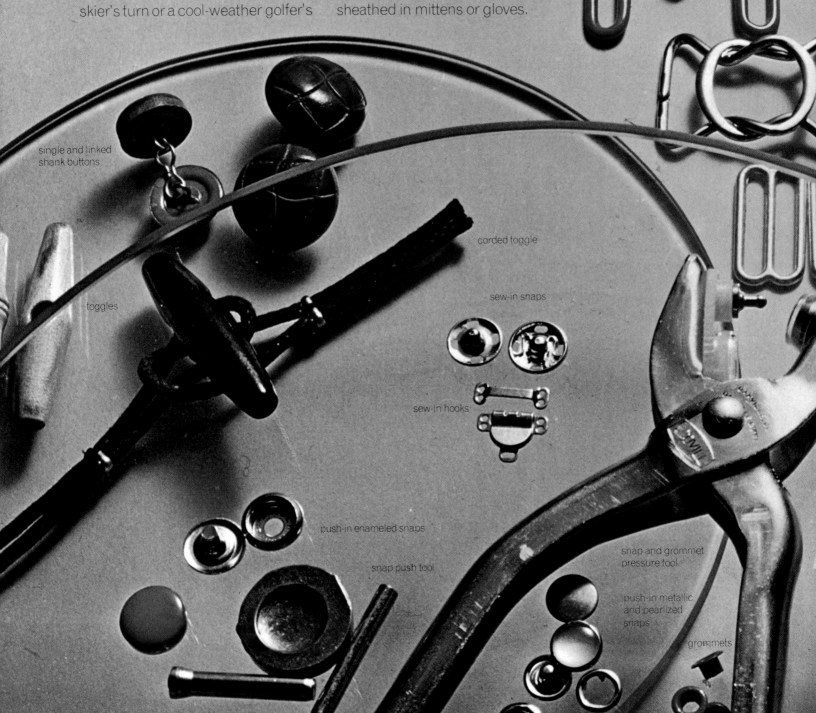

two-piece buckles

single and linked shank buttons

corded toggle

toggles

sew-in snaps

sew-in hooks

push-in enameled snaps

snap push tool

snap and grommet pressure tool

push-in metallic and pearlized snaps

grommets

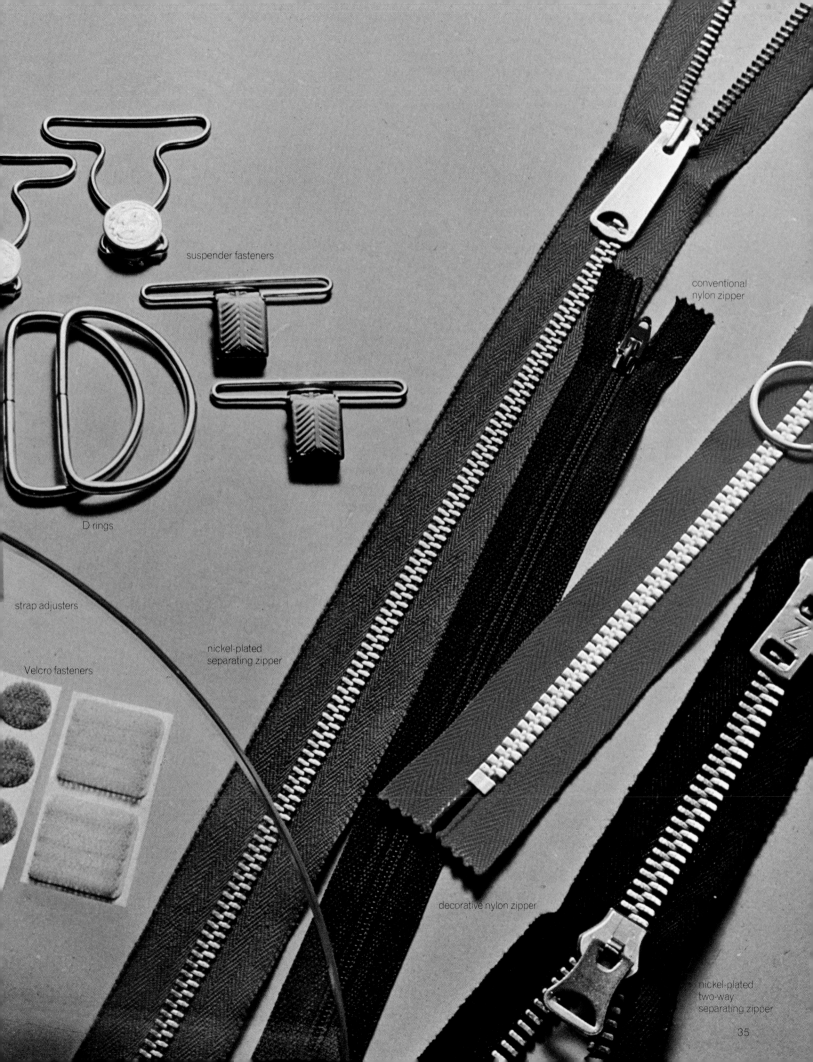

suspender fasteners

conventional
nylon zipper

D rings

strap adjusters

nickel-plated
separating zipper

Velcro fasteners

decorative nylon zipper

nickel-plated
two-way
separating zipper

35

polyester
stretch trim

cotton webbing

cotton and nylon
knit cuffs

cheesecloth

cotton webbing

cotton webbing

polyester stretch trim

elastic

cording

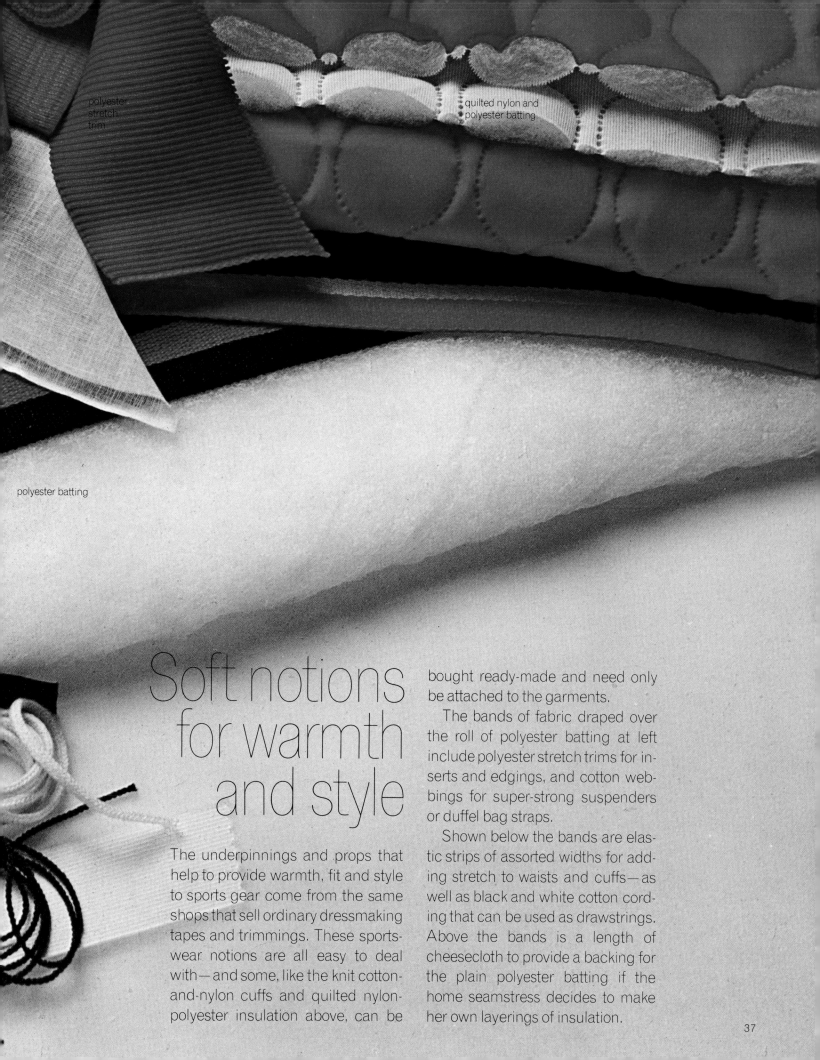

polyester
stretch
trim

quilted nylon and
polyester batting

polyester batting

Soft notions for warmth and style

The underpinnings and props that help to provide warmth, fit and style to sports gear come from the same shops that sell ordinary dressmaking tapes and trimmings. These sportswear notions are all easy to deal with—and some, like the knit cotton-and-nylon cuffs and quilted nylon-polyester insulation above, can be bought ready-made and need only be attached to the garments.

The bands of fabric draped over the roll of polyester batting at left include polyester stretch trims for inserts and edgings, and cotton webbings for super-strong suspenders or duffel bag straps.

Shown below the bands are elastic strips of assorted widths for adding stretch to waists and cuffs—as well as black and white cotton cording that can be used as drawstrings. Above the bands is a length of cheesecloth to provide a backing for the plain polyester batting if the home seamstress decides to make her own layerings of insulation.

37

The trim look of lightweight insulation

The light weight and slim lines of this ski parka hide the fact that it contains an interlining efficient enough to keep the wearer comfortable in subfreezing weather. The interlining is polyester batting *(pages 36 and 37),* a fluffy nonwoven substance about half an inch thick. In a garment like this, the batting is backed with muslin or cheesecloth, then quilted *(instructions, opposite)* and finally lined. Several layers of the batting can be stitched together for extra warmth in very cold weather.

Another popular interlining is prequilted polyester, which comes already backed with nylon. Though easier to sew, prequilted polyester is not as efficient an insulator as polyester batting.

Woolen coats, or jackets more fitted than a ski parka and not meant to be worn in such cold weather, can be interlined with a thin layer of lamb's wool or cotton flannelette, according to the instructions overleaf.

PADDING A JACKET

A | PREPARING THE PADDING

1. Use the pattern pieces for the outside of the garment to cut out the backing fabric. Then transfer the pattern markings to the fabric, using dressmaker's carbon paper and a tracing wheel.

2. Use the same pattern pieces to cut out the polyester batting.

3. Working on one garment section at a time, lay the backing, marked side up, over the corresponding batting piece.

4. Baste the backing and batting together. Make parallel rows of long stitches about 3 inches apart.

5. To quilt the padding, run parallel rows of horizontal machine basting—6 stitches to the inch—about 4 inches apart across the section. As you stitch, stretch the fabric slightly to reduce puckering.

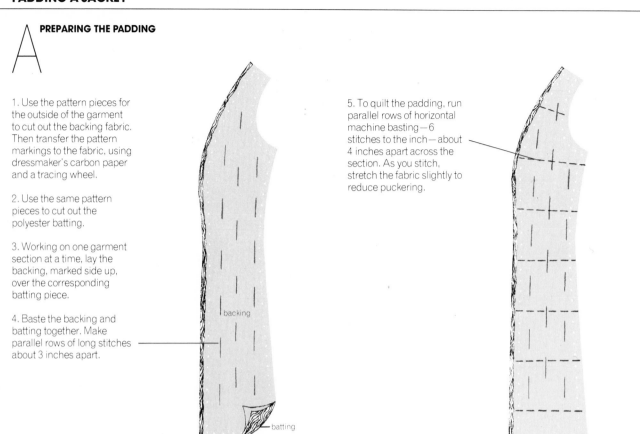

B | STITCHING THE PADDING TO THE GARMENT SECTIONS

6. Place the corresponding outside layer of the garment wrong side up. Then position the quilted padding, backing side up, over it. Pin around the edges.

7. Machine baste 1/4 inch outside the seam lines, removing the pins as you go.

8. Remove the vertical bastings made in Step 4.

9. Proceed to assemble the garment according to the pattern instructions.

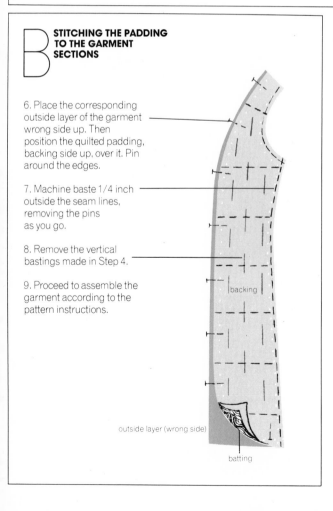

PADDING PANTS

1. Using the pattern pieces for the outside of the garment, cut out the prequilted padding. Then, with dressmaker's carbon paper and a tracing wheel, transfer the pattern markings to the padding.

2. Place the corresponding outside layer of the garment wrong side up. Position the padding, marked side up, over it. Pin.

3. Machine baste 1/4 inch outside the seam lines, removing the pins as you go.

4. Proceed to assemble the garment according to the pattern instructions.

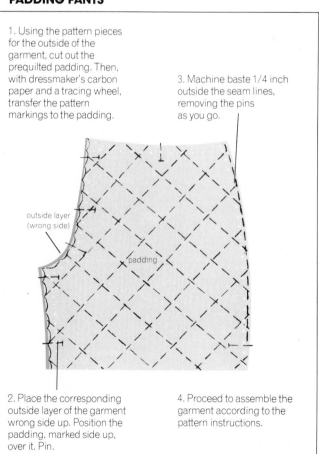

INTERLINING A GARMENT

A ATTACHING THE INTERLINING TO THE LINING

1. Use the lining pattern pieces to cut out the interlining as you did the lining itself—except at the hem edge. There, cut the interlining so that it extends 1/2 inch below the hem fold line.

2. With dressmaker's carbon paper and a tracing wheel, transfer all pattern markings to the interlining.

5. Turn the basted pieces over so that the interlining faces up. Then baste the pieces together again, this time stitching 1/4 inch outside all seam lines.

6. Now baste 1/4 inch inside all dart stitching lines.

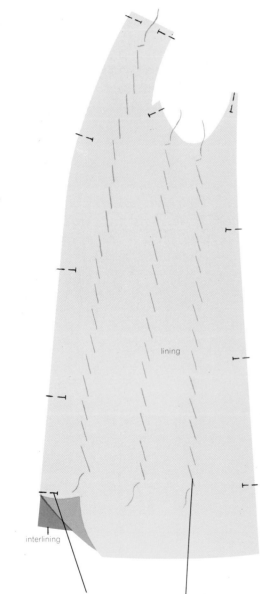

3. Working on one section at a time, place the interlining marked side down, and cover it with the corresponding lining section, wrong side down. Pin the two pieces together at the edges, keeping them as flat as possible.

4. Run parallel rows of diagonal basting stitches (Appendix) about 4 inches apart down the length of the section, smoothing the fabrics as you go.

7. Make long running stitches to secure the pieces 1/8 inch below the hem fold line.

8. Stay stitch (Glossary) the armholes, front openings and neck edges 1/8 inch outside the seam lines. Remove the basting.

9. Trim the interlining as close to the stay stitching as possible.

10. Machine stitch the darts, then remove the basting made in Step 6.

11. Make horizontal clips in the darts about 1 inch inside the points. Cut up to, but not through, the line of stitching.

15. Stitch together the combination lining-interlining sections along the seam lines. Then remove the bastings made in Step 5.

16. Trim the interlining as close to the stitched seams as possible.

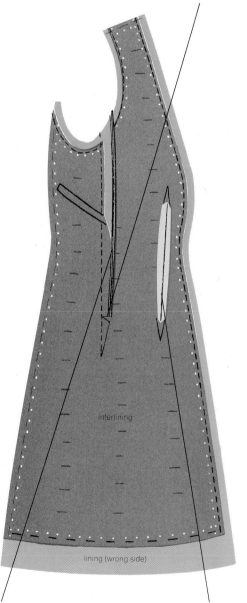

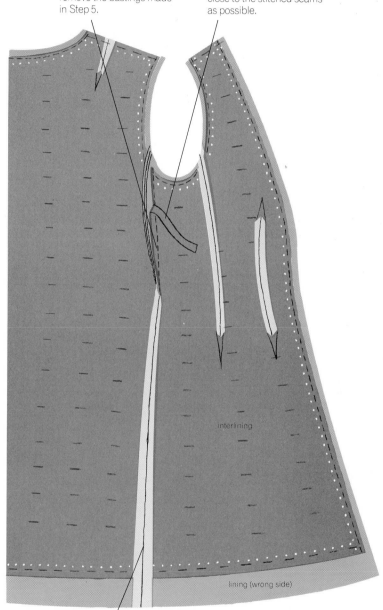

12. Slash the darts between the horizontal clips.

13. Trim the interlining in the slashed portion of the darts as close to the stitching line as possible.

14. Press open the darts, being careful to flatten the points.

17. Press open the seams.

18. Remove the diagonal bastings made in Step 4.

19. Attach the interlined lining to your garment, following your pattern instructions.

Strong seams and neat edgings

The stress and strain often put on sports clothes call for seams and edgings that are as toughly functional as the fabric. The heavyweight cotton pants shown here, for example, have flat felled seams (*opposite*), which provide reinforcement as well as a neat look.

Other designs and other fabrics dictate the seaming treatments explained on the following pages. For example, the French seam that encloses raw fabric edges is appropriate for lightweight and easily frayed materials like nylon. The topstitched seam is utilitarian and decorative on all sporting fabrics except those of the heaviest weight. The corded seam buffers stitches from abrasion. Edge stitching holds a crease in shape. The double stitched hem shelters the seam allowances on lined garments. And the shirttail hem reinforces and delineates the bottom edge of such garments as jackets and tennis dresses.

THE FLAT FELLED SEAM

A MAKING A PLAIN SEAM

1. Pin together the two pieces of fabric. If you want to have two lines of stitching visible on the finished flat felled seam, as in this example, pin the fabric pieces with the wrong sides together. If you want to have only one line of stitching visible, pin the pieces together wrong sides out.

2. Baste and remove the pins. Machine stitch 5/8 inch from the edge, and remove the basting.

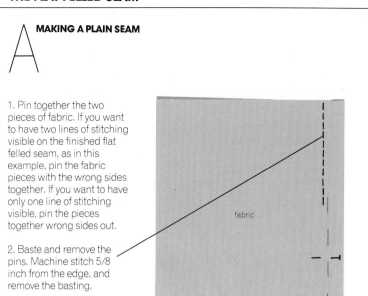

B PREPARING THE FLAT FELLED SEAM

3. Press open the seam. Then press both seam allowances in the direction in which the felled seam will fall according to your pattern.

4. Trim the underneath seam allowance to 1/8 inch.

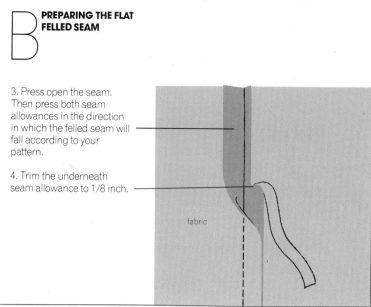

C FOLDING AND BASTING THE FLAT FELLED SEAM

5. Fold under the wider seam allowance 1/4 inch, then pin it to the garment. Baste 1/8 inch from the folded edge and remove the pins.

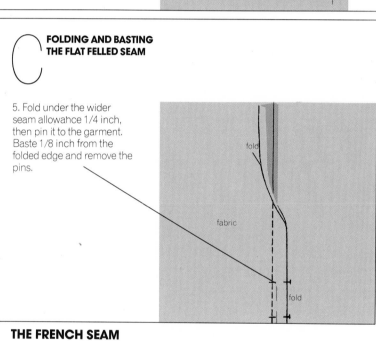

D STITCHING THE SEAM

6. Machine stitch close to the folded edge. Remove the basting and press.

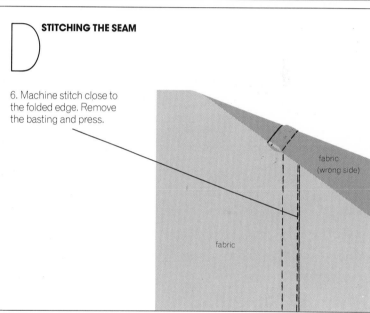

THE FRENCH SEAM

A PREPARING THE SEAM

1. With the wrong sides of the fabric together, align the seam lines of the two pieces to be seamed, and pin.

2. Baste 5/8 inch from the edge. Remove the pins.

3. Machine stitch 1/4 inch outside the basting. Remove the basting.

4. Trim the seam allowances 1/8 inch from the stitching.

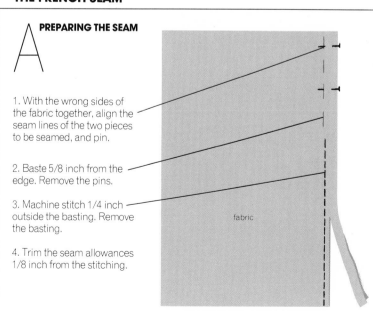

B FOLDING AND STITCHING THE SEAM

5. Turn the seamed fabric wrong side out, and fold along the seam.

6. Roll the seamed edge between your fingers to bring the stitching to the edge. Press.

7. Machine stitch along the seam line, making sure to enclose the seam allowances.

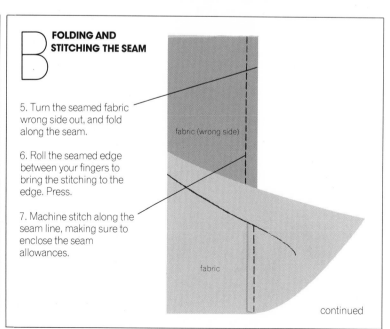

continued

C PRESSING THE SEAM

8. Open the fabric wrong side up, and press the seam flat to one side.

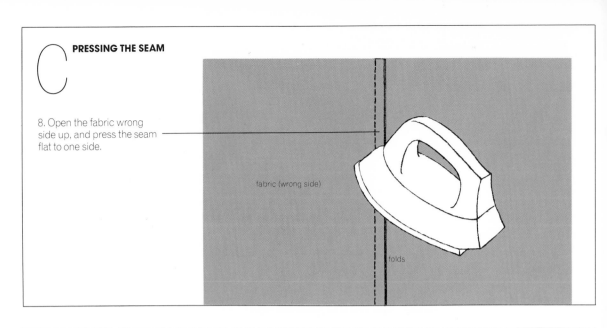

fabric (wrong side)

folds

THE CORDED SEAM

A MAKING THE CASING FOR THE CORD

1. To determine the total length of the casing you will require for the cording, measure the seam into which you will be sewing the cording. Add 2 inches.

2. Lay the casing fabric wrong side up on a flat surface. Fold up one corner diagonally so that a crosswise edge is aligned with a selvage edge. Pin the edges.

3. Cut the fabric along the fold. Remove the pins, and set aside the top piece of fabric.

4. Trim off both of the selvages.

5. Determine the number of bias strips of fabric you will need to make the casing for your seam. Be sure to add 1/2 inch for seam allowances on each strip.

6. Mark off the strips with a series of chalk lines parallel to the diagonal edge. Make each strip wide enough to fit around the cord, plus 1 inch for seam allowances.

7. Cut out the strips along the chalk lines.

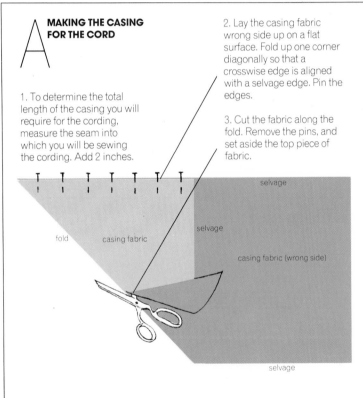

selvage

fold   casing fabric

selvage

casing fabric (wrong side)

selvage

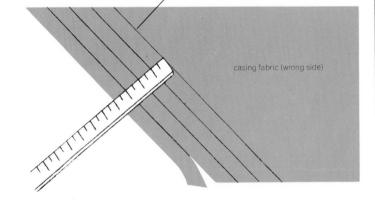

casing fabric (wrong side)

8. Mark a 1/4-inch seam allowance with chalk on the ends of each strip.

9. Place two of the strips together, wrong sides out, so that they form a V. Align the seam lines, and pin.

10. Machine stitch, and remove the pins.

11. Repeat Steps 8-10 until you have one long strip that is slightly longer than the total measurement determined in Step 1.

12. Press open the seams.

13. Cut off one end of the strip at a right angle to the long edges.

14. Mark the total measurement determined in Step 1, and cut off the other end of the strip. Again make the cut at a right angle to the long edge.

bias strip

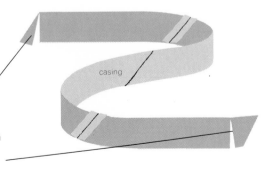

casing

B MAKING THE CORDING

15. Cut a piece of cord the length of the casing, plus 1 inch.

16. Fold the casing, wrong sides together, around the cord, and align the edges.

17. Using a zipper foot, machine baste (6 stitches to the inch) close to the cord but not up against it. Hold the edges of the casing to keep them aligned as you stitch.

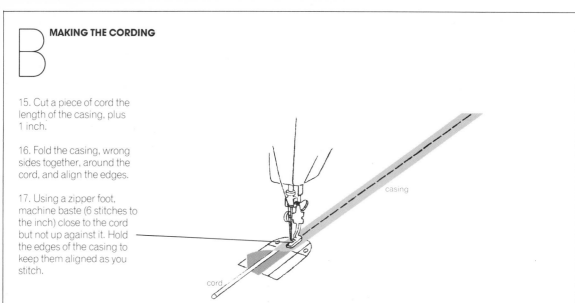

casing

cord

C ATTACHING THE CORDING

18. Lay one of the garment pieces to be joined wrong side down on a flat surface. Place the cording on the garment piece, with the edges of the casing 1/8 inch in from the edge of the garment piece. Pin.

19. To ensure that the cording will lie flat on any curves or corners, clip the outer edges of the casing up to but not through the machine basting.

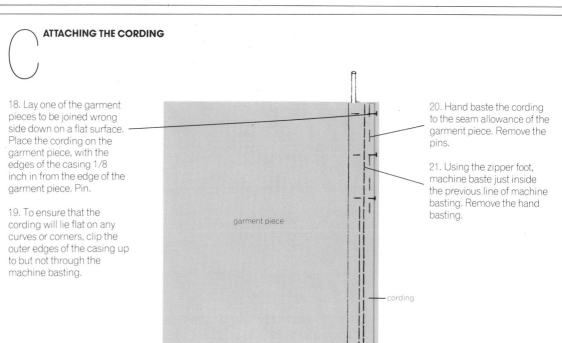

garment piece

cording

20. Hand baste the cording to the seam allowance of the garment piece. Remove the pins.

21. Using the zipper foot, machine baste just inside the previous line of machine basting. Remove the hand basting.

D CLOSING THE CORDED SEAM

22. Place the garment piece to which you have attached the cording wrong side down on a flat surface. Position the other garment piece over it, wrong side up. The cording should lie between the two pieces.

23. Align the outer edges of the garment pieces, and pin.

24. Hand baste. Remove the pins.

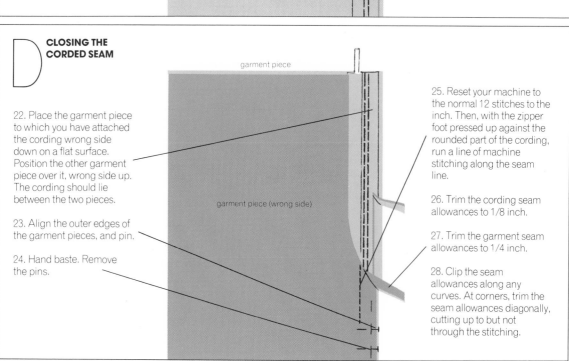

garment piece

garment piece (wrong side)

25. Reset your machine to the normal 12 stitches to the inch. Then, with the zipper foot pressed up against the rounded part of the cording, run a line of machine stitching along the seam line.

26. Trim the cording seam allowances to 1/8 inch.

27. Trim the garment seam allowances to 1/4 inch.

28. Clip the seam allowances along any curves. At corners, trim the seam allowances diagonally, cutting up to but not through the stitching.

THE TOPSTITCHED PLAIN SEAM

1. Make a plain seam, following the instructions for the flat felled seam *(page 43, Box A)*. Press open the seam. Then press both seam allowances to one side.

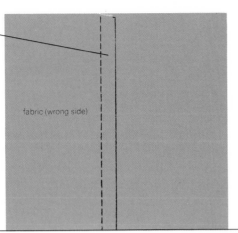

fabric (wrong side)

2. Turn the seamed fabric wrong side down and topstitch a short distance —usually 1/8 inch—from the folded edge of the seam. If you want a second line of topstitching, make it 1/4 inch from the first line.

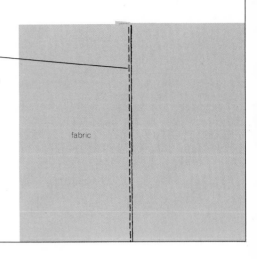

fabric

EDGE STITCHING

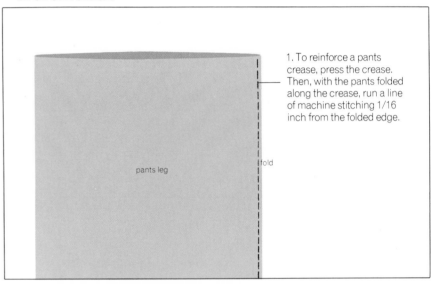

pants leg

fold

1. To reinforce a pants crease, press the crease. Then, with the pants folded along the crease, run a line of machine stitching 1/16 inch from the folded edge.

THE STITCHED DOUBLE HEM

A PREPARING THE GARMENT FABRIC AND THE LINING

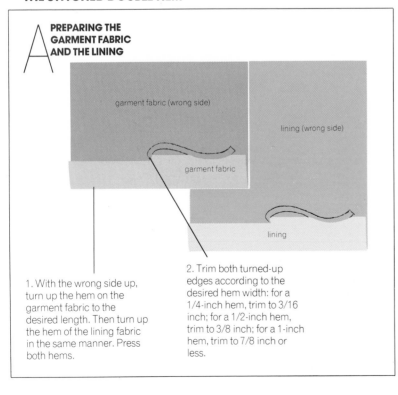

garment fabric (wrong side)

lining (wrong side)

garment fabric

lining

1. With the wrong side up, turn up the hem on the garment fabric to the desired length. Then turn up the hem of the lining fabric in the same manner. Press both hems.

2. Trim both turned-up edges according to the desired hem width: for a 1/4-inch hem, trim to 3/16 inch; for a 1/2-inch hem, trim to 3/8 inch; for a 1-inch hem, trim to 7/8 inch or less.

B JOINING THE GARMENT FABRIC TO THE LINING

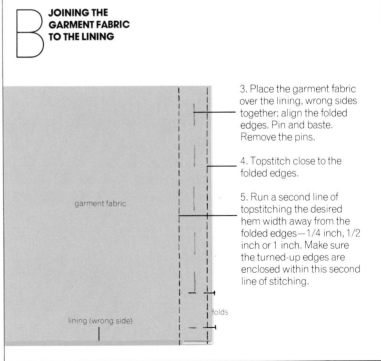

garment fabric

lining (wrong side)

folds

3. Place the garment fabric over the lining, wrong sides together; align the folded edges. Pin and baste. Remove the pins.

4. Topstitch close to the folded edges.

5. Run a second line of topstitching the desired hem width away from the folded edges—1/4 inch, 1/2 inch or 1 inch. Make sure the turned-up edges are enclosed within this second line of stitching.

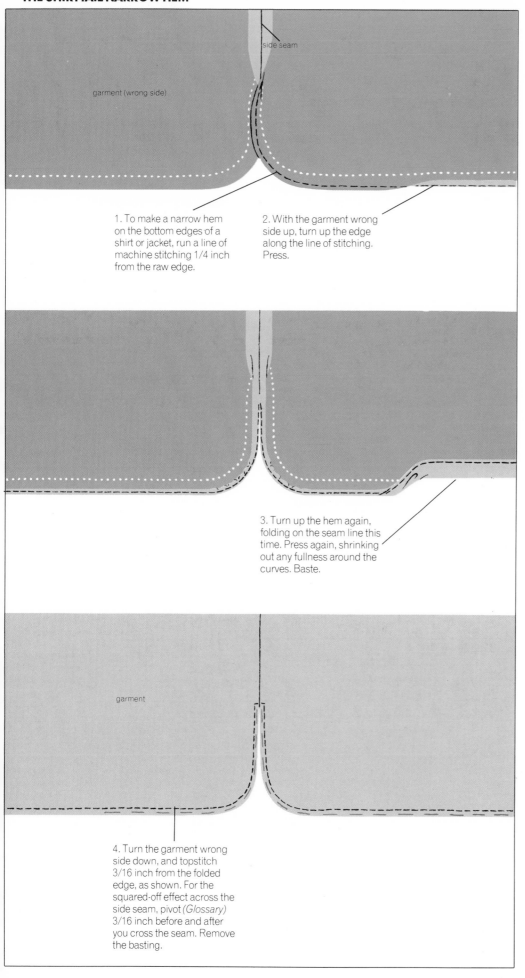

side seam

garment (wrong side)

1. To make a narrow hem on the bottom edges of a shirt or jacket, run a line of machine stitching 1/4 inch from the raw edge.

2. With the garment wrong side up, turn up the edge along the line of stitching. Press.

3. Turn up the hem again, folding on the seam line this time. Press again, shrinking out any fullness around the curves. Baste.

garment

4. Turn the garment wrong side down, and topstitch 3/16 inch from the folded edge, as shown. For the squared-off effect across the side seam, pivot (Glossary) 3/16 inch before and after you cross the seam. Remove the basting.

Casual closures

The buttoned plackets and so-called separating zippers demonstrated on the following pages provide handsome, unencumbering closures for sports clothes. The plackets—slits to which two strips of overlapping fabric are added—extend only partway down the front of a pullover or up the sleeve of a shirt or jacket. Usually they are closed with buttons as shown here. The stitching at the bottom reinforces the placket against the stress of active use.

Separating zippers—those whose bottom ends come apart when unzipped—open a garment to its full length. On a golf jacket, the zipper usually goes from the hemline to about collarbone level; but on a ski parka it may reach all the way to the chin. In either case, the zipper can be concealed with flaps or it can be displayed as part of the design.

THE FRONT PLACKET FOR COLLARS WITH A STAND

A · PREPARING THE GARMENT FRONT

1. To prevent the fabric from stretching as you work, machine stitch just outside the neck seam-line markings of the garment front. Then machine stitch just outside the seam-line markings for the front placket.

2. At the bottom of the opening for the placket, clip the seam allowance diagonally to the corners. Be careful to cut up to, but not into, the stitching.

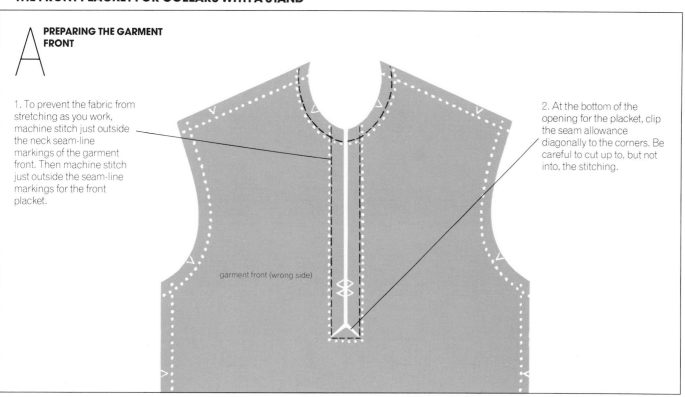

garment front (wrong side)

B · PREPARING THE FRONT PLACKETS

3. Fold the front placket pattern piece in half lengthwise. Then, using the notched portion, cut and mark two interfacing sections for the plackets.

4. With the wrong sides facing up, pin the interfacing to the notched half of each placket along the seam lines and the fold line. Make sure to match the notches and center-front lines.

5. Run a line of basting along the center-front line of each placket.

6. On each placket, baste just outside the seam lines. Remove the pins from the seam lines.

7. Catch stitch (Appendix) the interfacing to each placket along the center edge. Remove the pins.

8. Trim to 1/4 inch the long noninterfaced seam allowance of each placket.

9. Turn under the trimmed seam allowance of each placket along the seam line. Press.

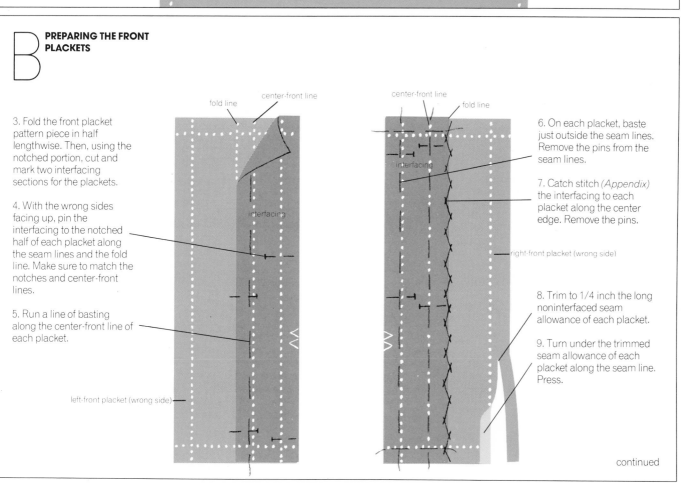

fold line
center-front line
center-front line
fold line
interfacing
interfacing
right-front placket (wrong side)
left-front placket (wrong side)

continued

C ATTACHING THE PLACKETS TO THE GARMENT FRONT

10. With the wrong sides out, pin the interfaced side of the right-front placket to the garment front along the right-front seam line. Match at the neck, the bottom of the front opening and the notches.

11. Baste and remove the pins.

12. Machine stitch from the neck edge to the intersection with the bottom seam line of the front opening. Remove the basting from the stitched seam.

13. Along the right-front seam, trim the interfacing seam allowance close to the stitching, the placket seam allowance to 1/8 inch and the garment seam allowance to 1/4 inch.

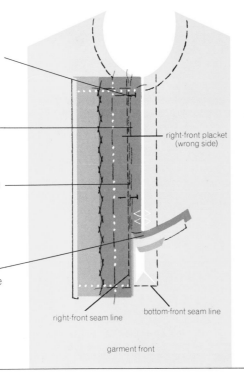

right-front placket (wrong side)

right-front seam line

bottom-front seam line

garment front

14. Turn the garment front wrong side up and extend the placket. Press the seam allowances of the right-front seam toward the placket.

15. Fold the placket in half lengthwise, wrong sides together, and align the unattached folded edge against the right-front seam. Pin in place.

16. Slip stitch (Appendix) the placket to the seam allowance of the right-front seam. Remove the pins and press.

17. Repeat Steps 10-16 to attach the left placket to the garment front.

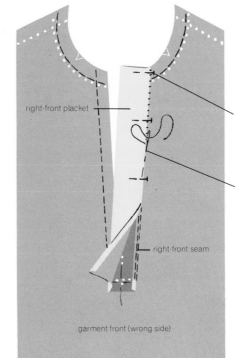

right-front placket

right-front seam

garment front (wrong side)

D TOPSTITCHING THE FRONT PLACKETS

18. Place the garment front wrong side down.

19. Topstitch each placket 1/8 inch to 1/4 inch inside the long edges and the basted neck and bottom seam markings. Begin and end the stitching at the inner bottom corner without backstitching. Then pull the threads through to the wrong side of the garment and tie them off.

20. Place the garment front wrong side up, and pull through the bottom ends of the plackets to the wrong side of the garment.

21. If you are making a man's garment as shown here, lap the right placket over the left one. For a woman's garment, lap the left placket over the right. Align the basted center-front markings, and pin the plackets together.

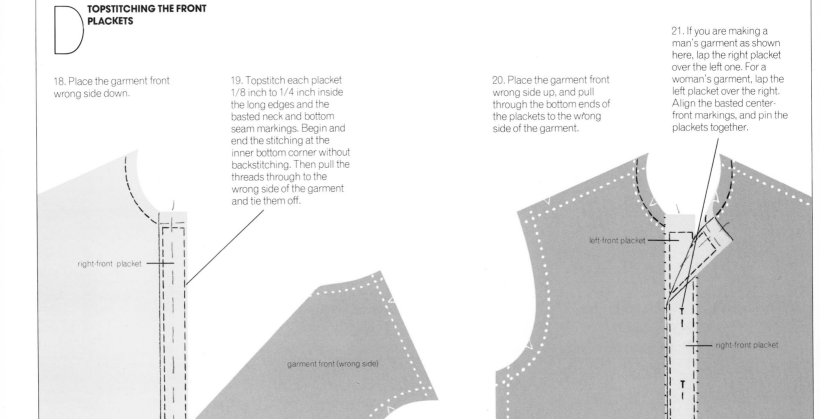

right-front placket

garment front (wrong side)

left-front placket

garment front

left-front placket

right-front placket

garment front (wrong side)

50

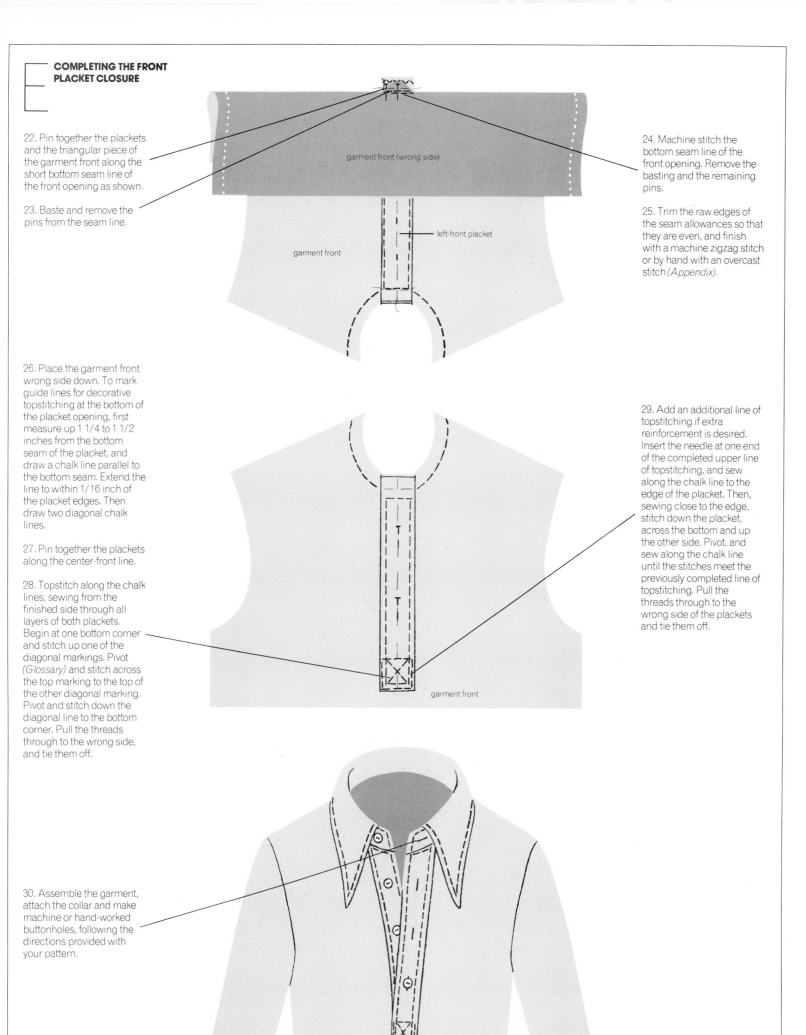

22. Pin together the plackets and the triangular piece of the garment front along the short bottom seam line of the front opening as shown.

23. Baste and remove the pins from the seam line.

garment front (wrong side)

left-front placket

garment front

24. Machine stitch the bottom seam line of the front opening. Remove the basting and the remaining pins.

25. Trim the raw edges of the seam allowances so that they are even, and finish with a machine zigzag stitch or by hand with an overcast stitch (Appendix).

26. Place the garment front wrong side down. To mark guide lines for decorative topstitching at the bottom of the placket opening, first measure up 1 1/4 to 1 1/2 inches from the bottom seam of the placket, and draw a chalk line parallel to the bottom seam. Extend the line to within 1/16 inch of the placket edges. Then draw two diagonal chalk lines.

27. Pin together the plackets along the center-front line.

28. Topstitch along the chalk lines, sewing from the finished side through all layers of both plackets. Begin at one bottom corner and stitch up one of the diagonal markings. Pivot (Glossary) and stitch across the top marking to the top of the other diagonal marking. Pivot and stitch down the diagonal line to the bottom corner. Pull the threads through to the wrong side, and tie them off.

29. Add an additional line of topstitching if extra reinforcement is desired. Insert the needle at one end of the completed upper line of topstitching, and sew along the chalk line to the edge of the placket. Then, sewing close to the edge, stitch down the placket, across the bottom and up the other side. Pivot, and sew along the chalk line until the stitches meet the previously completed line of topstitching. Pull the threads through to the wrong side of the plackets and tie them off.

garment front

30. Assemble the garment, attach the collar and make machine or hand-worked buttonholes, following the directions provided with your pattern.

THE FRONT PLACKET FOR CONVERTIBLE COLLARS

1. Prepare the garment front and the plackets, following the instructions for the front placket closure for collars with a stand *(page 49, Steps 1-9)*. Then attach the right-front placket to the garment along the right-front seam line, as in page 50, Steps 10-13.

2. Place the garment front wrong side up, and extend the placket. Press the seam allowances of the right-front seam toward the placket.

3. Fold the placket in half lengthwise along the fold line, wrong sides out. Match and pin along the neck seam-line marking.

4. Machine stitch along the neck line of the placket from the center-front marking to the folded edge. Remove the pins.

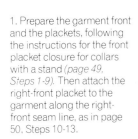
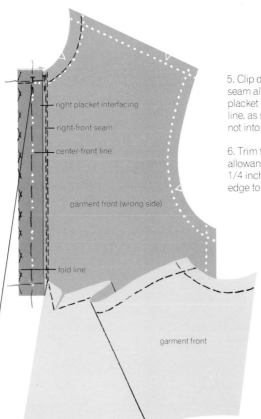

right placket interfacing
right-front seam
center-front line
garment front (wrong side)
fold line
garment front

5. Clip diagonally the neck seam allowances of the placket to the center-front line, as shown. Cut up to but not into the stitching.

6. Trim the neck seam allowances of the placket to 1/4 inch from the folded edge to the center-front line.

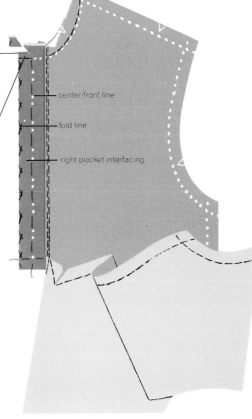

center-front line
fold line
right placket interfacing

7. Turn the placket right side out, and push out the corner at the neckline.

8. Align the unattached folded edge of the placket against the right-front seam. Pin in place.

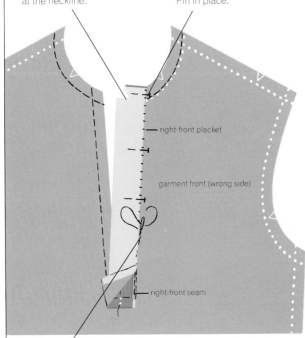

right-front placket
garment front (wrong side)
right-front seam

9. Slip stitch *(Appendix)* the placket to the seam allowance of the right-front seam. Remove the pins and press.

10. Repeat Steps 1-9 to attach the left placket to the garment front.

11. Complete the closure by following the directions in the front placket closure for collars with a stand *(pages 50 and 51, Boxes D and E)*.

12. Finish the garment following your pattern instructions.

THE SLEEVE PLACKET

A PREPARING THE SLEEVE

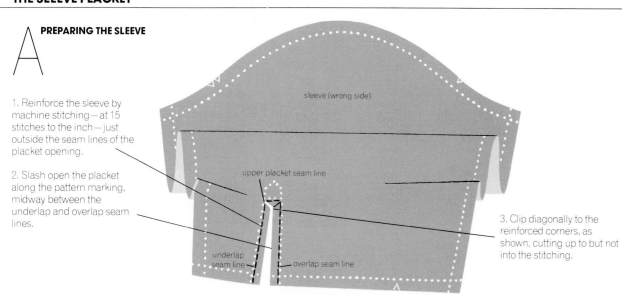

1. Reinforce the sleeve by machine stitching—at 15 stitches to the inch—just outside the seam lines of the placket opening.

2. Slash open the placket along the pattern marking, midway between the underlap and overlap seam lines.

sleeve (wrong side)

upper placket seam line

underlap seam line

overlap seam line

3. Clip diagonally to the reinforced corners, as shown, cutting up to but not into the stitching.

B ATTACHING THE UNDERLAP TO THE SLEEVE

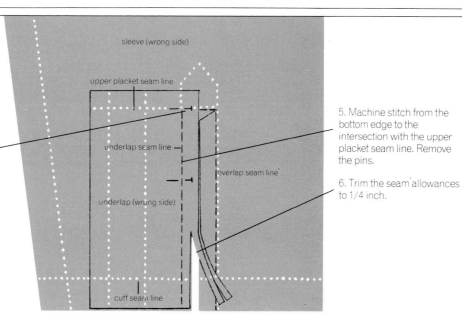

4. Cut out the underlap section following your pattern instructions. Position the underlap section, wrong side up, on the sleeve. Align one long seam line of the underlap section with the underlap seam line on the sleeve, matching the intersections at the cuff and upper placket seam lines. Pin.

sleeve (wrong side)

upper placket seam line

underlap seam line

overlap seam line

underlap (wrong side)

cuff seam line

5. Machine stitch from the bottom edge to the intersection with the upper placket seam line. Remove the pins.

6. Trim the seam allowances to 1/4 inch.

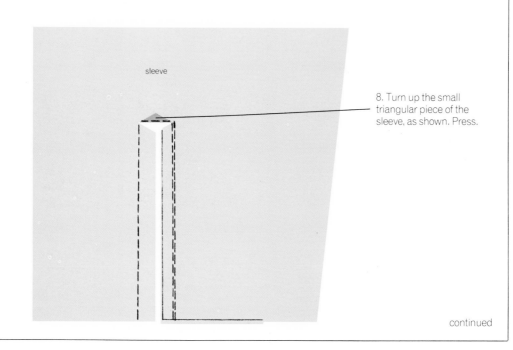

sleeve

7. Place the sleeve wrong side down.

8. Turn up the small triangular piece of the sleeve, as shown. Press.

continued

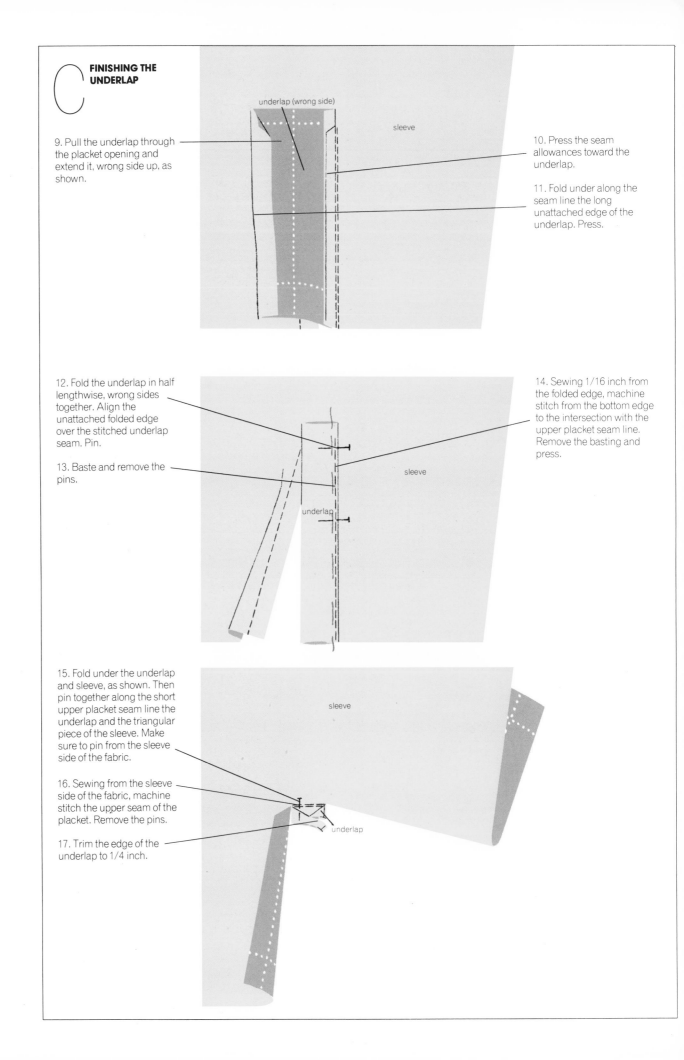

C FINISHING THE UNDERLAP

9. Pull the underlap through the placket opening and extend it, wrong side up, as shown.

10. Press the seam allowances toward the underlap.

11. Fold under along the seam line the long unattached edge of the underlap. Press.

12. Fold the underlap in half lengthwise, wrong sides together. Align the unattached folded edge over the stitched underlap seam. Pin.

13. Baste and remove the pins.

14. Sewing 1/16 inch from the folded edge, machine stitch from the bottom edge to the intersection with the upper placket seam line. Remove the basting and press.

15. Fold under the underlap and sleeve, as shown. Then pin together along the short upper placket seam line the underlap and the triangular piece of the sleeve. Make sure to pin from the sleeve side of the fabric.

16. Sewing from the sleeve side of the fabric, machine stitch the upper seam of the placket. Remove the pins.

17. Trim the edge of the underlap to 1/4 inch.

D ▶ ATTACHING THE OVERLAP TO THE SLEEVE

18. Turn the sleeve wrong side up.

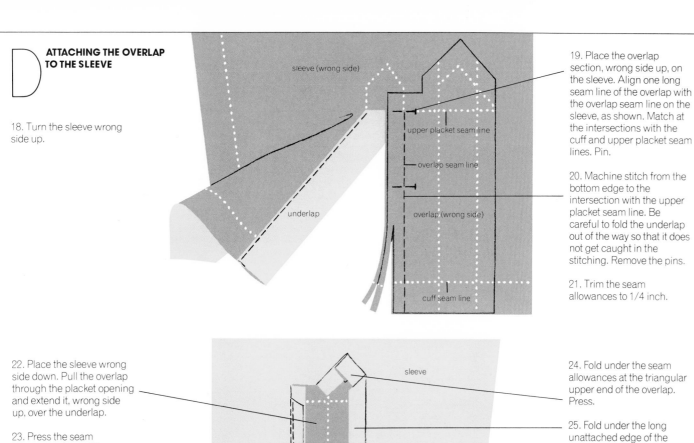

sleeve (wrong side)

underlap

upper placket seam line

overlap seam line

overlap (wrong side)

cuff seam line

19. Place the overlap section, wrong side up, on the sleeve. Align one long seam line of the overlap with the overlap seam line on the sleeve, as shown. Match at the intersections with the cuff and upper placket seam lines. Pin.

20. Machine stitch from the bottom edge to the intersection with the upper placket seam line. Be careful to fold the underlap out of the way so that it does not get caught in the stitching. Remove the pins.

21. Trim the seam allowances to 1/4 inch.

22. Place the sleeve wrong side down. Pull the overlap through the placket opening and extend it, wrong side up, over the underlap.

23. Press the seam allowances toward the overlap.

sleeve

overlap (wrong side)

24. Fold under the seam allowances at the triangular upper end of the overlap. Press.

25. Fold under the long unattached edge of the overlap. Press.

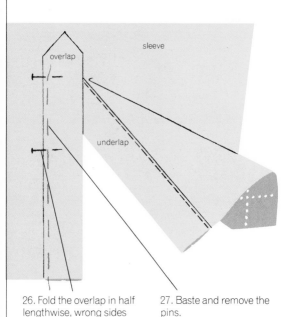

sleeve

overlap

underlap

26. Fold the overlap in half lengthwise, wrong sides together. Align the unattached folded edge with the stitched overlap seam. Pin, making sure not to catch the underlap.

27. Baste and remove the pins.

28. Position the unattached edge of the overlap on top of the stitched edge of the underlap and pin. Then pin the triangular upper portion of the overlap to the sleeve.

29. Baste across the overlap at the position of the upper placket seam line. Then baste around the edges of the triangular upper portion of the overlap. Remove the pins.

30. Machine stitch the upper portion of the overlap, sewing through all layers from the finished side. Stitch across the top of the overlap as shown. Pivot (Glossary) and stitch around the triangular upper portion of the overlap 1/16 inch from the folded edge.

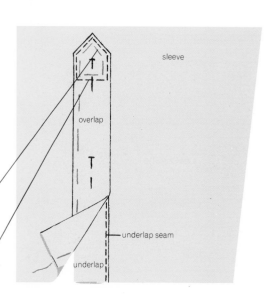

sleeve

overlap

underlap seam

underlap

31. When you reach the point at which the stitching began, stop the machine, leaving the needle in the fabric. Raise the presser foot.

continued

FINISHING THE PLACKET

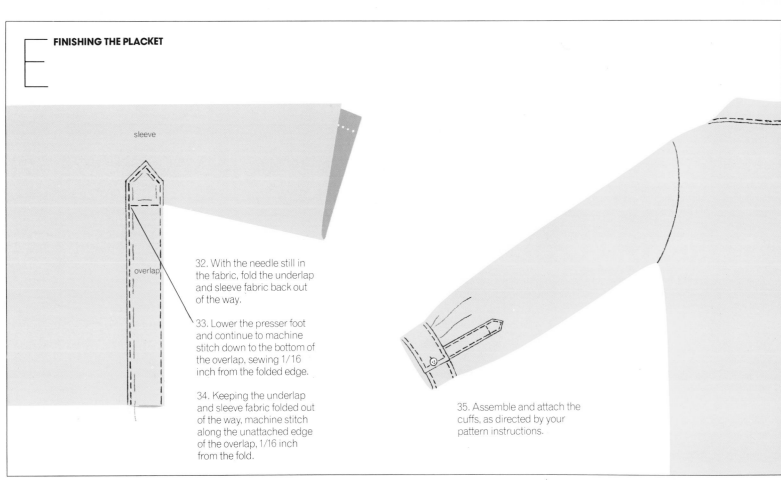

sleeve

overlap

32. With the needle still in the fabric, fold the underlap and sleeve fabric back out of the way.

33. Lower the presser foot and continue to machine stitch down to the bottom of the overlap, sewing 1/16 inch from the folded edge.

34. Keeping the underlap and sleeve fabric folded out of the way, machine stitch along the unattached edge of the overlap, 1/16 inch from the fold.

35. Assemble and attach the cuffs, as directed by your pattern instructions.

THE SEPARATING ZIPPER INSERTED TO THE NECKLINE

A PREPARING THE GARMENT AND THE FACING

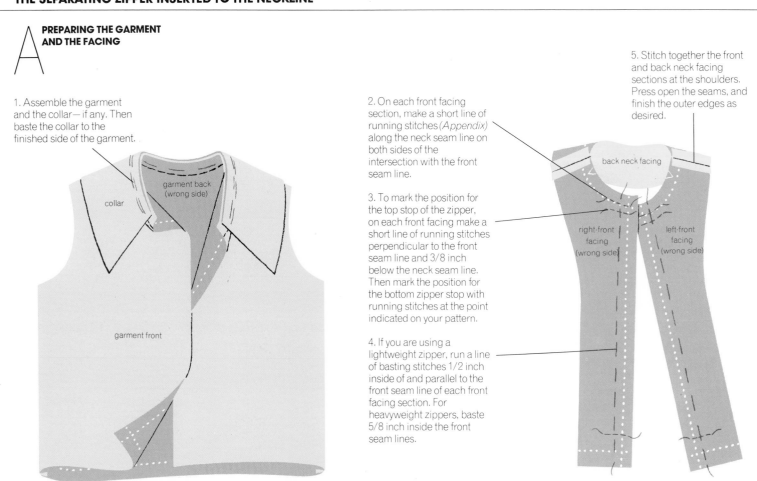

1. Assemble the garment and the collar—if any. Then baste the collar to the finished side of the garment.

collar

garment back (wrong side)

garment front

2. On each front facing section, make a short line of running stitches (*Appendix*) along the neck seam line on both sides of the intersection with the front seam line.

3. To mark the position for the top stop of the zipper, on each front facing make a short line of running stitches perpendicular to the front seam line and 3/8 inch below the neck seam line. Then mark the position for the bottom zipper stop with running stitches at the point indicated on your pattern.

4. If you are using a lightweight zipper, run a line of basting stitches 1/2 inch inside of and parallel to the front seam line of each front facing section. For heavyweight zippers, baste 5/8 inch inside the front seam lines.

5. Stitch together the front and back neck facing sections at the shoulders. Press open the seams, and finish the outer edges as desired.

back neck facing

right-front facing (wrong side)

left-front facing (wrong side)

B ATTACHING THE ZIPPER TO THE FACING

6. Turn the facing wrong side down.

7. Separate the zipper, and place the left-hand side of the zipper face up on the left-front facing. Line up the zipper teeth against the basted front marking, and align the top and bottom stops of the zipper with the horizontal running stitches, as shown. Pin.

8. Baste the zipper to the left-front facing. Remove the pins.

9. Using a zipper foot, machine stitch along the center of the zipper tape from the bottom to the neck seam line. Remove the basting and the basted markings—including the running stitches.

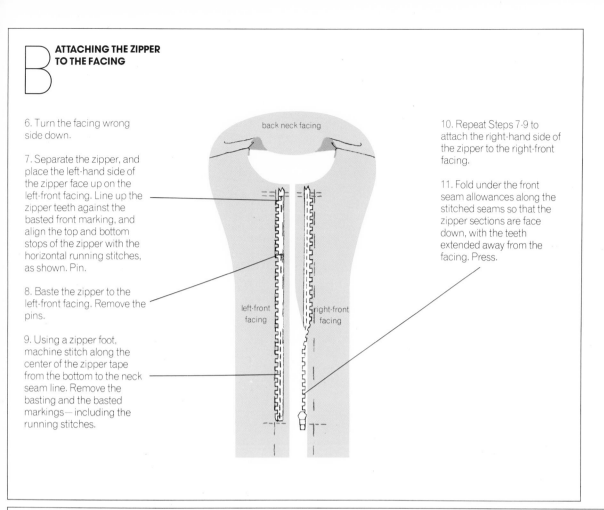

back neck facing

left-front facing

right-front facing

10. Repeat Steps 7-9 to attach the right-hand side of the zipper to the right-front facing.

11. Fold under the front seam allowances along the stitched seams so that the zipper sections are face down, with the teeth extended away from the facing. Press.

C ATTACHING THE FACING TO THE GARMENT

12. With the wrong sides out, pin the facing to the garment along the neck seam line, matching at the center back, shoulders and pattern notches. Be sure that the garment front seam allowances are extended and the front seam allowances of the facing are folded back, as shown.

13. Baste and remove the pins.

14. Machine stitch along the neck seam line. Remove the basting.

15. Fold down the top of the zipper tape so that it will be out of the way. Trim the facing seam allowance to 1/8 inch, the collar to 1/4 inch and the garment seam allowance to 3/8 inch. Be careful not to trim the zipper tape.

16. Clip the neck seam allowances at 1/2-inch intervals, cutting up to but not into the stitching.

17. Turn the facing and collar up, as shown. Press the neck seam allowances toward the garment.

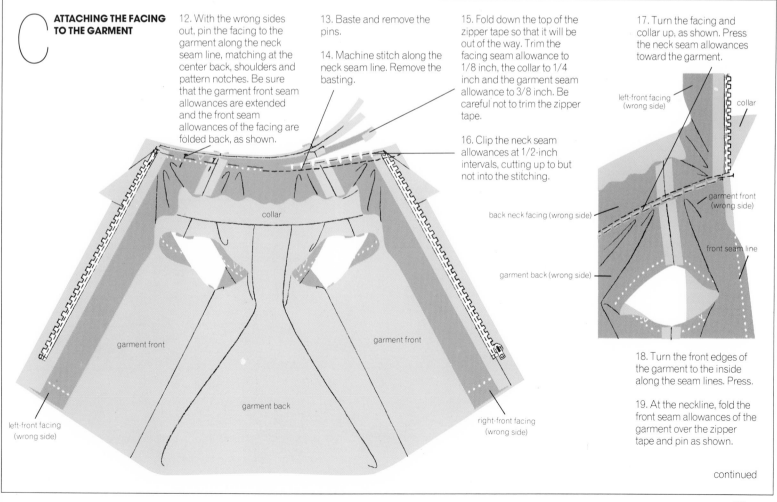

collar

garment front

garment front

garment back

left-front facing (wrong side)

right-front facing (wrong side)

left-front facing (wrong side)

collar

back neck facing (wrong side)

garment front (wrong side)

garment back (wrong side)

front seam line

18. Turn the front edges of the garment to the inside along the seam lines. Press.

19. At the neckline, fold the front seam allowances of the garment over the zipper tape and pin as shown.

continued

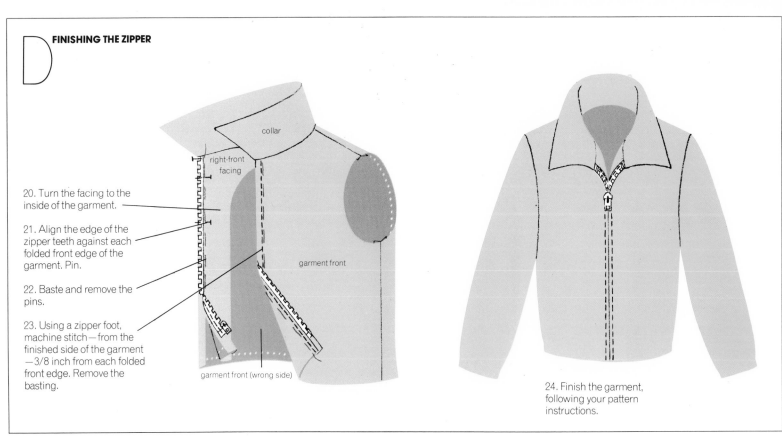

20. Turn the facing to the inside of the garment.

21. Align the edge of the zipper teeth against each folded front edge of the garment. Pin.

22. Baste and remove the pins.

23. Using a zipper foot, machine stitch—from the finished side of the garment—3/8 inch from each folded front edge. Remove the basting.

collar

right-front facing

garment front

garment front (wrong side)

24. Finish the garment, following your pattern instructions.

THE SEPARATING ZIPPER INSERTED INTO A ONE-PIECE COLLAR

A PREPARING THE GARMENT

1. On the collar section, mark the position for the top stop of the zipper by making a short line of running stitches (Appendix) perpendicular to each front seam line and 1/4 inch below the fold-line marking.

2. Baste along the front seam-line markings of the collar and garment—1/4 inch inside the seam lines for lightweight zippers or 3/8 inch inside the seam lines for heavyweight zippers.

3. On each garment front, make a short line of running stitches—perpendicular to the front seam line—at the pattern marking for the bottom stop of the zipper.

4. Assemble the garment and attach the collar, as shown, following your pattern instructions.

5. Around the neckline, trim the collar seam allowance to 1/4 inch. Then trim the garment seam allowance to 3/8 inch.

6. Press the neck seam allowances toward the collar.

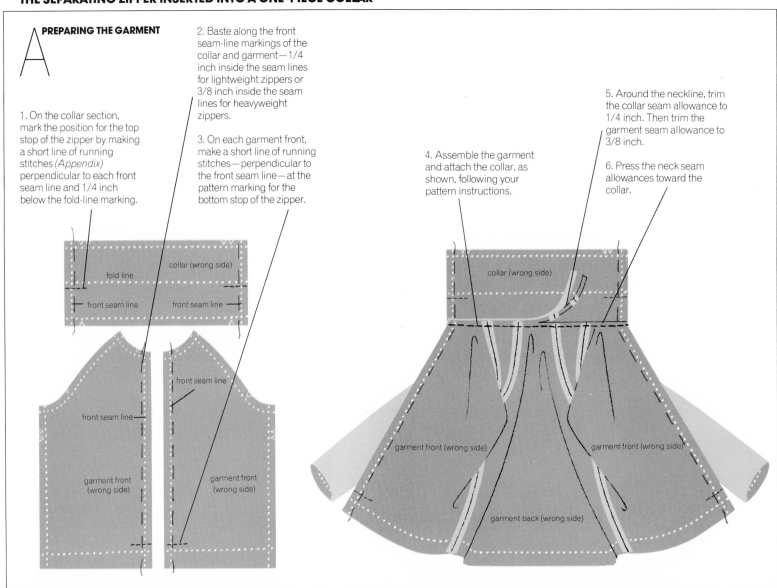

collar (wrong side)

fold line

front seam line   front seam line

front seam line

front seam line

garment front (wrong side)

garment front (wrong side)

collar (wrong side)

garment front (wrong side)

garment front (wrong side)

garment back (wrong side)

ATTACHING THE ZIPPER TO THE GARMENT

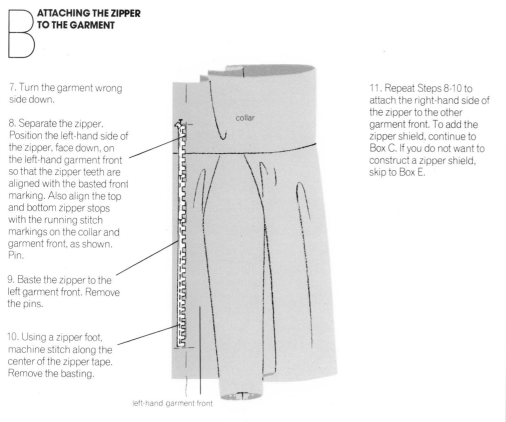

collar

left-hand garment front

7. Turn the garment wrong side down.

8. Separate the zipper. Position the left-hand side of the zipper, face down, on the left-hand garment front so that the zipper teeth are aligned with the basted front marking. Also align the top and bottom zipper stops with the running stitch markings on the collar and garment front, as shown. Pin.

9. Baste the zipper to the left garment front. Remove the pins.

10. Using a zipper foot, machine stitch along the center of the zipper tape. Remove the basting.

11. Repeat Steps 8-10 to attach the right-hand side of the zipper to the other garment front. To add the zipper shield, continue to Box C. If you do not want to construct a zipper shield, skip to Box E.

C PREPARING THE ZIPPER SHIELD

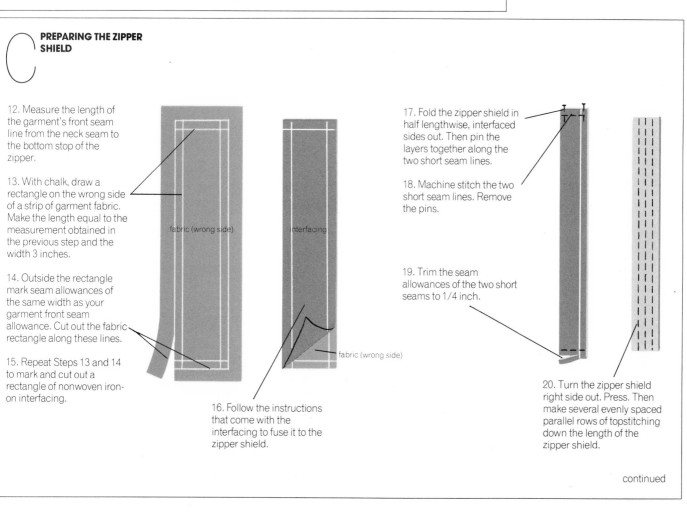

fabric (wrong side)

interfacing

fabric (wrong side)

12. Measure the length of the garment's front seam line from the neck seam to the bottom stop of the zipper.

13. With chalk, draw a rectangle on the wrong side of a strip of garment fabric. Make the length equal to the measurement obtained in the previous step and the width 3 inches.

14. Outside the rectangle mark seam allowances of the same width as your garment front seam allowance. Cut out the fabric rectangle along these lines.

15. Repeat Steps 13 and 14 to mark and cut out a rectangle of nonwoven iron-on interfacing.

16. Follow the instructions that come with the interfacing to fuse it to the zipper shield.

17. Fold the zipper shield in half lengthwise, interfaced sides out. Then pin the layers together along the two short seam lines.

18. Machine stitch the two short seam lines. Remove the pins.

19. Trim the seam allowances of the two short seams to 1/4 inch.

20. Turn the zipper shield right side out. Press. Then make several evenly spaced parallel rows of topstitching down the length of the zipper shield.

continued

D ATTACHING THE ZIPPER SHIELD TO THE GARMENT

21. If you are making a woman's garment, as shown here, place the zipper shield on top of the zipper on the left-hand front edge of the garment. For a man's garment, place the shield on the right-hand front edge.

22. Line up the raw edge of the shield against the front edge of the garment. Align the top of the shield with the neck seam and the bottom of the shield with the bottom zipper stop, as shown. Pin in place.

23. Machine stitch 1/4 inch inside the front edge if you have a 3/8 inch seam allowance. Stitch 1/2 inch inside the front edge if you have a 5/8-inch seam allowance. Remove the pins.

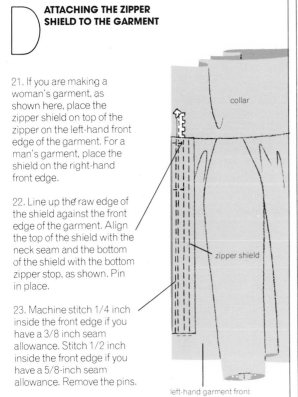

collar

zipper shield

left-hand garment front

E ATTACHING THE FACINGS TO THE GARMENT

24. Finish the outer edges of the front facing sections, following your pattern instructions.

25. With the wrong sides out, pin the front facing sections to the long, unattached edge of the collar along the neck seam line.

26. Baste and remove the pins.

27. Machine stitch and remove the basting.

28. Trim the neck seam allowance of each facing to 3/8 inch. Trim the collar seam allowance along the stitched portion of the seam to 1/4 inch.

29. Press the seam allowances toward the collar.

30. With the wrong sides out, pin the front facings to the garment fronts along the hem seam-line markings, aligning the front seams.

31. Machine stitch along the hem seam lines. Remove the pins.

32. Press the seam allowances as shown.

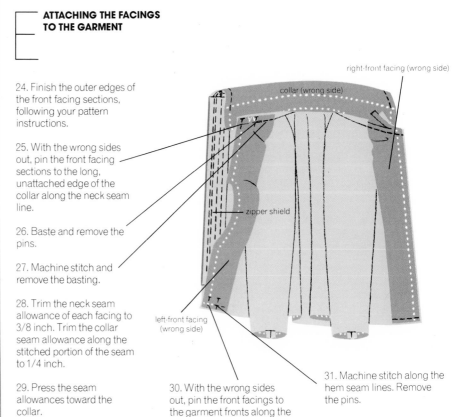

right-front facing (wrong side)

collar (wrong side)

zipper shield

left-front facing (wrong side)

F FINISHING THE ZIPPER

33. Fold the collar along the fold line. Then pin together the layers along each front seam line, matching the neck seams.

34. Pin each front facing to the garment along the front seam lines. Pin down to the folded hem edge.

35. Baste and remove the pins.

36. Using a zipper foot, machine stitch along each front seam line. Sew from the folded top edge of the collar to the folded bottom edge of the hem. Remove the basting.

37. Turn the facings and the underside of the collar to the inside of the garment.

38. Extend the zipper teeth and the visible portion of the zipper tapes away from the front seams. Press along the seams.

39. Using a zipper foot, machine stitch from the finished side of the garment 1/8 inch outside each front seam.

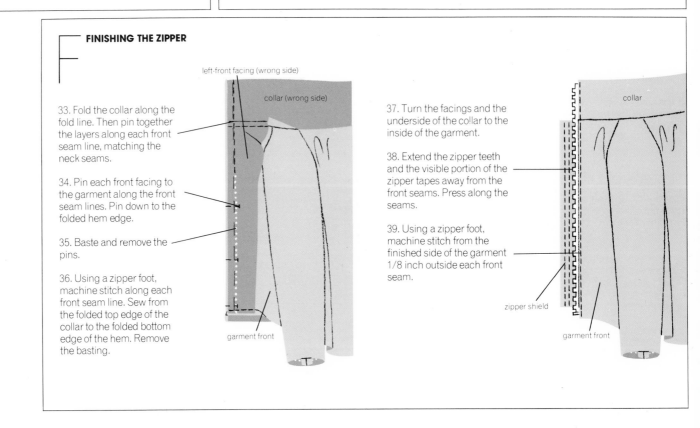

left-front facing (wrong side)

collar (wrong side)

garment front

collar

zipper shield

garment front

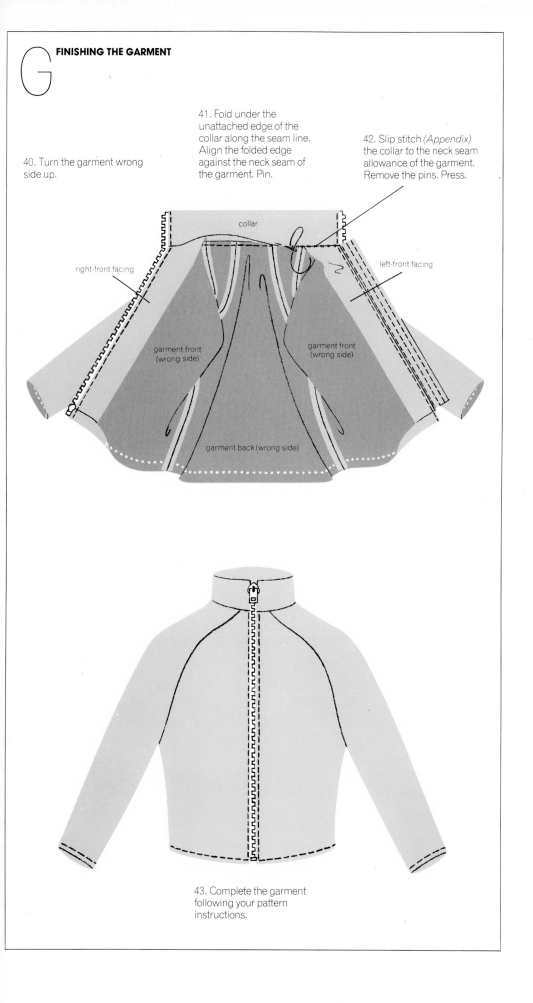

40. Turn the garment wrong side up.

41. Fold under the unattached edge of the collar along the seam line. Align the folded edge against the neck seam of the garment. Pin.

42. Slip stitch (*Appendix*) the collar to the neck seam allowance of the garment. Remove the pins. Press.

collar

right-front facing

left-front facing

garment front (wrong side)

garment front (wrong side)

garment back (wrong side)

43. Complete the garment following your pattern instructions.

A trio of functional pockets

On sportswear, pockets are hard workers—used primarily for convenience rather than for decoration —and each of the styles described on the following pages does its particular job well. For safari and hunting jackets, the accordion pocket shown here has expandable folds at the sides and bottom so that its capacity—for film, cartridges, food snacks and the like—can be increased when necessary.

For sweat shirts and jogging suits, the kangaroo pocket, sewed onto the front to provide a space almost as roomy as the marsupial's pouch, opens at the sides to serve as a convenient muff for cold hands. On ski wear and other apparel for rough sports, the best pocket is the flat, narrow-mouthed slash design, equipped with a zipper to keep loose change, lipstick and car keys from spilling when the wearer does.

A MAKING THE PATTERN
FOR THE POCKET

1. In the center of a piece of paper at least 14 inches square, draw a rectangle that measures 7 inches by 8 inches. Mark one of the shorter lines as the upper edge and the other shorter line as the lower edge.

2. Extend all lines a few inches.

3. To make the pocket wider at the bottom, first measure out 1/2 inch from the lower corners along the extended lower edge line. Make markings on the line.

6. To mark accordion folds on the side and the bottom edges, draw two lines 1 inch apart outside of and parallel to each of the three edges, as shown. Mark the inner parallel lines as the inner fold lines, and the outer parallel lines as the cutting lines.

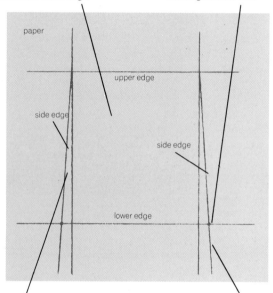

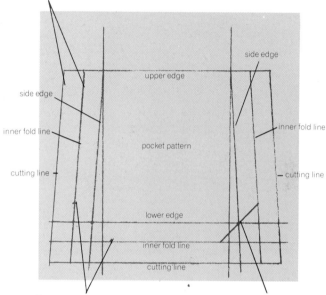

4. Connect the markings to the upper corners of the rectangle. Mark these diagonal lines as the side edges.

5. Extend the side edge lines a few inches downward.

7. To indicate mitered corners, first make markings on each inner fold line 2 inches from the intersections of the fold lines.

8. Next, connect each pair of markings made in the preceding step. Each line should touch its respective lower corner of the pocket.

9. From each end of the lines made in the preceding step, draw perpendicular lines to the cutting lines. Mark these lines as the seam lines for the mitered corners.

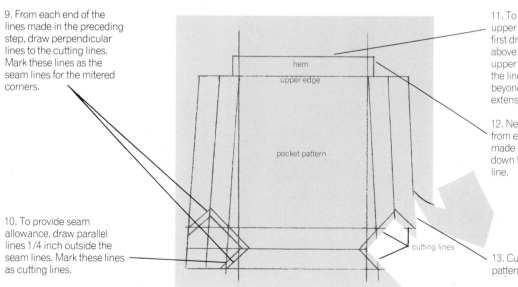

11. To mark the hem for the upper edge of the pocket, first draw a line 3/4 inch above and parallel to the upper edge line. Make sure the line extends 1/4 inch beyond both vertical extension lines.

12. Next draw a vertical line from each end of the line made in the preceding step down to the upper edge line.

10. To provide seam allowance, draw parallel lines 1/4 inch outside the seam lines. Mark these lines as cutting lines.

13. Cut out the pocket pattern along the outline.

continued

B MAKING THE PATTERN FOR THE POCKET FLAP

14. Place a piece of tracing paper over the top of the pocket pattern as shown, and pin.

15. Trace the upper edge line of the pocket on the paper.

16B. If you prefer a flap with a curved, V-shaped lower edge, measure down 2 1/2 inches along the side edge lines. Mark. Then mark the lower point of the V midway between the side edge lines and 3 1/2 inches from the upper edge line.

17B. Draw the V-shaped lower edge by connecting the markings made in Step 16B with curved lines. Extend the lines 1/8 inch beyond the side edge lines.

18. Connect the ends of the upper and lower edge lines.

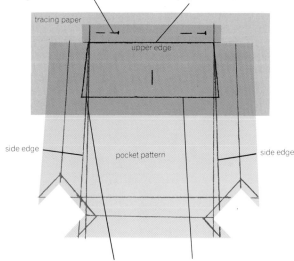

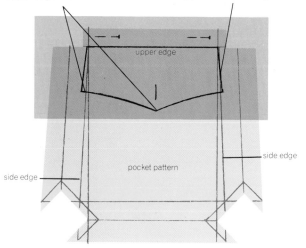

16A. If you want a flap with a straight lower edge—as shown in the photograph on page 62—measure down 2 3/4 inches along the side edge lines. Mark.

17A. Draw the straight lower edge of the flap by connecting the markings made in Step 16A. Extend the line 1/8 inch beyond the side edge lines.

19. To mark a vertical buttonhole line, first measure up from the center of the lower edge a distance equal to the radius of your button, plus 1/4 inch. Then draw a line equal in length to the diameter of the button plus its thickness.

20. Remove the tracing paper from the pocket pattern.

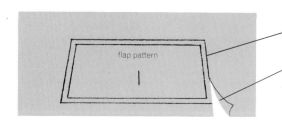

21. Draw cutting lines 1/4 inch outside of and parallel to each line of the flap.

22. Cut out the flap pattern.

C CUTTING OUT AND MARKING THE POCKET AND FLAP PIECES

23. Use the pattern pieces to cut out the number of pockets desired. For each pocket, cut out two flap pieces.

24. Transfer to the wrong side of one of the flap pieces all lines—except the buttonhole line. The marked piece will be the front of the finished flap; the unmarked piece will be the facing. Remove the pattern piece.

25. On the wrong side of the pocket piece, transfer the upper, side, lower, inner fold and seam lines. Remove the pattern piece.

D MAKING THE MITERED CORNERS

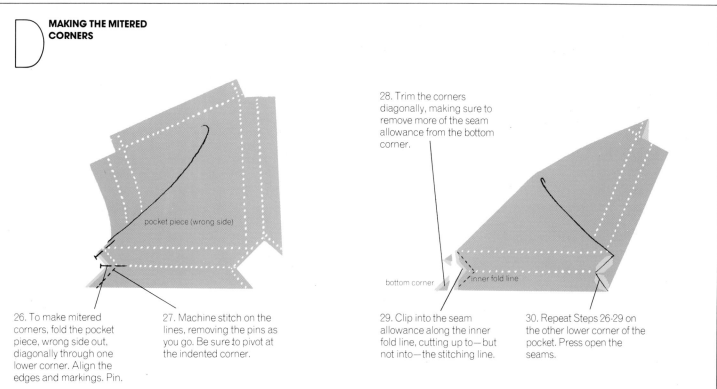

pocket piece (wrong side)

28. Trim the corners diagonally, making sure to remove more of the seam allowance from the bottom corner.

bottom corner

inner fold line

26. To make mitered corners, fold the pocket piece, wrong side out, diagonally through one lower corner. Align the edges and markings. Pin.

27. Machine stitch on the lines, removing the pins as you go. Be sure to pivot at the indented corner.

29. Clip into the seam allowance along the inner fold line, cutting up to—but not into—the stitching line.

30. Repeat Steps 26-29 on the other lower corner of the pocket. Press open the seams.

E PRESSING IN THE ACCORDION FOLDS AND THE HEM

31. Place the pocket piece wrong side up on an ironing board.

32. Fold in along the side and lower edge lines. Press.

33. Fold out along the inner fold lines. Press.

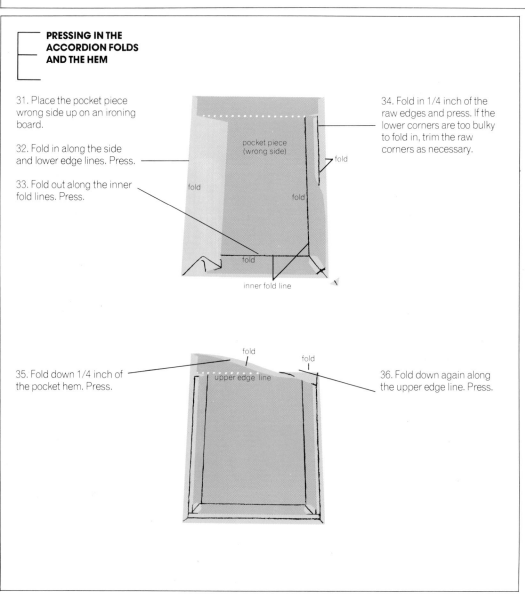

pocket piece (wrong side)

fold

fold

fold

fold

inner fold line

34. Fold in 1/4 inch of the raw edges and press. If the lower corners are too bulky to fold in, trim the raw corners as necessary.

35. Fold down 1/4 inch of the pocket hem. Press.

fold

upper edge line

fold

36. Fold down again along the upper edge line. Press.

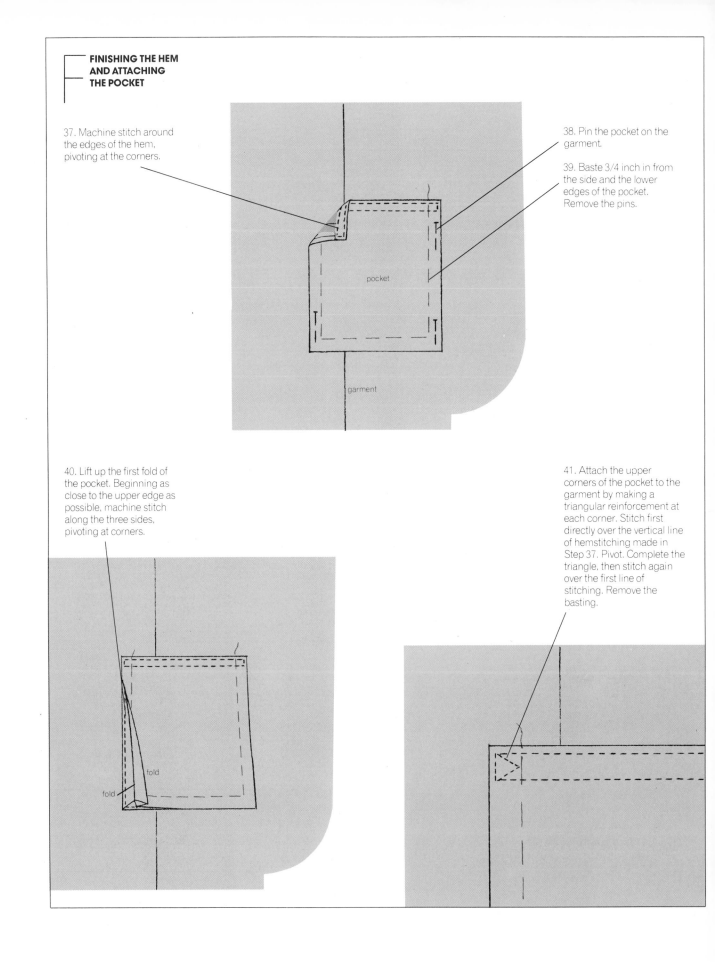

37. Machine stitch around the edges of the hem, pivoting at the corners.

38. Pin the pocket on the garment.

39. Baste 3/4 inch in from the side and the lower edges of the pocket. Remove the pins.

pocket

garment

40. Lift up the first fold of the pocket. Beginning as close to the upper edge as possible, machine stitch along the three sides, pivoting at corners.

41. Attach the upper corners of the pocket to the garment by making a triangular reinforcement at each corner. Stitch first directly over the vertical line of hemstitching made in Step 37. Pivot. Complete the triangle, then stitch again over the first line of stitching. Remove the basting.

fold

fold

42. Place the two flap pieces together, wrong sides out.

43. Ease in the top flap piece 1/8 inch from the side and lower edges of the bottom piece. Pin.

44. Baste along the side and lower edges. Make sure to distribute evenly the ease on the top piece. Remove the pins.

45. Trim the seam allowances of the facing so that they are even with the flap front.

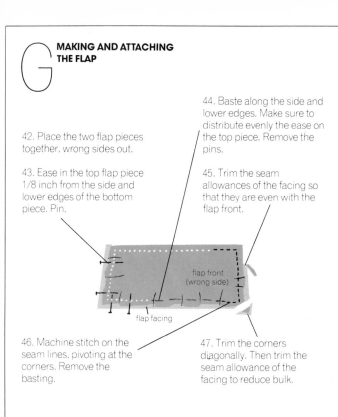

flap front
(wrong side)

flap facing

46. Machine stitch on the seam lines, pivoting at the corners. Remove the basting.

47. Trim the corners diagonally. Then trim the seam allowance of the facing to reduce bulk.

48. Turn the flap inside out through the unstitched upper edge. Pull out the corners with a needle. Press.

49. Machine stitch 1/4 inch inside the side and lower edges, pivoting at the corners.

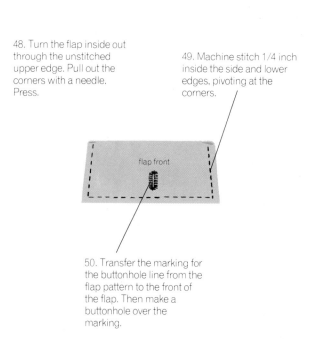

flap front

50. Transfer the marking for the buttonhole line from the flap pattern to the front of the flap. Then make a buttonhole over the marking.

51. Measure up 1/2 inch from the top of the pocket and make chalk marks on the garment.

52. Place the flap—facing side up—on the garment, with the unfinished edge toward the pocket. Align the unfinished edge of the flap with the markings made in Step 51. Pin.

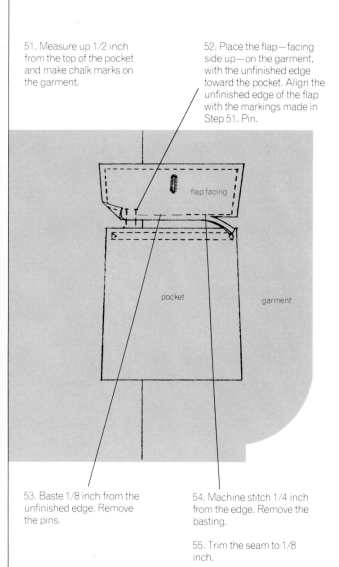

flap facing

pocket

garment

53. Baste 1/8 inch from the unfinished edge. Remove the pins.

54. Machine stitch 1/4 inch from the edge. Remove the basting.

55. Trim the seam to 1/8 inch.

56. Turn the flap down. Press.

57. Machine stitch 1/4 inch from the upper edge of the flap.

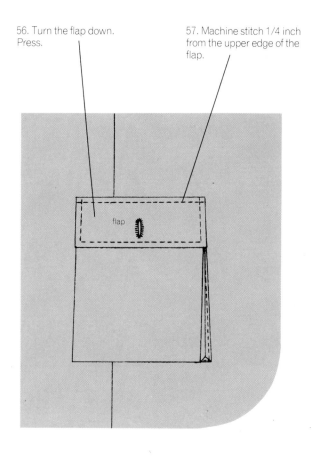

flap

58. Sew the button onto the pocket at the position directly under the buttonhole opening.

59. Finish the garment according to your pattern instructions.

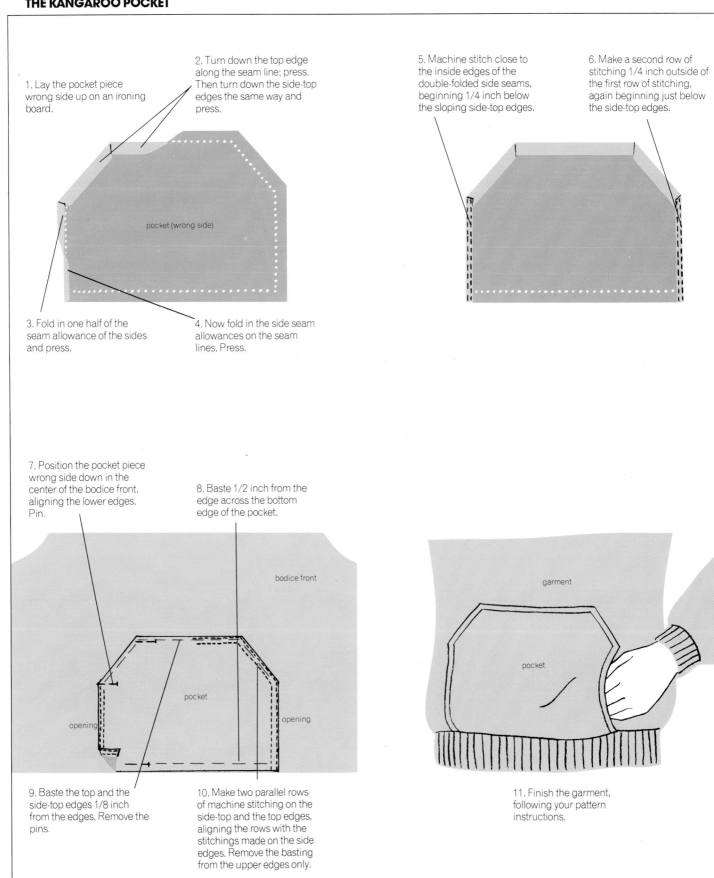

1. Lay the pocket piece wrong side up on an ironing board.

2. Turn down the top edge along the seam line; press. Then turn down the side-top edges the same way and press.

pocket (wrong side)

3. Fold in one half of the seam allowance of the sides and press.

4. Now fold in the side seam allowances on the seam lines. Press.

5. Machine stitch close to the inside edges of the double-folded side seams, beginning 1/4 inch below the sloping side-top edges.

6. Make a second row of stitching 1/4 inch outside of the first row of stitching, again beginning just below the side-top edges.

7. Position the pocket piece wrong side down in the center of the bodice front, aligning the lower edges. Pin.

8. Baste 1/2 inch from the edge across the bottom edge of the pocket.

bodice front

pocket

opening

opening

9. Baste the top and the side-top edges 1/8 inch from the edges. Remove the pins.

10. Make two parallel rows of machine stitching on the side-top and the top edges, aligning the rows with the stitchings made on the side edges. Remove the basting from the upper edges only.

garment

pocket

11. Finish the garment, following your pattern instructions.

THE ZIPPERED POCKET FOR A PADDED GARMENT

A PREPARING THE POCKET OPENING

1. Determine how wide you want the pocket to be. The following instructions are based on a 6-inch-wide pocket.

2. With chalk, mark two dots, 6 inches apart, on the garment section where you want the pocket to be. Position the dot that is closer to the center front higher than the other dot, as shown. The angle between the dots should be about 45°.

3. Draw a line—which will be the center line of the pocket—connecting the dots.

4. To mark the outer ends of the pocket opening, draw chalk lines, about 2 inches long, perpendicular to each end of the center line and bisected by it.

5. Complete the opening outline by drawing lines 3/8 inch from and parallel to the center line.

6. Stay stitch *(Glossary)* just inside the outline, pivoting at corners.

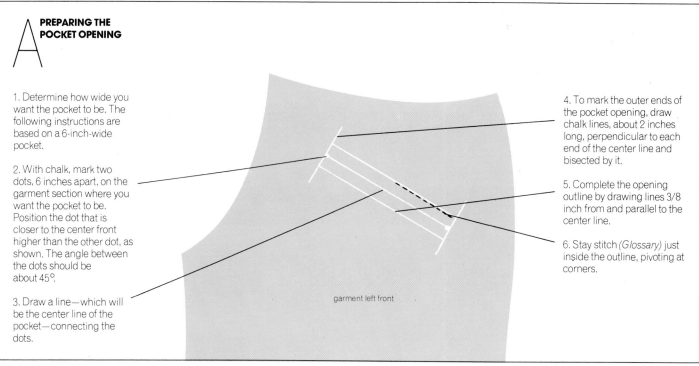

garment left front

B CUTTING OUT AND MAKING THE PIPING STRIPS

7. Cut from garment fabric two piping strips 2 inches longer than the center line and 1 1/2 inches wide.

8. Cut from nonwoven fusible interfacing two strips that are 1 inch less in length and width than the piping strips.

11. Fold the strips in half lengthwise with the interfaced sides together. Press.

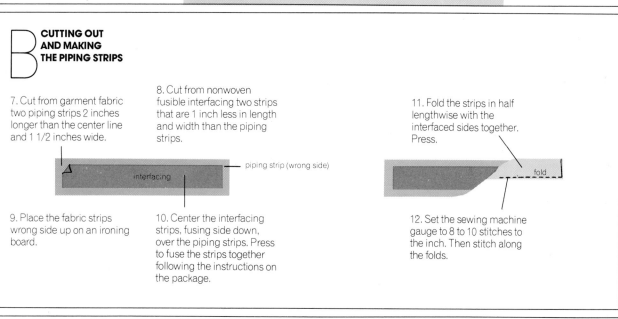

interfacing

piping strip (wrong side)

fold

9. Place the fabric strips wrong side up on an ironing board.

10. Center the interfacing strips, fusing side down, over the piping strips. Press to fuse the strips together following the instructions on the package.

12. Set the sewing machine gauge to 8 to 10 stitches to the inch. Then stitch along the folds.

C ATTACHING THE PIPING STRIPS TO THE ZIPPER

16. Turn over the zipper piece.

13. Lay face side up a closed zipper 2 to 3 inches longer than the center line. Over it, place one piping strip. Align its stitched side with the center of the zipper, and one short end to the tab end. Pin.

14. Baste, making sure the strip does not shift its position on the zipper. Remove the pins.

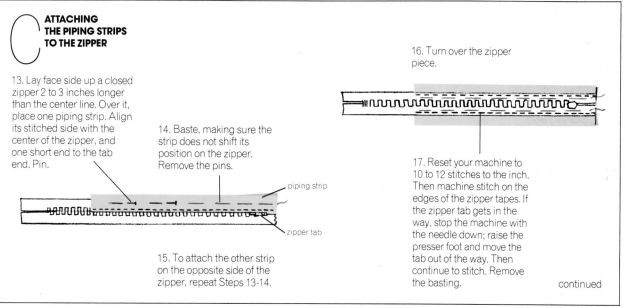

piping strip

zipper tab

17. Reset your machine to 10 to 12 stitches to the inch. Then machine stitch on the edges of the zipper tapes. If the zipper tab gets in the way, stop the machine with the needle down; raise the presser foot and move the tab out of the way. Then continue to stitch. Remove the basting.

15. To attach the other strip on the opposite side of the zipper, repeat Steps 13-14.

continued

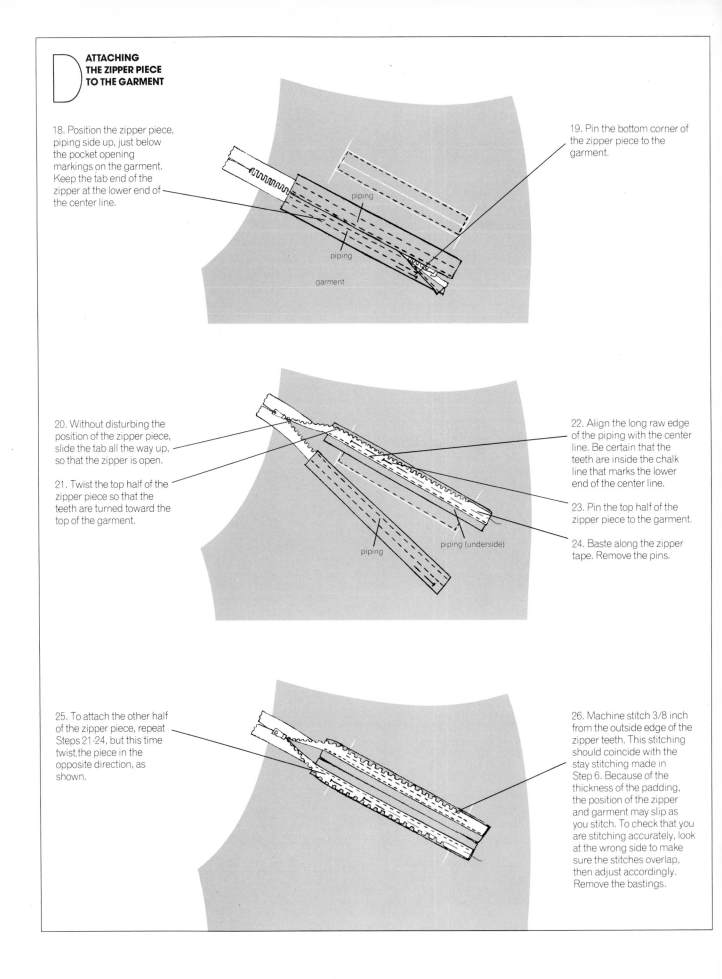

18. Position the zipper piece, piping side up, just below the pocket opening markings on the garment. Keep the tab end of the zipper at the lower end of the center line.

19. Pin the bottom corner of the zipper piece to the garment.

piping

piping

garment

20. Without disturbing the position of the zipper piece, slide the tab all the way up, so that the zipper is open.

21. Twist the top half of the zipper piece so that the teeth are turned toward the top of the garment.

22. Align the long raw edge of the piping with the center line. Be certain that the teeth are inside the chalk line that marks the lower end of the center line.

23. Pin the top half of the zipper piece to the garment.

24. Baste along the zipper tape. Remove the pins.

piping

piping (underside)

25. To attach the other half of the zipper piece, repeat Steps 21-24, but this time twist the piece in the opposite direction, as shown.

26. Machine stitch 3/8 inch from the outside edge of the zipper teeth. This stitching should coincide with the stay stitching made in Step 6. Because of the thickness of the padding, the position of the zipper and garment may slip as you stitch. To check that you are stitching accurately, look at the wrong side to make sure the stitches overlap, then adjust accordingly. Remove the bastings.

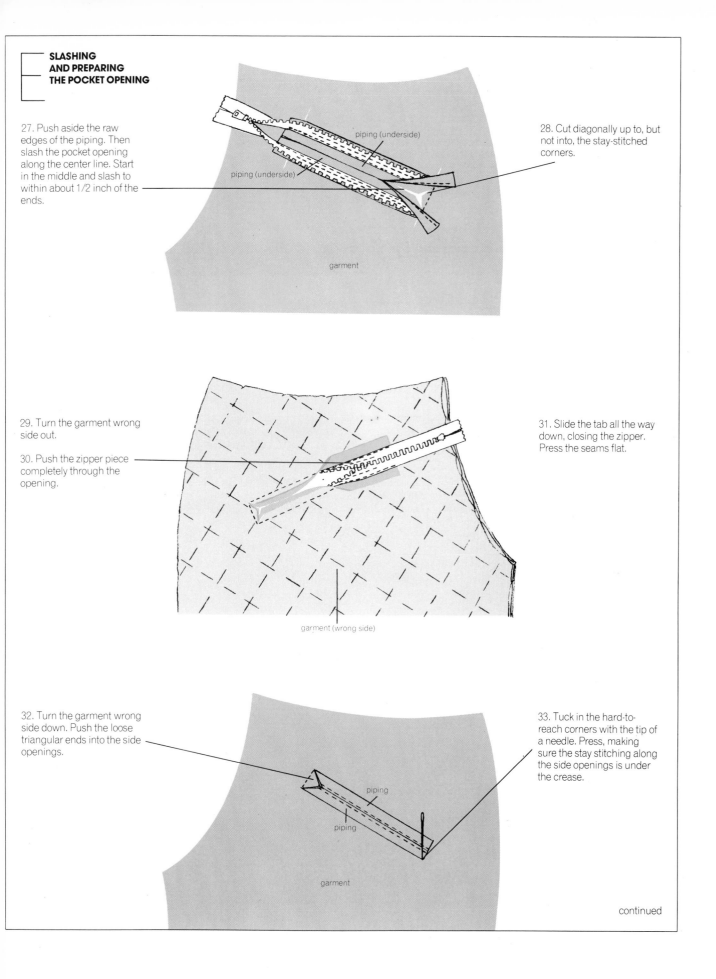

27. Push aside the raw edges of the piping. Then slash the pocket opening along the center line. Start in the middle and slash to within about 1/2 inch of the ends.

piping (underside)

piping (underside)

garment

28. Cut diagonally up to, but not into, the stay-stitched corners.

29. Turn the garment wrong side out.

30. Push the zipper piece completely through the opening.

garment (wrong side)

31. Slide the tab all the way down, closing the zipper. Press the seams flat.

32. Turn the garment wrong side down. Push the loose triangular ends into the side openings.

piping

piping

garment

33. Tuck in the hard-to-reach corners with the tip of a needle. Press, making sure the stay stitching along the side openings is under the crease.

continued

34. Cut from a double layer of pocket fabric two rectangles that measure 10 inches in length and 2 inches more than the center line in width.

35. To shape the rectangles, first determine the angle of the slant of the pocket opening. Then mark the angle on one long edge. Connect the mark to the top of the rectangle on the opposite side.

36. Cut through both thicknesses along the line.

37. On the wrong side of the garment, position one of the pocket pieces, wrong side up, over the pocket openings. The slanted side of the pocket piece should be aligned with the bottom edge of the piping below the pocket opening. The longest edge should be toward the top of the garment. Pin.

38. Pin the pocket piece above the opening as shown, to prevent the piece from flopping down.

39. Baste along the slanted edge. Remove the pins, except the one placed in Step 38.

40. Turn the garment wrong side down.

41. Reset the machine to 8 to 10 stitches to the inch. Then stitch along the bottom edge, just outside the piping.

42. Pull the thread ends through to the other side and tie. Remove the basting.

43. Unpin the pocket piece and turn it down. Press.

44. Position the remaining pocket piece wrong side up on the pocket opening, so the slanted side is aligned to the top of the pocket opening. The vertical side edges of both pocket pieces should also be aligned.

45. Pin and baste along the top edge. Remove the pins.

46. Trim the bottom pocket piece so that it is the same length as the top piece.

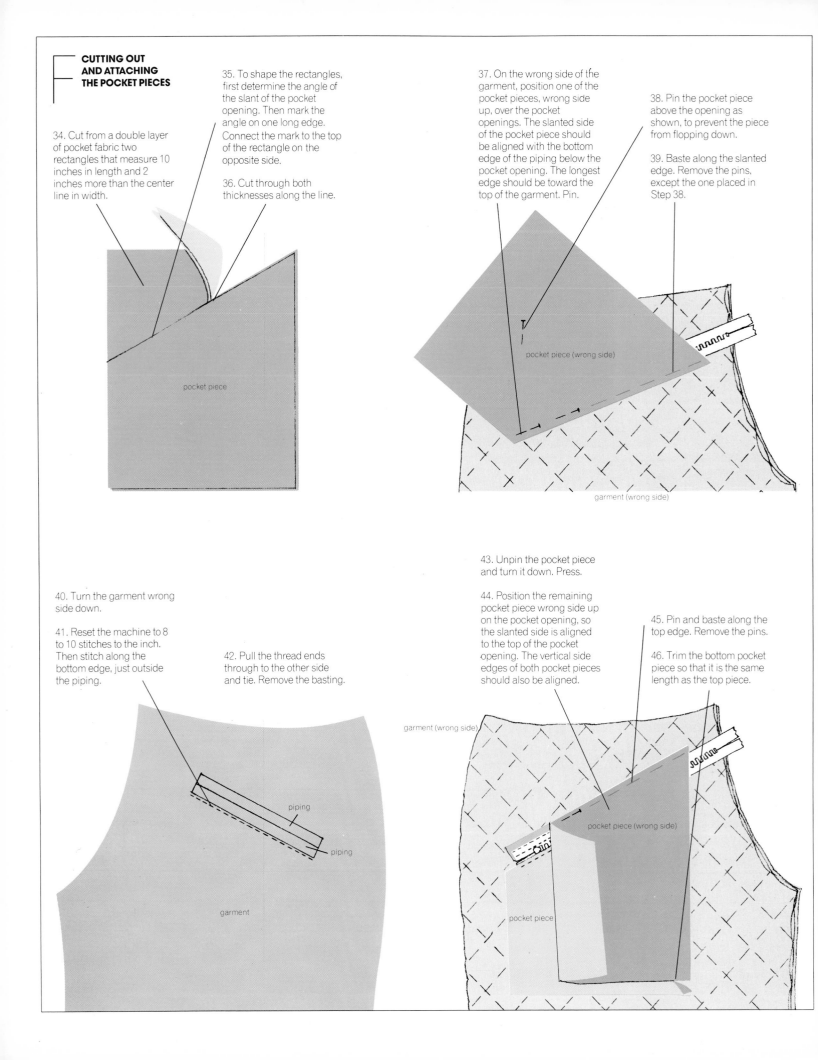

pocket piece

pocket piece (wrong side)

garment (wrong side)

piping

piping

garment

garment (wrong side)

pocket piece (wrong side)

pocket piece

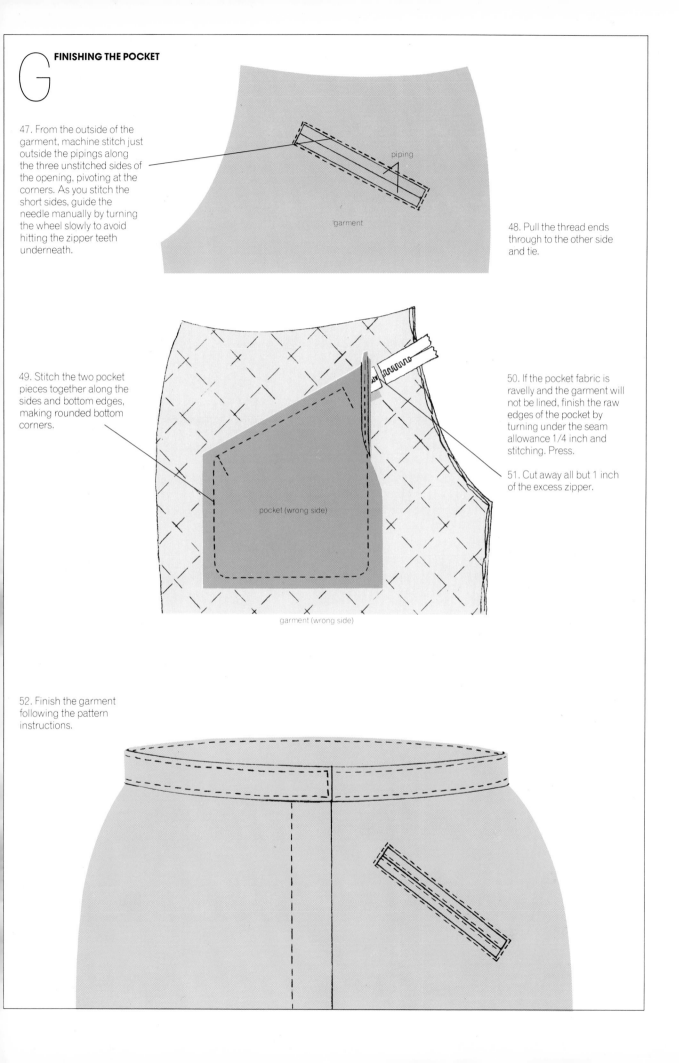

G FINISHING THE POCKET

47. From the outside of the garment, machine stitch just outside the pipings along the three unstitched sides of the opening, pivoting at the corners. As you stitch the short sides, guide the needle manually by turning the wheel slowly to avoid hitting the zipper teeth underneath.

piping

garment

48. Pull the thread ends through to the other side and tie.

49. Stitch the two pocket pieces together along the sides and bottom edges, making rounded bottom corners.

pocket (wrong side)

garment (wrong side)

50. If the pocket fabric is ravelly and the garment will not be lined, finish the raw edges of the pocket by turning under the seam allowance 1/4 inch and stitching. Press.

51. Cut away all but 1 inch of the excess zipper.

52. Finish the garment following the pattern instructions.

Snug and supple waistlines

For comfort as well as good looks, the waist on an outdoor jacket has to fit neatly—all the time. That means it not only needs to be snug enough to hug the waistline and shut out the wind, but it also must be flexible enough to move easily with the wearer's body motions. Getting such a fit can be done in any of the ways shown on the following pages; the particular method chosen will depend on the style of the jacket.

On a waist-length design like the one shown here, the hem itself can serve as a tunnel for a band of elastic that will cinch the waistline firmly. For a more adjustable fit, the hem may hold a side-tied drawstring.

On a hip-length style, elastic can be used inside the jacket as an insert across the back at the waistline, or outside the garment as part of a belt made from the same fabric as the jacket. And if drawstrings are desired they can be fitted into an invisible waistline casing to tie in the front, over the zipper.

THE ELASTICIZED WAIST

A MAKING THE CASING TUNNEL

1. Construct the jacket to the point at which you would insert the zipper. Then try on the jacket and mark the desired finished length —which will also be the position for the casing —with a row of pins or chalk marks.

2. To mark the fold line for the casing, connect the markings with a line of basting stitches. Remove any pins.

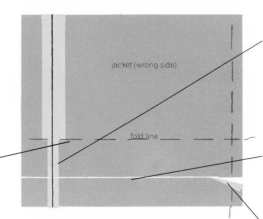

jacket (wrong side)

fold line

3. With the jacket wrong side out, trim to 1/4 inch the vertical seam allowances of any seams below the basted fold line.

4. To determine the depth of the casing, add 1/2 inch to the width of the elastic you plan to use.

5. Measure down from the basting the distance determined in the previous step, and draw a chalk line around the edge.

6. Trim off the jacket edge along the chalk line.

7. Fold up the bottom edge toward the wrong side of the jacket, along the bastings. Then baste along the fold.

8. Pin the top folded edge to the jacket at 1-inch intervals.

9. Baste the top edge to the jacket and remove the pins.

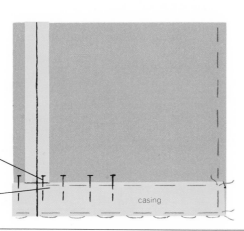

casing

10. To complete the casing, machine stitch 1/8 inch from both folded edges. Remove the bastings.

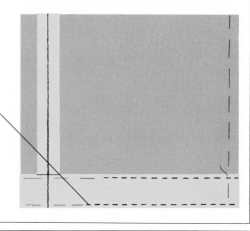

B INSERTING THE ELASTIC

12. Pin the elastic to the casing 1 to 1 1/2 inches from the center-front seam line. Catch the elastic 1/2 inch from its end.

13. Make a vertical row of machine stitches across the casing, and remove the pin.

14. Try on the jacket, and stretch the elastic until it is secure and comfortable.

11. Without cutting the elastic to its final length, attach a small safety pin to one end. Then insert the pinned end of the elastic into one end of the casing, and work it through. Remove the pin.

15. Pin the end of the elastic to the casing opening.

16. Make a row of machine stitches across the casing at a distance from its end equal to that used on the first side. Remove the pin.

17. Cut off the excess elastic 1/2 inch from the stitches.

18. Finish the jacket according to your pattern instructions.

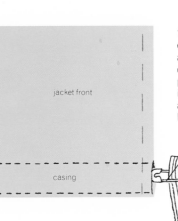

jacket front

casing

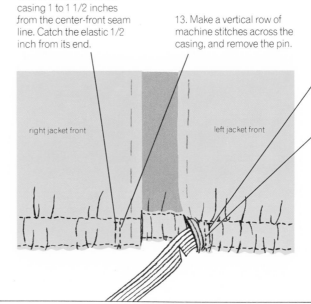

right jacket front

left jacket front

MAKING THE CASING TUNNEL

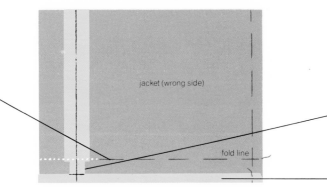

jacket (wrong side)

fold line

1. Construct the jacket to the point at which you would insert the zipper. Then turn the jacket wrong side out —and make a line of basting stitches along the pattern markings for the casing fold line. If the pattern does not have a fold line, follow the instructions for the elasticized waist *(page 75, Steps 1-6).*

2. With the jacket wrong side out, trim to 1/4 inch the seam allowances of any vertical seams below the bastings.

3. Fold the bottom edge 1/4 inch. Press.

5. Turn the jacket wrong side down. To provide an opening for the drawstring, mark the position for eyelets between the bastings and the pins. Make a mark 1 inch from each side of each side seam.

6. Apply four large eyelets through the single outer jacket layer at the marks made in Step 5.

7. Complete the casing tunnel, following the instructions for the elasticized waist *(page 75, Steps 7-10).*

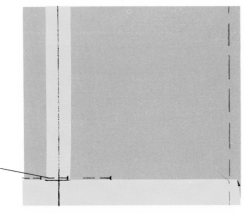

jacket

eyelet

fold line

4. At the side seams, fold up the edge along the bastings, and place three or four pins in the jacket body just outside the folded edge. Do not catch the fold.

MAKING THE DRAWSTRING

8A. If you are making the drawstring from garment fabric, cut out a strip of fabric on the grain—that is, parallel to either the lengthwise or the selvage edge. The strip should be twice the width of the casing between the two parallel rows of stitching, plus 1/4 inch. The strip should be at least two times your waist measurement.

8B. If you are using a purchased drawstring, cut it so that it is the width of the casing and at least twice your waist measurement. Cut the drawstring in half. Cut one of the pieces in half again. Skip to Step 16.

9. By the same token, if the drawstring is to be made of garment fabric, cut the fabric in half. Then cut one of the pieces in half again.

10. On the long fabric piece, fold over 1/4 inch at each short end toward the wrong side. Press.

11. Fold over the two lengthwise edges 1/4 inch toward the wrong side. Pin at 1-inch intervals. Baste and remove the pins.

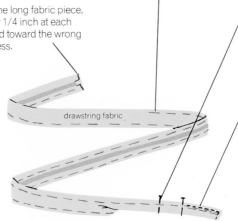

drawstring fabric

12. Fold the strip in half lengthwise with the folded edges inside. Pin the edges together at 1-inch intervals along the length of the strip. Baste and remove the pins.

13. Starting at the fold made in Step 10, machine stitch across one short end. Pivot *(Glossary)* and stitch as close to the long folded edges as possible. Then pivot and stitch across the other short end.

14. On the short fabric pieces, fold over 1/4 inch at one short end and press.

15. To finish the short drawstring sections, repeat Steps 11-13, stitching only along the folded edges.

C INSERTING THE DRAWSTRING

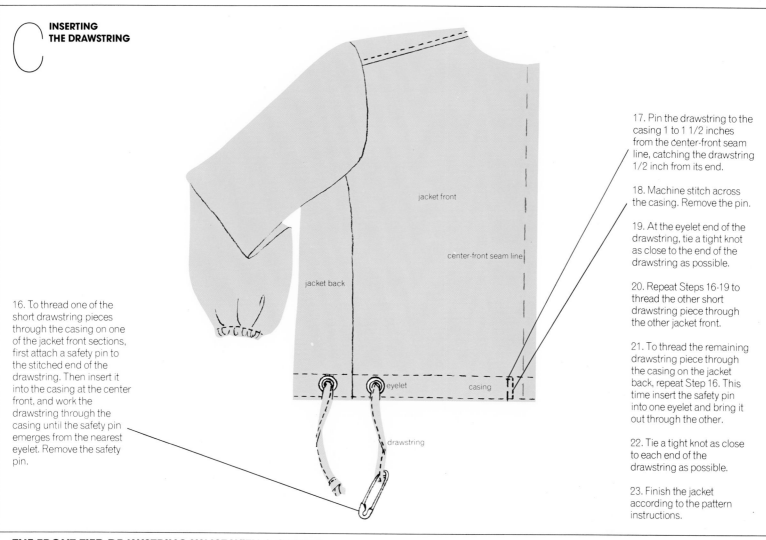

16. To thread one of the short drawstring pieces through the casing on one of the jacket front sections, first attach a safety pin to the stitched end of the drawstring. Then insert it into the casing at the center front, and work the drawstring through the casing until the safety pin emerges from the nearest eyelet. Remove the safety pin.

17. Pin the drawstring to the casing 1 to 1 1/2 inches from the center-front seam line, catching the drawstring 1/2 inch from its end.

18. Machine stitch across the casing. Remove the pin.

19. At the eyelet end of the drawstring, tie a tight knot as close to the end of the drawstring as possible.

20. Repeat Steps 16-19 to thread the other short drawstring piece through the other jacket front.

21. To thread the remaining drawstring piece through the casing on the jacket back, repeat Step 16. This time insert the safety pin into one eyelet and bring it out through the other.

22. Tie a tight knot as close to each end of the drawstring as possible.

23. Finish the jacket according to the pattern instructions.

THE FRONT-TIED DRAWSTRING WAIST WITH A CASING

A MAKING THE CASING

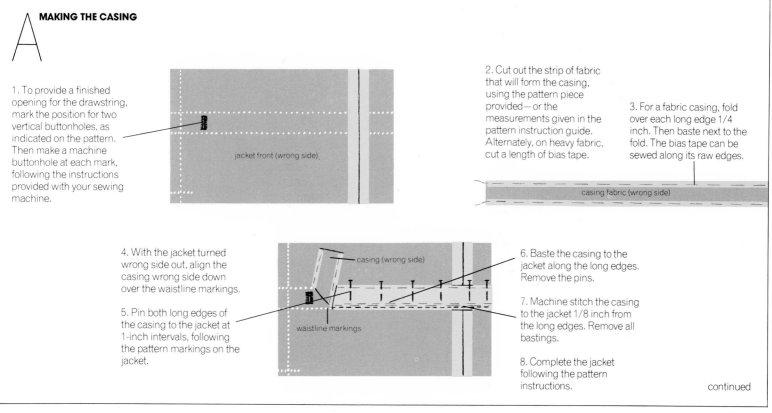

1. To provide a finished opening for the drawstring, mark the position for two vertical buttonholes, as indicated on the pattern. Then make a machine buttonhole at each mark, following the instructions provided with your sewing machine.

2. Cut out the strip of fabric that will form the casing, using the pattern piece provided—or the measurements given in the pattern instruction guide. Alternately, on heavy fabric, cut a length of bias tape.

3. For a fabric casing, fold over each long edge 1/4 inch. Then baste next to the fold. The bias tape can be sewed along its raw edges.

4. With the jacket turned wrong side out, align the casing wrong side down over the waistline markings.

5. Pin both long edges of the casing to the jacket at 1-inch intervals, following the pattern markings on the jacket.

6. Baste the casing to the jacket along the long edges. Remove the pins.

7. Machine stitch the casing to the jacket 1/8 inch from the long edges. Remove all bastings.

8. Complete the jacket following the pattern instructions.

continued

9. Make a drawstring following the instructions for the side-tied drawstring waist *(page 76, Steps 8-13)*, but make the drawstring only 1 1/2 times your waist measurement, and do not cut it.

10. Attach a safety pin to one end of the drawstring, and insert the pin into one buttonhole. Then work the pin through the casing until the drawstring emerges from the other buttonhole. Remove the safety pin.

11. Tie a tight knot as close to each end of the drawstring as possible.

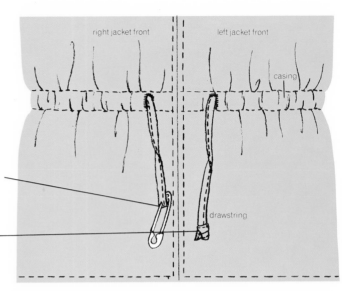

right jacket front

left jacket front

casing

drawstring

THE PARTIALLY TUNNELED ELASTICIZED BACK

jacket back (wrong side)

casing

elastic

1. Make a casing and attach it to the unstitched jacket back section, following the instructions for the front-tied drawstring waist with a casing *(page 77, Steps 2-7)*.

2. Cut a length of elastic that is one third your waistline measurement, plus 1 inch.

3. Attach a safety pin to one end of the elastic. Then insert the pin into one end of the casing. Work the elastic through to the other end.

4. Pin both ends of the elastic to the casing at the side seam lines. Then remove the safety pin.

5. Make a vertical row of machine stitches across the ends of the casing within the seam allowance, and remove the pins.

6. Finish the jacket according to your pattern instructions.

THE ADJUSTABLE BELT

A MAKING THE BELT PATTERNS

1. To make the belt, you will need the following: four snaps; a set of D rings and two rectangular or oval rings of the same size; garment fabric; heavyweight, nonwoven interfacing; and a strip of firm, nonroll elastic that is as wide as the rings.

2. Try on the jacket and measure the waistline, placing the tape loosely around your waist.

3. Increase the waistline measurement by one half. Then divide the total by three.

4. To make patterns for one half of the front and for the back, first draw a rectangle. Use the figure determined in Step 3 for the length, and the width of the elastic plus 1/8 inch for the width. Then add a 1/4-inch seam allowance around all sides of the pattern.

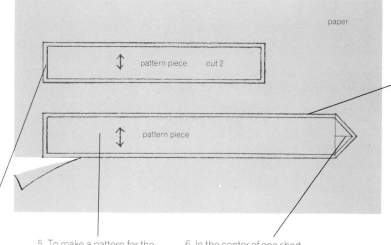

5. To make a pattern for the other half of the front —which will include the overlap—draw a second rectangle that is the same width as the one drawn in Step 4, but 6 inches longer.

6. In the center of one short side of the longer rectangle, draw a 1-inch line at a right angle to the short side. Then connect with two diagonal lines the end of the line drawn in the previous step to the sides of the rectangle.

7. Add a 1/4-inch seam allowance around all sides of the pattern.

8. If the fabric has no definite weave, place grain-line arrows across the pattern pieces as shown. If there is a weave to the fabric, place the grain-line arrows parallel to the long edges.

9. Mark the short rectangle to be cut twice.

10. Cut out the rectangles.

B CUTTING OUT THE BELT SECTIONS

11. Fold the fabric with the wrong sides out as shown. Place on the folded fabric the pattern piece that is marked to be cut twice. Then pin the pattern to both fabric layers at the corners and in the center.

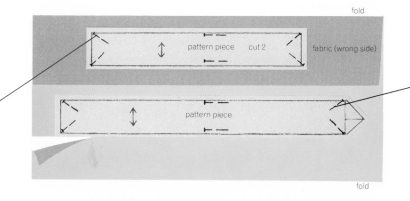

12. Pin the other pattern piece to a single fabric thickness.

13. Cut out the fabric pieces.

14. Remove the pattern pieces, and indicate with chalk the wrong sides of each fabric piece.

15. On the interfacing, draw one rectangle that is the length determined in Step 3 — the length of the short pattern piece without the seam allowances—and one half the width, minus 1/16 inch. Then indicate a 1/4-inch seam allowance at each short end.

16. Draw another rectangle that is the length determined in Step 5 and half the width, minus 1/16 inch.

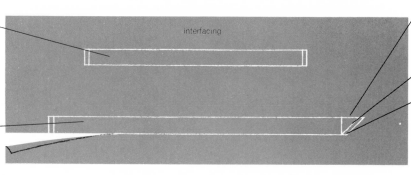

17. Extend one long side of the rectangle 1 inch.

18. Draw a diagonal line to connect the end of the extended line to the bottom edge of the rectangle.

19. Add a 1/4-inch seam allowance to each short end.

20. Cut out the interfacing pieces.

continued

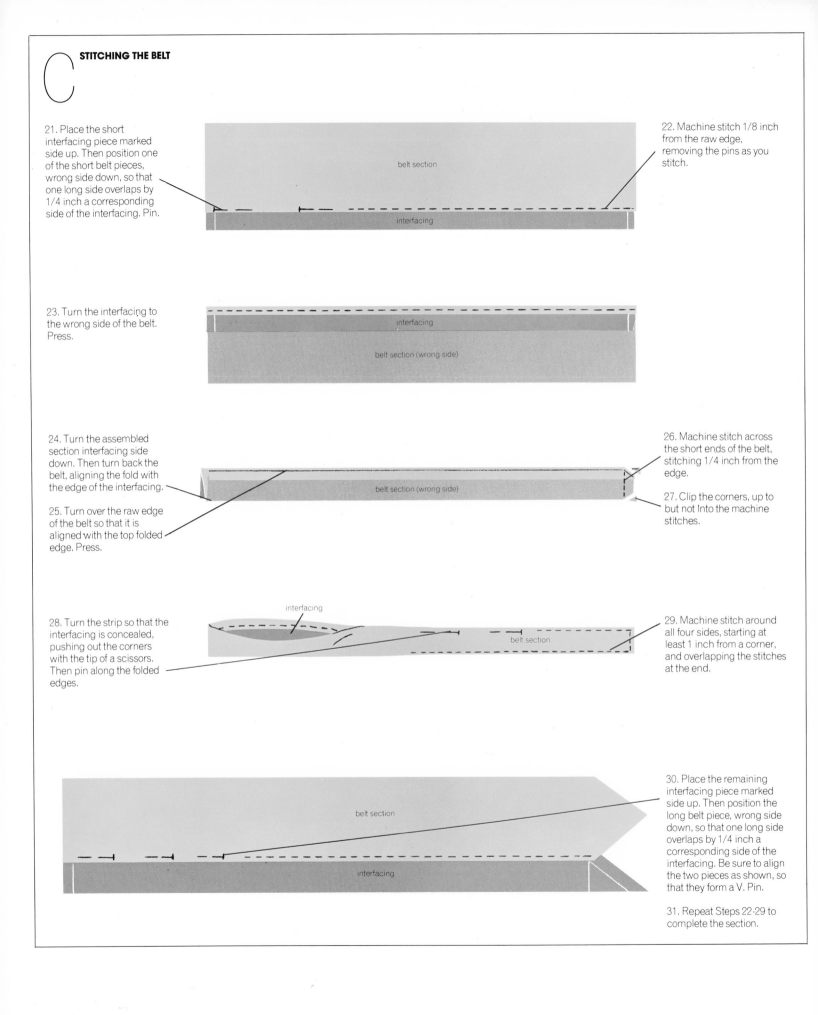

21. Place the short interfacing piece marked side up. Then position one of the short belt pieces, wrong side down, so that one long side overlaps by 1/4 inch a corresponding side of the interfacing. Pin.

belt section

interfacing

22. Machine stitch 1/8 inch from the raw edge, removing the pins as you stitch.

23. Turn the interfacing to the wrong side of the belt. Press.

interfacing

belt section (wrong side)

24. Turn the assembled section interfacing side down. Then turn back the belt, aligning the fold with the edge of the interfacing.

25. Turn over the raw edge of the belt so that it is aligned with the top folded edge. Press.

belt section (wrong side)

26. Machine stitch across the short ends of the belt, stitching 1/4 inch from the edge.

27. Clip the corners, up to but not into the machine stitches.

28. Turn the strip so that the interfacing is concealed, pushing out the corners with the tip of a scissors. Then pin along the folded edges.

interfacing

belt section

29. Machine stitch around all four sides, starting at least 1 inch from a corner, and overlapping the stitches at the end.

belt section

interfacing

30. Place the remaining interfacing piece marked side up. Then position the long belt piece, wrong side down, so that one long side overlaps by 1/4 inch a corresponding side of the interfacing. Be sure to align the two pieces as shown, so that they form a V. Pin.

31. Repeat Steps 22-29 to complete the section.

STITCHING THE BELT BACK

32. Fold the remaining belt piece, which will become a casing for the elastic, wrong side out, and pin together the raw edges. Then machine stitch 1/4 inch from the edges, removing the pins as you go.

33. Center the seam on the casing and press open the seam allowance.

34. Attach a safety pin to one end of the casing, and insert it into the same end. Then turn the casing by working the pin through to the other end. Remove the safety pin.

belt casing (wrong side)

35. Press the seam flat, making sure that it is still centered on the casing.

36. Cut a piece of elastic one half the length of the casing.

37. Attach a safety pin to one end of the elastic, and insert it into the casing. Work the elastic through, making sure to pin the free end of the elastic to the end of the casing. Then pin the other end of the elastic to the casing, and remove the safety pin.

belt casing

38. Machine stitch 1/4 inch from both edges, and remove the pins.

FINISHING THE BELT

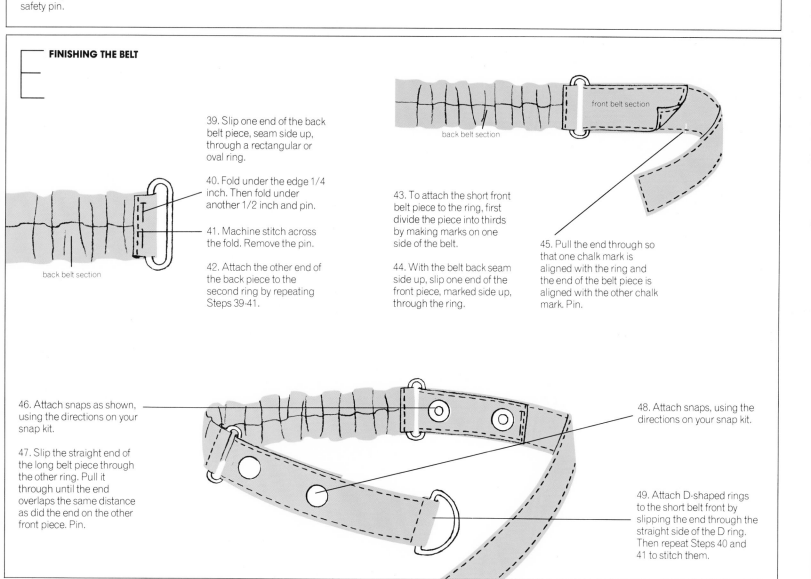

39. Slip one end of the back belt piece, seam side up, through a rectangular or oval ring.

40. Fold under the edge 1/4 inch. Then fold under another 1/2 inch and pin.

41. Machine stitch across the fold. Remove the pin.

42. Attach the other end of the back piece to the second ring by repeating Steps 39-41.

back belt section

43. To attach the short front belt piece to the ring, first divide the piece into thirds by making marks on one side of the belt.

44. With the belt back seam side up, slip one end of the front piece, marked side up, through the ring.

front belt section

back belt section

45. Pull the end through so that one chalk mark is aligned with the ring and the end of the belt piece is aligned with the other chalk mark. Pin.

46. Attach snaps as shown, using the directions on your snap kit.

47. Slip the straight end of the long belt piece through the other ring. Pull it through until the end overlaps the same distance as did the end on the other front piece. Pin.

48. Attach snaps, using the directions on your snap kit.

49. Attach D-shaped rings to the short belt front by slipping the end through the straight side of the D ring. Then repeat Steps 40 and 41 to stitch them.

4
THE SMASHING
LOOK OF
ACTION WEAR

Along with many another young sportswoman, professional golfer Laura Baugh, shown on the preceding pages unwinding after a long drive, has strong notions about the look and the role of clothing in her active life. "How you look affects your game. If I shoot a 75 one day and need a 70 the next, I get a lift by wearing a pretty outfit."

Laura's interest in fashion—"second only to playing golf"—has given her another

WHEN PRETTY IS AS PRETTY DOES

promising career. She is designing golf clothes that incorporate her ideas of how a woman should put together her wardrobe for the outdoors. "The colors are bright," she says, "because women who are active have tans and look well in bright colors. And lines are trim, because sportswomen are usually trim, no matter what their age."

Laura's simple yet striking styles include short culottes, short shorts and skirts cut on the bias—"they flatter more figures." And they are easy to make. So are her pantsuits, which come in pink and blue plaids.

Besides being attractive and simple, her clothes are designed to be functional. For example, everything is made of machine-washable double knit except golf shirts, which are cotton "because it breathes." But no cloth is used if it doesn't look right. "Function doesn't have to mean drab," she says. "It's taken for granted that no skirt will flare up, or sleeve restrict a stroke."

This kind of sound guidance for the home seamstress—with stress on good looks—is heartily seconded by other top sportswear creators. "First be pretty. Be current. Most of all be yourself," says Monika Tilley, a former ski instructor and competitive swimmer turned designer. While aware of the need to be practical, she cautions: "When the whole emphasis is on function, you can end up with ticky-tacky pockets everywhere."

Monika's carefully structured ski outfits include such flattering ideas as topping a one-piece, one-color stretch suit with a quilted vest that combines three shades of a contrasting color. For swim suits, by choosing curving vertical stripes in body-hugging maillots, she manages to make one style look attractive on virtually any woman.

Alex Schuster, president of Head Sportswear, is another style setter whose techniques for melding practicality with flair set standards for sports clothes. And though he professes a strong preference for the practical ("Between function and fashion there is no choice," he says. "Function always comes first."), his ski and tennis wear is as stylish as it is functional.

Schuster often makes a new sport fashion spring from the solution to a functional problem. For example, to prevent a fallen skier from sliding dangerously in a suit of slippery synthetics, he attaches nonskid panels down the pants legs where they can grip the snow. But then he continues the strips up the sides of the parka where they are only style elements.

Monika Tilley also has some imaginative thoughts on colors; she chooses them for the environment in which they will be worn. Her ski and swim wear alike come in bright shades. "Skiing and swimming both take place against a basically no-color background," says Monika. "Whatever color you use should stand out." With the same reasoning, Laura Baugh dislikes green clothes in golf's green world.

The home seamstress, too, should think of choosing the colors of her creations with awareness of the place in the sun where they will be worn. But first she must work out her basic design. Perhaps the most practical way is to adapt standard clothing patterns into patterns for sports garments, changing them just enough to meet the requirements of the game.

The projects on the following pages all evolve that way. The warm-up suits start with patterns for slacks and a jacket. The tennis dress is adapted from a shirt, the reversible shirts from a jacket pattern and the ski overalls from workman's overalls. By making such simple conversions the home seamstress, like the top professional designers, can create clothing that not only looks good, but works well in its sport.

A half century of swinging tennis styles

Women's tennis apparel—like the players who wear it—has come a long way since the turn of the century when corseted ladies in ankle-length skirts delicately lobbed while remaining almost stationary. The woman who first triggered the revolution in both clothes and style of play was Suzanne Lenglen, a free-spirited Frenchwoman who dominated the game by winning a series of international championships after World War I. Unrestricted by corsets or petticoats, she danced joyfully across the court in daring sleeveless, calf-length frocks. Long hose were her only concession to convention.

For the next 25 years, except for the disappearance of stockings, tennis styles remained relatively stable. Then, in 1949, the tennis world was again scandalized when British player-turned-designer Teddy Tinling created highly visible lace panties for Gertrude "Gorgeous Gussie" Moran to wear at Wimbledon. Tinling has continued to produce innovative court styles that have often won as much attention as the players who wore them. His assault on the all-white uniform has been aided by television's recent love affair with the game. When such photogenic stars as Chris Evert wore color for the camera, they inspired weekend players everywhere to break another tradition and add color to their tennis wardrobes.

Suzanne Lenglen's short costume liberated court fashion.

Sensibly visored Helen Wills Moody typified the '30s.

Gussie Moran's lace pants were a '49 *cause célèbre*.

Chris Evert's colorful frocks made a '70s break with white.

Brazilian Maria Bueno's A-line dress was a '60s favorite.

A slick and colorful switch for warm-ups

Today's vividly striped and stream-lined warm-up suits bear almost no visible resemblance to their direct ancestor, the baggy gray sweat suit. Made in bright-hued double knits, warm-up suits now provide a dash of style and color for bike riders, joggers, dabblers at tennis and a host of other weekend sportsmen.

Both the suits shown here are derived from familiar patterns—a shirt-style jacket and straight-legged trousers—restyled into a warm-up jacket and tapered pants. Before sewing begins, the patterns are modified, as explained on the following pages.

The jacket, for example, is shortened, converted to a zipper closure and outfitted with pockets that tuck conveniently into the side seams where they anchor shut with Velcro fasteners. Stretch-knit ribbing replaces the old wrist cuffs and the waistband on the jacket and an elastic casing tops the pants. For both outfits, double-knit fabrics provide the requisite warmth, absorbency and stretch; the method for figuring yardage is described overleaf.

MODIFYING THE JACKET PATTERN

A SHORTENING THE JACKET

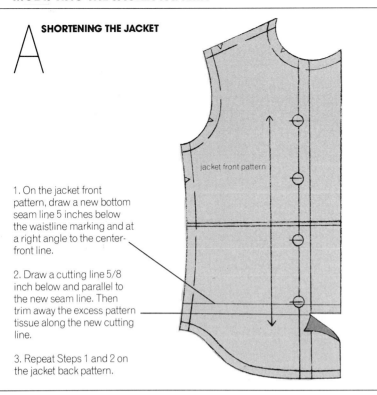

1. On the jacket front pattern, draw a new bottom seam line 5 inches below the waistline marking and at a right angle to the center-front line.

2. Draw a cutting line 5/8 inch below and parallel to the new seam line. Then trim away the excess pattern tissue along the new cutting line.

3. Repeat Steps 1 and 2 on the jacket back pattern.

B CONVERTING THE BUTTON CLOSURE TO A ZIPPER FRONT

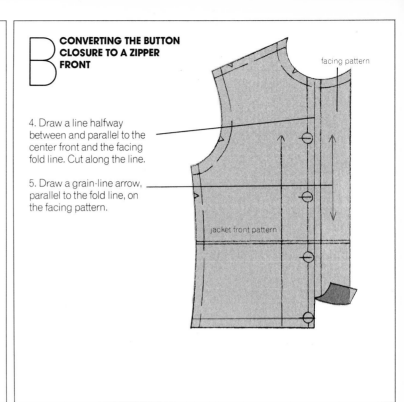

4. Draw a line halfway between and parallel to the center front and the facing fold line. Cut along the line.

5. Draw a grain-line arrow, parallel to the fold line, on the facing pattern.

C ADDING THE POCKET FACING

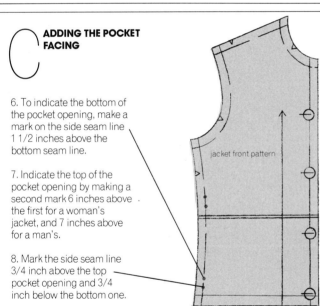

6. To indicate the bottom of the pocket opening, make a mark on the side seam line 1 1/2 inches above the bottom seam line.

7. Indicate the top of the pocket opening by making a second mark 6 inches above the first for a woman's jacket, and 7 inches above for a man's.

8. Mark the side seam line 3/4 inch above the top pocket opening and 3/4 inch below the bottom one.

9. Tape a piece of paper under the pattern. The paper should extend at least 2 inches beyond the edge of the pattern between the marks made in Step 8.

10. To make the pocket facing, draw 1 1/2-inch-long lines out from the top and bottom marks on the side seam line. Then connect the ends of the lines.

11. Trim away the excess paper along the pocket facing edges.

12. Repeat Steps 6 and 7 on the jacket back pattern.

D TAPERING THE SLEEVE PATTERN

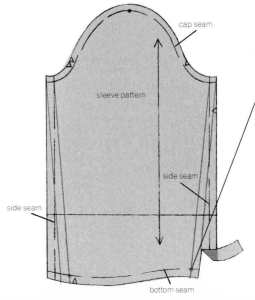

13. Measure the width of the sleeve pattern between the side seam lines at the point that they intersect the cap seam line. Subtract 2 1/2 inches.

14. Measure the bottom seam line between the side seam lines.

15. Subtract the measurement taken in Step 14 from the number obtained in Step 13. Then divide the difference by two.

16. Make a mark inside each end of the bottom seam line the distance obtained in Step 15.

17. On each side of the pattern, connect the marks made in the preceding step with the intersection of the cap and side seam lines. These are the new side seam lines.

18. Draw new cutting lines 5/8 inch outside the seam lines. Then trim away the excess pattern tissue along the new cutting lines.

E MARKING GUIDE LINES FOR THE STRIPES

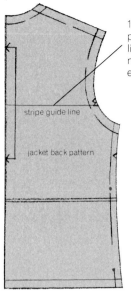

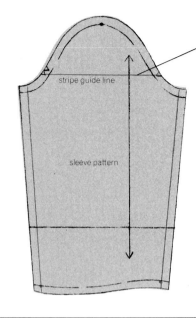

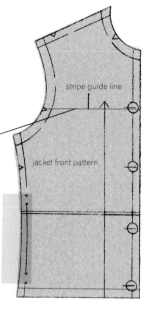

19. On the jacket back pattern, draw a horizontal line from the lower armhole notch to the center-back edge.

stripe guide line

jacket back pattern

stripe guide line

sleeve pattern

20. On the sleeve pattern, draw a line from the notch on the front of the sleeve cap to the lower notch at the back of the cap.

21. On the jacket front pattern, draw a horizontal line from the armhole notch to the center-front edge.

stripe guide line

jacket front pattern

F DRAFTING THE POCKET PATTERN

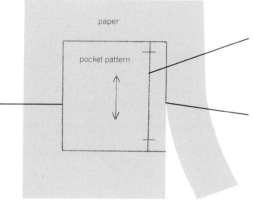

paper

pocket pattern

22. On the jacket front pattern, measure the distance between the pocket marks made in Step 8.

23. Draw a square of the dimensions determined in the preceding step.

24. Draw a line 1 inch inside one side of the square. Then make cross marks on the line, 3/4 inch inside both ends.

25. Draw a grain-line arrow parallel to the line drawn in Step 24. Then cut around the edges of the pocket pattern.

G DRAFTING THE COLLAR PATTERN

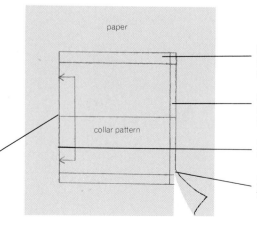

paper

collar pattern

26. Using a tape measure turned on its edge, measure the neck stitching line —discounting the seam allowances—on the jacket front and back patterns. Add the measurements together.

27. Draw a rectangle. Use the figure determined in Step 26 for the length, and make it 8 inches wide. Divide the rectangle in half lengthwise.

28. Add 5/8-inch seam allowances outside the top and bottom edges.

29. Add a 3/8-inch seam allowance outside the right-hand edge.

30. Mark the left-hand edge "place on fold."

31. Cut around the edges of the collar pattern.

continued

DRAFTING THE JACKET WAISTBAND PATTERN

32. Measure your hips 6 inches below the waist. Subtract 2 inches. Then divide the remainder by two.

33. Using the figure determined in Step 32 for the length, draw a rectangle that measures 6 inches in width. Divide the rectangle in half lengthwise.

34A. If the ribbing fabric you plan to use is more than twice as wide as the rectangle is long, repeat Steps 28-31 to complete the waistband pattern.

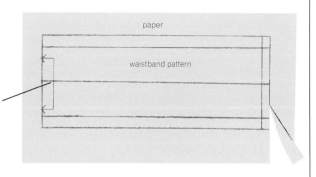

34B. If the ribbing fabric you plan to use is less than twice as wide as the rectangle is long, repeat Steps 28 and 29. Then add a 3/8-inch seam allowance to the left-hand edge, draw a grain-line arrow parallel to it and cut out the pattern.

DRAFTING THE CUFF PATTERN

35. Measure your wrist. Subtract 1 inch.

36. Using the figure determined in Step 35 for the length, draw a rectangle that measures 6 inches in width. Divide the rectangle in half lengthwise.

37. Draw a grain-line arrow parallel to the 6-inch-wide edges.

38. Add 5/8-inch seam allowances outside the top and bottom edges. Then add 3/8-inch seam allowances outside the side edges.

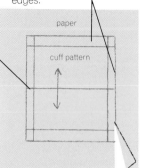

39. Cut out the cuff pattern.

MODIFYING THE PANTS PATTERN

A TAPERING THE LEGS

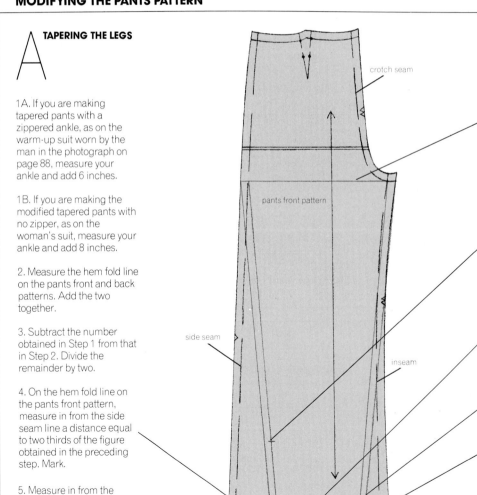

1A. If you are making tapered pants with a zippered ankle, as on the warm-up suit worn by the man in the photograph on page 88, measure your ankle and add 6 inches.

1B. If you are making the modified tapered pants with no zipper, as on the woman's suit, measure your ankle and add 8 inches.

2. Measure the hem fold line on the pants front and back patterns. Add the two together.

3. Subtract the number obtained in Step 1 from that in Step 2. Divide the remainder by two.

4. On the hem fold line on the pants front pattern, measure in from the side seam line a distance equal to two thirds of the figure obtained in the preceding step. Mark.

5. Measure in from the inseam a distance equal to one third the figure obtained in Step 3. Mark.

6. Draw a horizontal line from the intersection of the crotch seam and the inseam to the side seam.

7. Draw new side seam and inseam lines by connecting the ends of the line drawn in the preceding step with the marks made on the hem fold line in Steps 4 and 5. If your pants are to have zippered ankles, also mark the zipper opening with a cross mark 7 1/2 inches above the hem fold line on the new side seam line.

8. To add a 1-inch hem, extend the new side and inseam lines 1 inch below, and perpendicular to, the hem fold line.

9. Draw cutting lines 5/8 inch outside the side seam and inseam stitching lines.

10. Connect the ends of the lines to indicate a new hem cutting line.

11. Trim away the excess pattern tissue along the cutting lines.

12. Repeat Steps 4-11 on the pants back pattern.

B ADDING ELASTIC CASING AT THE WAIST

13. On the pants front pattern, eliminate the dart points from the waist seam line as shown.

14. Tape a piece of paper under the pattern so that the paper extends 2 1/2 inches above the waist edge.

15. On the paper, draw a fold line 1 inch above, and parallel to, the waist seam line.

16. Draw a second line parallel to the first and 1 1/4 inches above it.

17. Trim the paper along the line drawn in the preceding step.

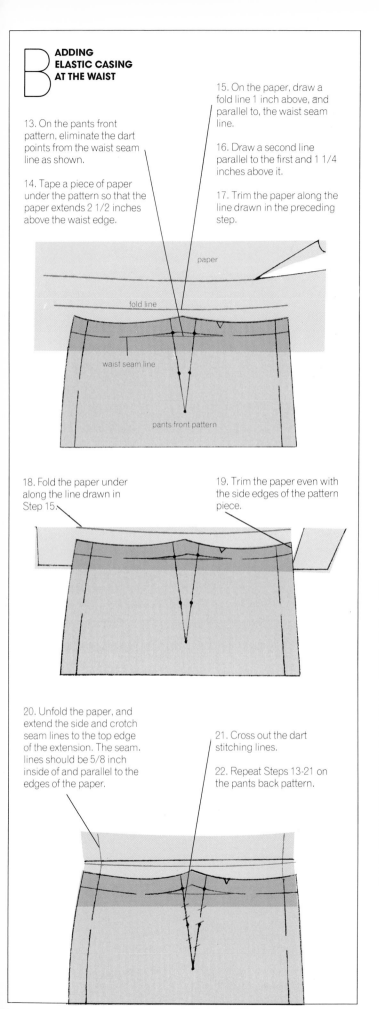

18. Fold the paper under along the line drawn in Step 15.

19. Trim the paper even with the side edges of the pattern piece.

20. Unfold the paper, and extend the side and crotch seam lines to the top edge of the extension. The seam lines should be 5/8 inch inside of and parallel to the edges of the paper.

21. Cross out the dart stitching lines.

22. Repeat Steps 13-21 on the pants back pattern.

LAYOUT, CUTTING AND MARKING

A DETERMINING FABRIC REQUIREMENTS

1. To estimate the amount of fabric you will need, use string to form a rectangle that is half the width of the fabric you plan to use and several yards long.

2. Arrange the jacket front, jacket back, jacket facing, sleeve, collar, pocket, pants front and pants back pattern pieces within the rectangle, keeping the grain-line arrows parallel to the lengthwise strings.

3. Align with one of the lengthwise strings the edges of patterns designed to be placed on the fold of fabric.

4. Adjust the length of the rectangle so that it just accommodates the pattern pieces. Then measure the length.

5. Repeat the procedure, using the waistband and cuff patterns to determine how much ribbing fabric is required.

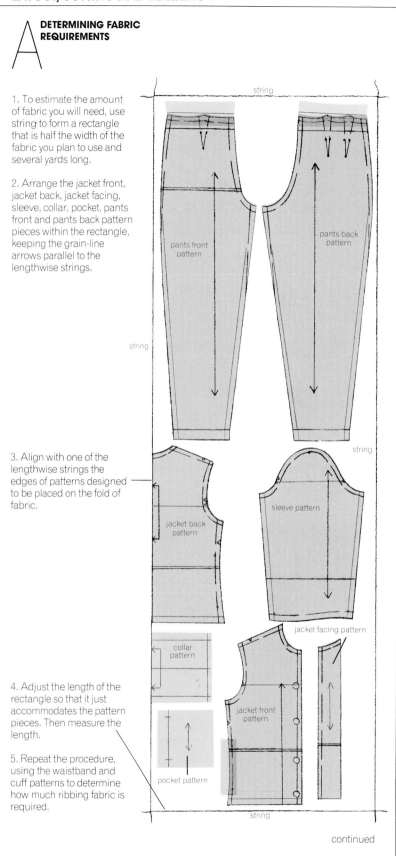

continued

93

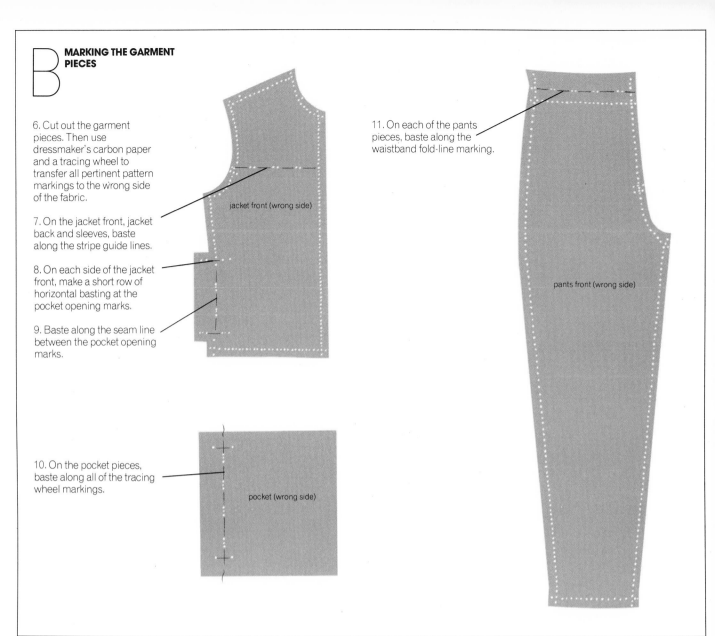

B MARKING THE GARMENT PIECES

6. Cut out the garment pieces. Then use dressmaker's carbon paper and a tracing wheel to transfer all pertinent pattern markings to the wrong side of the fabric.

7. On the jacket front, jacket back and sleeves, baste along the stripe guide lines.

8. On each side of the jacket front, make a short row of horizontal basting at the pocket opening marks.

9. Baste along the seam line between the pocket opening marks.

10. On the pocket pieces, baste along all of the tracing wheel markings.

11. On each of the pants pieces, baste along the waistband fold-line marking.

jacket front (wrong side)

pocket (wrong side)

pants front (wrong side)

ASSEMBLING THE JACKET

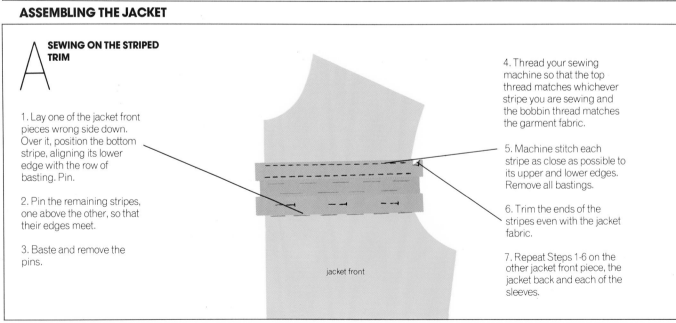

A SEWING ON THE STRIPED TRIM

1. Lay one of the jacket front pieces wrong side down. Over it, position the bottom stripe, aligning its lower edge with the row of basting. Pin.

2. Pin the remaining stripes, one above the other, so that their edges meet.

3. Baste and remove the pins.

4. Thread your sewing machine so that the top thread matches whichever stripe you are sewing and the bobbin thread matches the garment fabric.

5. Machine stitch each stripe as close as possible to its upper and lower edges. Remove all bastings.

6. Trim the ends of the stripes even with the jacket fabric.

7. Repeat Steps 1-6 on the other jacket front piece, the jacket back and each of the sleeves.

jacket front

Velcro

8. Cut a 5-inch strip of Velcro fastener (6 inches for a man's jacket). Separate the pieces.

9. Rethread your sewing machine so that the top thread matches your garment fabric. Then finish the edges of one of the pocket pieces with machine zigzag stitches.

pocket

10. Place the pocket piece wrong side down. Align the outer edge of the fuzzy Velcro strip against the row of vertical basting on the pocket. The strip should be centered between the horizontal bastings. Pin.

11. Machine stitch around the strip, removing the pins as you go.

jacket front

12. Finish the side seam edges of the jacket front piece with machine zigzag stitches. Then lay the piece wrong side down.

13. Arrange the needled Velcro strip 3/8 inch outside of, and parallel to, the vertical row of basting on the pocket facing. The strip should be centered between the horizontal rows of basting. Pin, then machine stitch and remove the pins.

Velcro

pocket facing

jacket back

14. Finish the side seam edge of the jacket back piece with machine zigzag stitches. Then lay the piece wrong side down. Over it position the pocket piece, wrong side up, matching the pocket opening marks. Pin.

15. Machine stitch between the pocket opening marks, 5/8 inch inside the edges of the fabric.

jacket back

pocket opening mark

pocket (wrong side)

pocket opening mark

16. Fold the pocket piece away from the jacket back piece. Lay the jacket front piece over the jacket back, matching the side seam edges.

17. Pin along the side seam from the armhole edge to the upper pocket opening, taking care not to catch the pocket piece with the pins. Then pin from the lower pocket opening mark to the bottom edge of the jacket.

18. Machine stitch, and remove the pins.

19. Press open the seam. Then press the pocket toward the jacket front.

jacket front (wrong side)

pocket opening mark

pocket

pocket opening mark

20. Turn the garment wrong side down. Press the folded front edge of the pocket opening along the line of basting.

21. Pin the pocket flat against the jacket front.

22. Using tailor's chalk, draw lines—6 inches long and at right angles to the side seam—from each of the pocket opening marks onto the jacket front. Connect the ends of the lines.

23. Starting and ending at the side seam, topstitch along the chalk lines. Remove the pins.

24. Make a second row of topstitching 1/4 inch outside of, and parallel to, the first line.

jacket front

jacket back

pocket opening mark

fold

pocket opening mark

25. Remove all bastings from the pocket area.

26. Repeat Steps 8-25 to attach the other pocket.

27. Pin, then machine stitch the shoulder seams, removing the pins as you go.

28. Press open the seams. Then finish the edges with machine zigzag stitches.

continued

C ATTACHING THE COLLAR

29. Stay stitch *(Glossary)* around the neck edge, just outside the seam line.

30. Make 1/4-inch clips at 1-inch intervals around the neck edge.

31. With their wrong sides facing out, match the neck edge of the jacket with one long edge of the collar. Pin, starting at the center back and working toward the center-front edges. Baste, then remove the pins.

32. Machine stitch, and remove the basting.

33. Trim the collar seam allowance to 1/4 inch. Trim the jacket seam allowance to 3/8 inch.

34. Turn the collar away from the jacket. Press the seam allowance toward the collar.

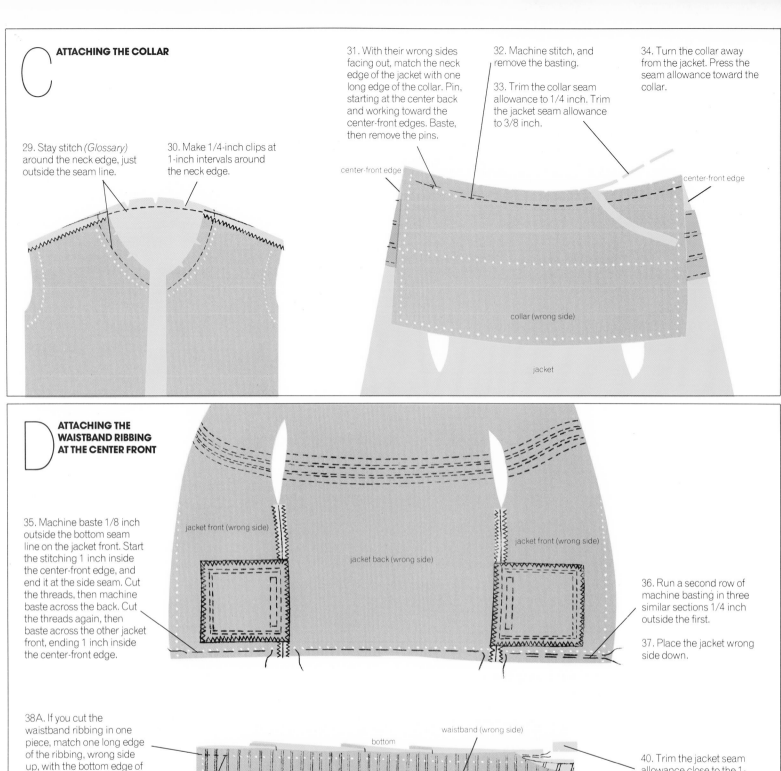

center-front edge

center-front edge

collar (wrong side)

jacket

D ATTACHING THE WAISTBAND RIBBING AT THE CENTER FRONT

35. Machine baste 1/8 inch outside the bottom seam line on the jacket front. Start the stitching 1 inch inside the center-front edge, and end it at the side seam. Cut the threads, then machine baste across the back. Cut the threads again, then baste across the other jacket front, ending 1 inch inside the center-front edge.

36. Run a second row of machine basting in three similar sections 1/4 inch outside the first.

37. Place the jacket wrong side down.

jacket front (wrong side)

jacket front (wrong side)

jacket back (wrong side)

38A. If you cut the waistband ribbing in one piece, match one long edge of the ribbing, wrong side up, with the bottom edge of the jacket. Pin at the center-front edges.

38B. If you cut the waistband ribbing in two pieces, first pin, then stitch the two pieces together. Now match one long edge of the ribbing, wrong side up, with the bottom edge of the jacket. Pin at the center-front edges.

39. Starting at the center-front edge, machine stitch for 1 inch on each side of the jacket opening. Remove the pins.

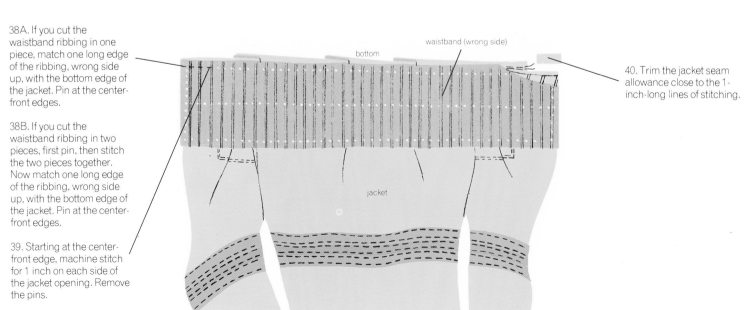

bottom

waistband (wrong side)

40. Trim the jacket seam allowance close to the 1-inch-long lines of stitching.

jacket

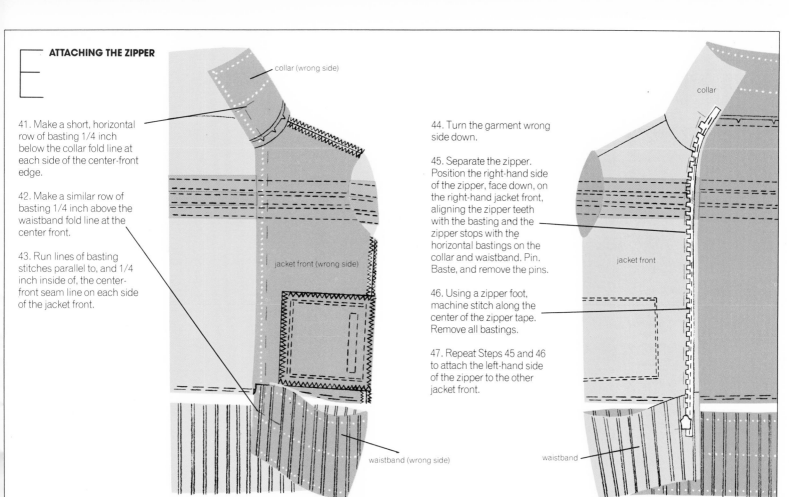

E ATTACHING THE ZIPPER

41. Make a short, horizontal row of basting 1/4 inch below the collar fold line at each side of the center-front edge.

42. Make a similar row of basting 1/4 inch above the waistband fold line at the center front.

43. Run lines of basting stitches parallel to, and 1/4 inch inside of, the center-front seam line on each side of the jacket front.

44. Turn the garment wrong side down.

45. Separate the zipper. Position the right-hand side of the zipper, face down, on the right-hand jacket front, aligning the zipper teeth with the basting and the zipper stops with the horizontal bastings on the collar and waistband. Pin. Baste, and remove the pins.

46. Using a zipper foot, machine stitch along the center of the zipper tape. Remove all bastings.

47. Repeat Steps 45 and 46 to attach the left-hand side of the zipper to the other jacket front.

collar (wrong side)

jacket front (wrong side)

waistband (wrong side)

collar

jacket front

waistband

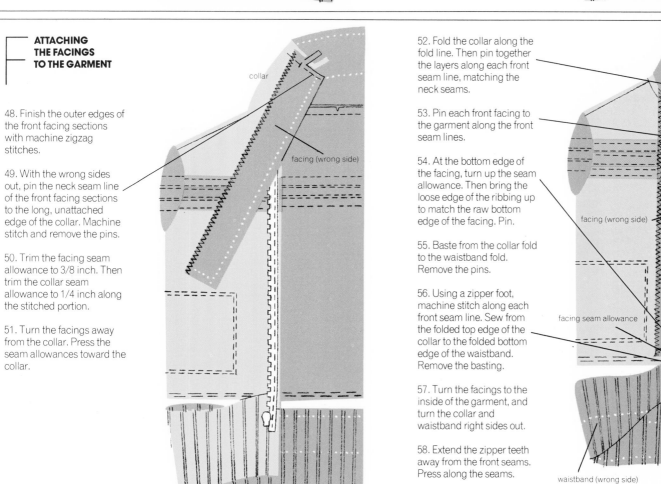

F ATTACHING THE FACINGS TO THE GARMENT

48. Finish the outer edges of the front facing sections with machine zigzag stitches.

49. With the wrong sides out, pin the neck seam line of the front facing sections to the long, unattached edge of the collar. Machine stitch and remove the pins.

50. Trim the facing seam allowance to 3/8 inch. Then trim the collar seam allowance to 1/4 inch along the stitched portion.

51. Turn the facings away from the collar. Press the seam allowances toward the collar.

52. Fold the collar along the fold line. Then pin together the layers along each front seam line, matching the neck seams.

53. Pin each front facing to the garment along the front seam lines.

54. At the bottom edge of the facing, turn up the seam allowance. Then bring the loose edge of the ribbing up to match the raw bottom edge of the facing. Pin.

55. Baste from the collar fold to the waistband fold. Remove the pins.

56. Using a zipper foot, machine stitch along each front seam line. Sew from the folded top edge of the collar to the folded bottom edge of the waistband. Remove the basting.

57. Turn the facings to the inside of the garment, and turn the collar and waistband right sides out.

58. Extend the zipper teeth away from the front seams. Press along the seams.

collar

facing (wrong side)

collar (wrong side)

facing (wrong side)

facing seam allowance

fold

waistband (wrong side)

continued

G FINISHING THE COLLAR AND THE WAISTBAND

59. Turn the jacket wrong side up.

60. Fold under the unattached edge of the collar. Align the folded edge against the neck seams of the garment. Pin.

61. Slip stitch (*Appendix*) the collar to the neck seam allowance of the garment. Remove the pins. Press.

62. Gather the bottom edge of the jacket so that it is the same size as the waistband ribbing.

63. Match the raw bottom edges of the ribbing with the raw bottom edge of the garment. Pin. Then baste, and remove the pins.

64. Machine stitch, using the narrowest zigzag setting on your machine. Remove the basting.

65. Trim the seam allowances to 3/8 inch. Then zigzag the edges together.

66. Press the seam allowance toward the jacket.

67. Slip stitch the bottom edge of the facing to the waistband.

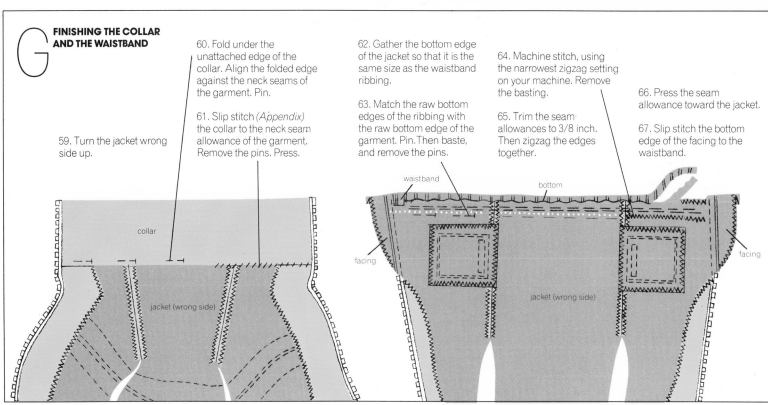

H SETTING IN THE SLEEVES

68. Gather the sleeve cap, stitch the side seam, and gather the bottom edge of the sleeve following your pattern instructions.

69. Pin the ribbing for the cuff along the side seam lines. Machine stitch, then remove the pins.

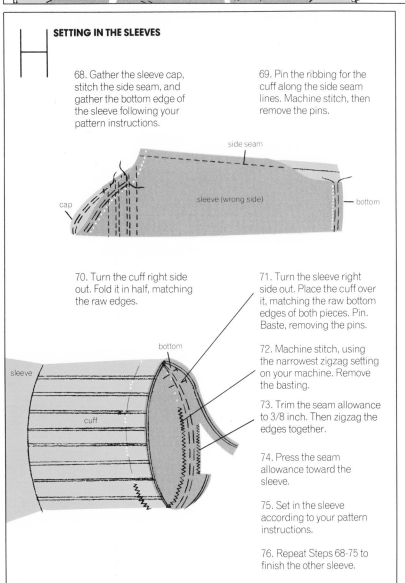

70. Turn the cuff right side out. Fold it in half, matching the raw edges.

71. Turn the sleeve right side out. Place the cuff over it, matching the raw bottom edges of both pieces. Pin. Baste, removing the pins.

72. Machine stitch, using the narrowest zigzag setting on your machine. Remove the basting.

73. Trim the seam allowance to 3/8 inch. Then zigzag the edges together.

74. Press the seam allowance toward the sleeve.

75. Set in the sleeve according to your pattern instructions.

76. Repeat Steps 68-75 to finish the other sleeve.

ASSEMBLING THE PANTS

A SEWING THE SIDE SEAM

1. Lay one of the pants back pieces wrong side down. Over it, position the corresponding pants front piece, wrong side up. Match the side seams and pin.

2. Baste, and remove the pins.

3A. If you are making pants with a zippered ankle, machine stitch from the waistline edge to the top of the zipper opening. Then backstitch twice. Adjust the stitch length on your sewing machine for basting—6 stitches to the inch—then stitch to the bottom edge of the side seam.

4A. Press open the seam, and finish the edges with zigzag stitches. Then proceed to Box B to insert a lapped zipper.

3B. If you are making pants without an ankle zipper, machine stitch from the waistline to the bottom edge of the side seam.

4B. Press open the seam, then finish the edges with zigzag stitches. Skip to Box C.

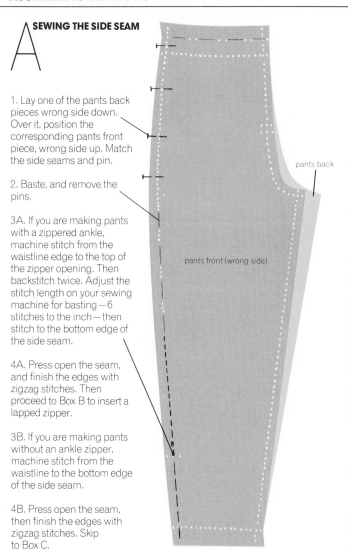

B | INSERTING A LAPPED ZIPPER

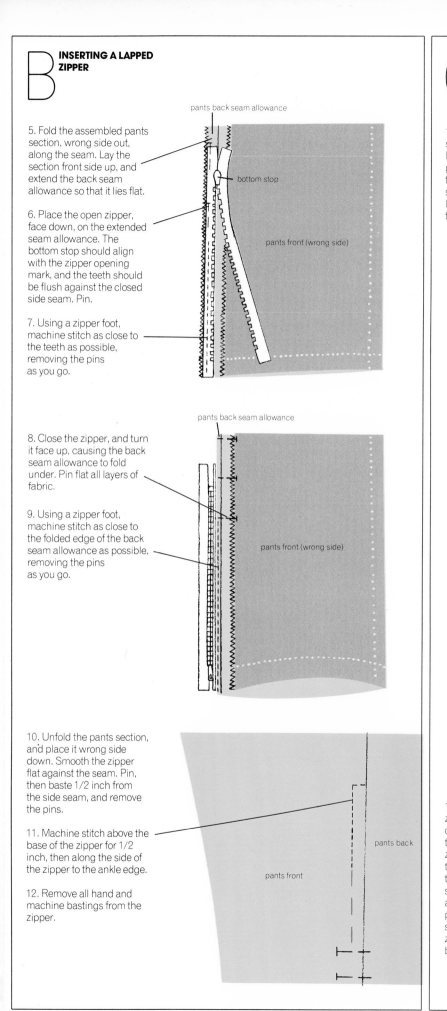

pants back seam allowance

5. Fold the assembled pants section, wrong side out, along the seam. Lay the section front side up, and extend the back seam allowance so that it lies flat.

bottom stop

6. Place the open zipper, face down, on the extended seam allowance. The bottom stop should align with the zipper opening mark, and the teeth should be flush against the closed side seam. Pin.

pants front (wrong side)

7. Using a zipper foot, machine stitch as close to the teeth as possible, removing the pins as you go.

pants back seam allowance

8. Close the zipper, and turn it face up, causing the back seam allowance to fold under. Pin flat all layers of fabric.

9. Using a zipper foot, machine stitch as close to the folded edge of the back seam allowance as possible, removing the pins as you go.

pants front (wrong side)

10. Unfold the pants section, and place it wrong side down. Smooth the zipper flat against the seam. Pin, then baste 1/2 inch from the side seam, and remove the pins.

11. Machine stitch above the base of the zipper for 1/2 inch, then along the side of the zipper to the ankle edge.

pants back

pants front

12. Remove all hand and machine bastings from the zipper.

C | SEWING ON THE STRIPE

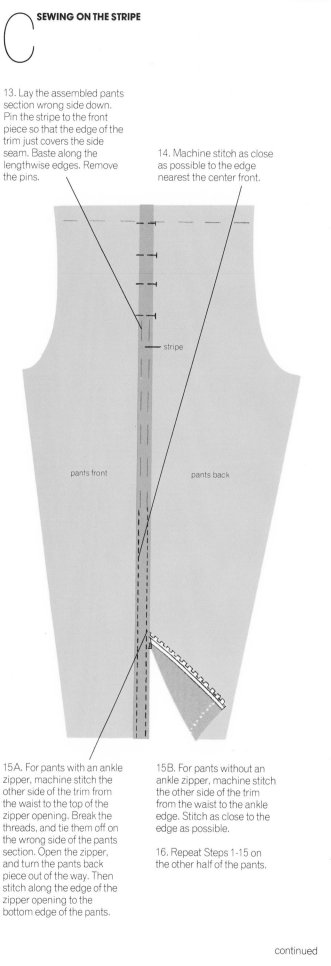

13. Lay the assembled pants section wrong side down. Pin the stripe to the front piece so that the edge of the trim just covers the side seam. Baste along the lengthwise edges. Remove the pins.

14. Machine stitch as close as possible to the edge nearest the center front.

stripe

pants front

pants back

15A. For pants with an ankle zipper, machine stitch the other side of the trim from the waist to the top of the zipper opening. Break the threads, and tie them off on the wrong side of the pants section. Open the zipper, and turn the pants back piece out of the way. Then stitch along the edge of the zipper opening to the bottom edge of the pants.

15B. For pants without an ankle zipper, machine stitch the other side of the trim from the waist to the ankle edge. Stitch as close to the edge as possible.

16. Repeat Steps 1-15 on the other half of the pants.

continued

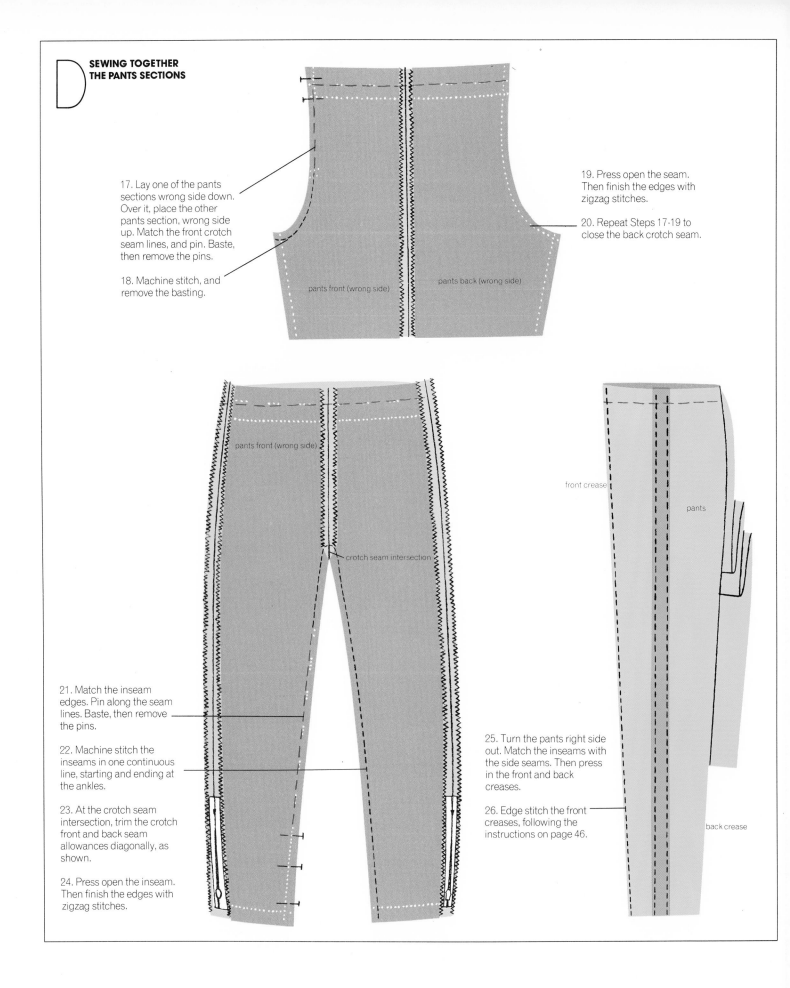

D SEWING TOGETHER THE PANTS SECTIONS

17. Lay one of the pants sections wrong side down. Over it, place the other pants section, wrong side up. Match the front crotch seam lines, and pin. Baste, then remove the pins.

18. Machine stitch, and remove the basting.

19. Press open the seam. Then finish the edges with zigzag stitches.

20. Repeat Steps 17-19 to close the back crotch seam.

pants front (wrong side)

pants back (wrong side)

pants front (wrong side)

crotch seam intersection

front crease

pants

back crease

21. Match the inseam edges. Pin along the seam lines. Baste, then remove the pins.

22. Machine stitch the inseams in one continuous line, starting and ending at the ankles.

23. At the crotch seam intersection, trim the crotch front and back seam allowances diagonally, as shown.

24. Press open the inseam. Then finish the edges with zigzag stitches.

25. Turn the pants right side out. Match the inseams with the side seams. Then press in the front and back creases.

26. Edge stitch the front creases, following the instructions on page 46.

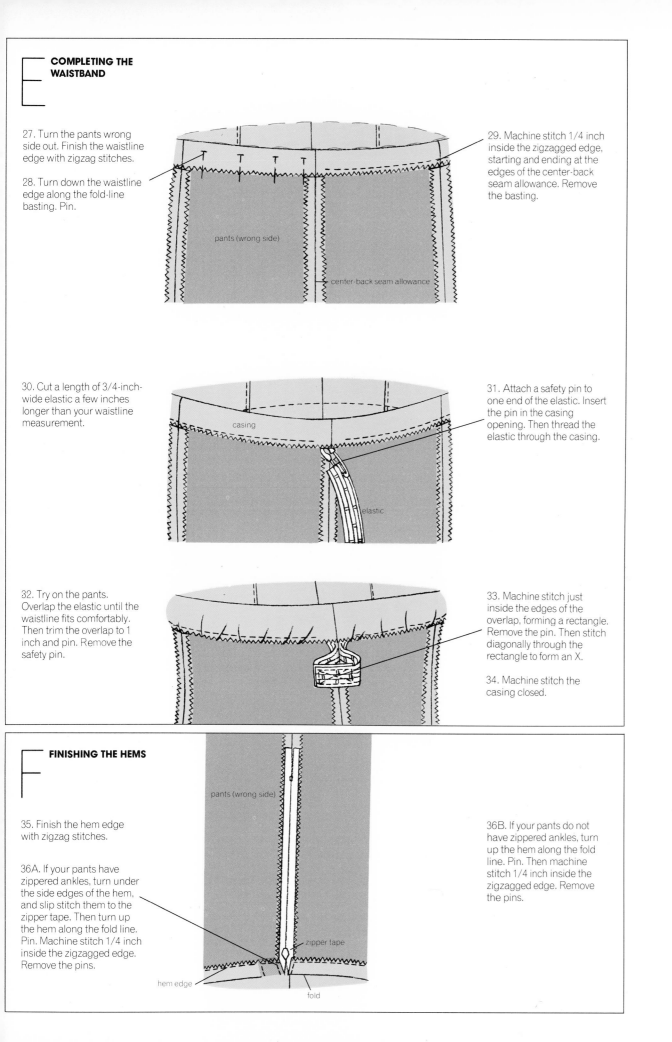

E COMPLETING THE WAISTBAND

27. Turn the pants wrong side out. Finish the waistline edge with zigzag stitches.

28. Turn down the waistline edge along the fold-line basting. Pin.

29. Machine stitch 1/4 inch inside the zigzagged edge, starting and ending at the edges of the center-back seam allowance. Remove the basting.

30. Cut a length of 3/4-inch-wide elastic a few inches longer than your waistline measurement.

31. Attach a safety pin to one end of the elastic. Insert the pin in the casing opening. Then thread the elastic through the casing.

32. Try on the pants. Overlap the elastic until the waistline fits comfortably. Then trim the overlap to 1 inch and pin. Remove the safety pin.

33. Machine stitch just inside the edges of the overlap, forming a rectangle. Remove the pin. Then stitch diagonally through the rectangle to form an X.

34. Machine stitch the casing closed.

F FINISHING THE HEMS

35. Finish the hem edge with zigzag stitches.

36A. If your pants have zippered ankles, turn under the side edges of the hem, and slip stitch them to the zipper tape. Then turn up the hem along the fold line. Pin. Machine stitch 1/4 inch inside the zigzagged edge. Remove the pins.

36B. If your pants do not have zippered ankles, turn up the hem along the fold line. Pin. Then machine stitch 1/4 inch inside the zigzagged edge. Remove the pins.

A shirt converted for playtime

By adding a bit here and subtracting a little there, a standard pattern for a tailored, convertible-collared shirt can produce a tennis dress as pert and practical as this one. The open neckline, loose waist and front buttons are all preserved from the original easy-to-wear design.

For even greater freedom of movement the sleeves are eliminated and the armholes are scooped even deeper—before being faced with the same fabric as the dress. A new band of fabric over the buttonholes strengthens the closure and adds decoration with its zigzag topstitching. And deep side pockets, sensibly backed with dark-colored fabric, provide a handy place for tennis balls.

Despite this restyling, the dress requires little more fabric than that specified in the original shirt pattern: roughly two yards of a polyester-and-cotton knit—plus an extra 1/4 yard of the darker color for the pockets and 1/4 yard of pocket lining.

MODIFYING THE PATTERN

A TAKING YOUR MEASUREMENTS

1. To establish the finished length of the tennis dress, measure from the top of your spine to the point on your leg where you want the hem to fall.

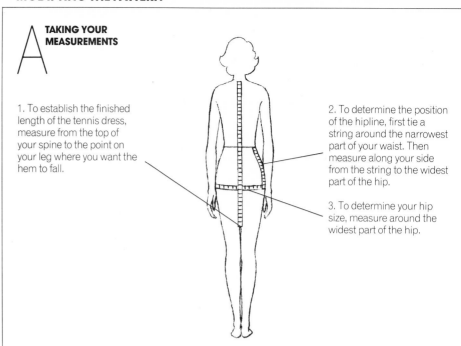

2. To determine the position of the hipline, first tie a string around the narrowest part of your waist. Then measure along your side from the string to the widest part of the hip.

3. To determine your hip size, measure around the widest part of the hip.

B LENGTHENING THE PATTERN

4. Tape paper to the bottom half of the back pattern piece. Then, starting at the neck seam line, measure down the center back a distance equal to the desired dress length, as determined in Step 1. Make a pencil mark on the paper.

5. Measure the distance between the bottom edge of the pattern piece and the mark made on the paper in the previous step. Then take that measurement and make a series of pencil marks across the paper, following the shape of the bottom edge of the pattern piece, as shown. Connect the marks to create a new hemline.

6. Measure down 5/8 inch from the new hemline, and make marks across the paper. Connect the marks to make a new cutting line.

7. Extend the center-back line to the new bottom cutting line.

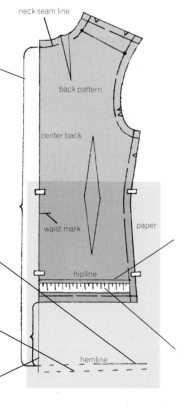

8. On the center-back line, measure down from the pattern mark indicating the waistline, to a point equal to the position of the hipline determined in Step 2. Make a mark.

9. Measure up from the bottom edge of the pattern to the mark made in the previous step. Now take that distance and measure up from the bottom of the pattern piece at the side seam line. Make a mark. Then connect that mark with the one made in Step 8 to draw in the hipline.

10. Measure along the hipline from the side seam line to the center-back line.

11. To measure the hipline on the front pattern piece, repeat Steps 8-10.

12. Add the width of the hipline on the back pattern piece to that of the front pattern piece. Then multiply the sum by two.

13. Compare the measurement determined in Step 12 to your hip measurement found in Step 3. If the pattern is at least 3 inches wider than your hip measurement, extend the back side seam line and cutting line down to the bottom cutting line. Then skip to Step 18.

14. If the pattern is less than 3 inches wider than your hip measurement, divide the difference by four.

15. At the hipline, measure out from the side seam line the distance determined in Step 14. Make a mark.

16. Indicate a new seam line by drawing a tapered line that starts on the original seam line about 2 inches above the mark, passes through the mark and continues to the bottom cutting line.

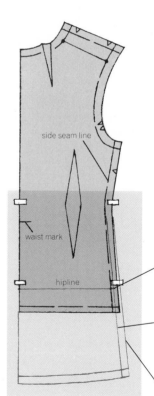

17. Draw a new cutting line 5/8 inch outside the new seam line.

C MAKING THE CURVED SIDE SLIT

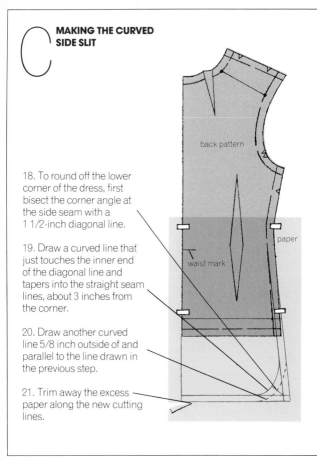

18. To round off the lower corner of the dress, first bisect the corner angle at the side seam with a 1 1/2-inch diagonal line.

19. Draw a curved line that just touches the inner end of the diagonal line and tapers into the straight seam lines, about 3 inches from the corner.

20. Draw another curved line 5/8 inch outside of and parallel to the line drawn in the previous step.

21. Trim away the excess paper along the new cutting lines.

back pattern

paper

waist mark

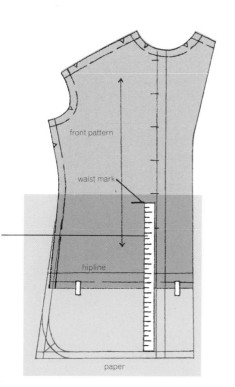

front pattern

waist mark

hipline

paper

22. On the center-back line of the back pattern piece, measure from the waistline mark to the bottom cutting line.

23. Tape paper to the bottom of the front pattern piece. Then take the length found in Step 22, and measure down at the center front from the waist. Make a mark.

24. Repeat Steps 5-21 on the shirt front pattern, adding the same amount of ease to the side seam that was added to the shirt back pattern.

D MAKING THE PATTERN FOR THE POCKET BACKING

side seam line

front pattern

center front

25. Working on the dress front pattern, make a pencil mark on the side seam line, 1 inch above the top of the curved side seam line. This mark will indicate the bottom edge of the pocket.

26. Draw a straight line across the pattern from the mark made in the previous step and at a right angle to the center-front line. The end of the line, indicating the front edge of the pocket, should be at least 3 inches from the center front.

27. Draw a line from the end of the one drawn in the previous step. This line —which will be the depth of the pocket—should be parallel to the center front, and 7 to 8 inches long.

28. Draw a straight line to connect the end of that line to the side seam line.

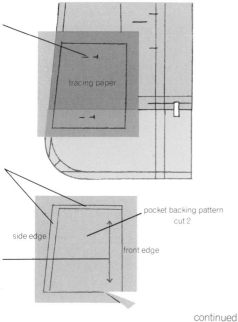

tracing paper

pocket backing pattern cut 2

side edge

front edge

29. Pin a piece of tracing paper over the outline of the pocket backing pattern, and trace the outline. Remove the tracing paper.

30. Add a 5/8-inch seam allowance along the side of the pattern that corresponds to the side seam line of the dress. Mark a 3/8-inch seam allowance along the top edge.

31. Mark the pattern to be cut twice. Then draw a grain-line arrow parallel to the front edge of the pattern.

32. Cut out the pattern.

continued

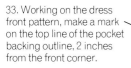

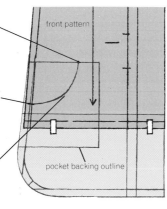

33. Working on the dress front pattern, make a mark on the top line of the pocket backing outline, 2 inches from the front corner.

34. Measure up along the side seam line 4 inches from the bottom line of the pocket backing outline. Make a mark.

35. To complete the pocket outline, draw a curved line to connect the marks made in Steps 33 and 34.

36. Repeat Step 29 to trace the pocket outline.

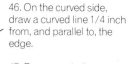

37. Draw a line that bisects the lower-front corner of the pocket outline and the center of the curved edge.

38. Cut around the outline.

39. Slash along the line drawn in Step 37.

40. Lay the cut pieces on a piece of paper so that the cut edges meet at the corner and are spread apart 2 1/2 inches at the curved edge. Tape the cut edges to the paper.

41. Join the cut edges with a curved line across the attached paper. The line will cut through the corners of the pattern.

42. Trim off the excess paper.

43. Pin the pattern to another piece of paper. Then trace around the edges of the pattern.

44. Remove the pattern, then add a 5/8-inch seam allowance on the side that corresponds to the dress side seam.

45. Add a 3/8-inch seam allowance on the other straight sides of the pattern.

46. On the curved side, draw a curved line 1/4 inch from, and parallel to, the edge.

47. Draw a grain-line arrow parallel to the front side of the pocket pattern. Then mark the pattern to be cut twice.

48. Cut out the finished pattern.

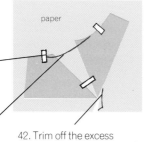

MAKING THE BAND PATTERN

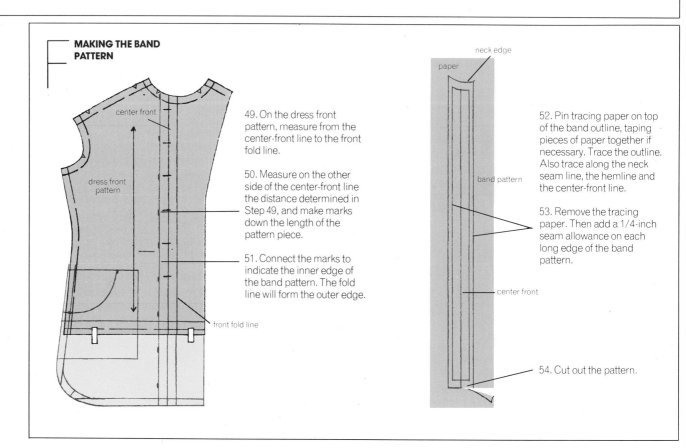

49. On the dress front pattern, measure from the center-front line to the front fold line.

50. Measure on the other side of the center-front line the distance determined in Step 49, and make marks down the length of the pattern piece.

51. Connect the marks to indicate the inner edge of the band pattern. The fold line will form the outer edge.

52. Pin tracing paper on top of the band outline, taping pieces of paper together if necessary. Trace the outline. Also trace along the neck seam line, the hemline and the center-front line.

53. Remove the tracing paper. Then add a 1/4-inch seam allowance on each long edge of the band pattern.

54. Cut out the pattern.

G ADJUSTING THE ARMHOLE

55. Pin the front and back pattern pieces together so that the yoke seam lines are aligned at the armhole.

56. Measure in on the shoulder line 1/2 inch from the armhole seam line. Make a mark.

57. With a curved ruler, draw a new seam line from the mark made in the previous step. Taper the line into the original seam line at the armhole notches on the front pattern piece and at the side seam line on the back pattern piece.

58. Draw another curved line 5/8 inch outside of, and parallel to, the line drawn in the previous step. Then trim the pattern along this line.

59. To make the armhole facing, first measure down 2 inches along the side seam line of the front pattern. Make a mark. Then measure down 2 inches on the side seam line of the back pattern. Make a mark.

60. Make a series of marks 2 inches from the armhole seam line around both pattern pieces. Connect the marks to indicate the position of the facing.

61. Make cross marks to indicate notches on the new seam line.

62. Pin a piece of tracing paper over the armhole facing outline.

63. Trace the outline. Make sure to trace over the side and armhole seam and cutting lines. Also trace the armhole notches.

64. Draw a grain-line arrow at a right angle to the shoulder seam line. Also mark the pattern to be cut twice.

65. Remove the paper and cut out the pattern along the outline.

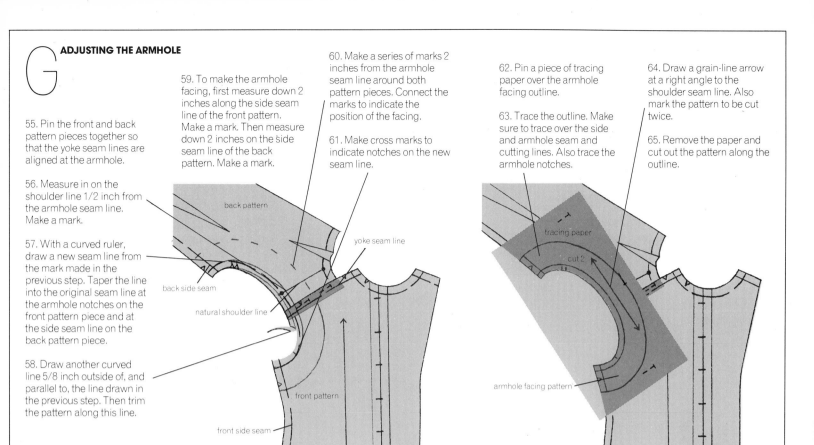

ASSEMBLING THE TENNIS DRESS

A CUTTING THE FABRIC

1. Fold over one side of the contrasting fabric, wrong sides out. Pin the pocket backing pattern to the double fabric thickness. Cut.

2. Fold over one side of the lining fabric, wrong sides out. Pin the pocket pattern to the double fabric thickness. Cut out the lining pieces. Then, using dressmaker's carbon paper and a tracing wheel, lightly transfer all pattern markings to the wrong side of the lining pieces. Remove the pattern.

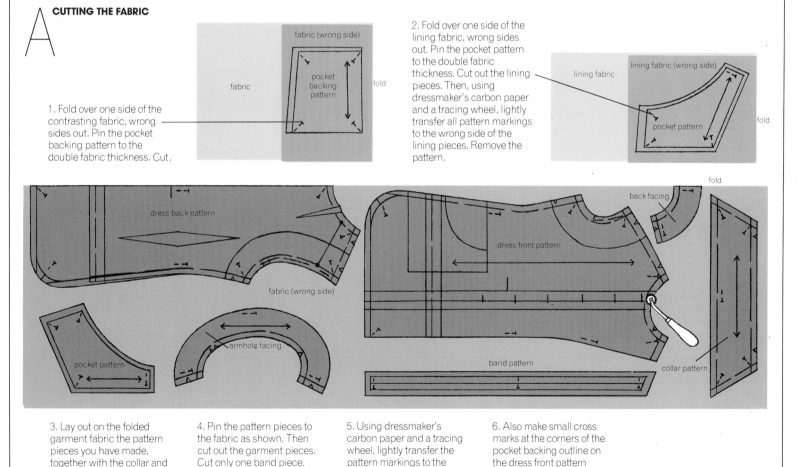

3. Lay out on the folded garment fabric the pattern pieces you have made, together with the collar and back neck facing pieces from the commercial pattern.

4. Pin the pattern pieces to the fabric as shown. Then cut out the garment pieces. Cut only one band piece.

5. Using dressmaker's carbon paper and a tracing wheel, lightly transfer the pattern markings to the wrong sides of the garment pieces. Do not trace the inner band line.

6. Also make small cross marks at the corners of the pocket backing outline on the dress front pattern pieces. Do not trace the waistline darts or buttonhole placement marks.

continued

B ATTACHING THE BAND

7. Cut a strip of iron-on interfacing, using the band pattern piece. Then trim off 1/4 inch along both long edges of the interfacing.

8. With dressmaker's carbon paper and a tracing wheel, lightly transfer all pattern markings.

9. Place the right-hand dress front wrong side up. Then center the interfacing, marked side up, over the center front, aligning the center-front lines. Use a medium-hot iron and a damp cloth to fuse the interfacing to the dress front.

10. Baste along the center-front line that is marked on the interfacing.

11. Turn the band piece wrong side up. Then turn over 1/4 inch along both long raw edges. Press.

12. Turn the right-hand dress front wrong side down. Position the band over it, aligning the center-front lines and the neckline curves. Pin. Then baste 1/4 inch from the folded edges and remove the pins.

13. Using contrasting thread and a large zigzag setting, machine stitch along both folded edges. Remove the bastings.

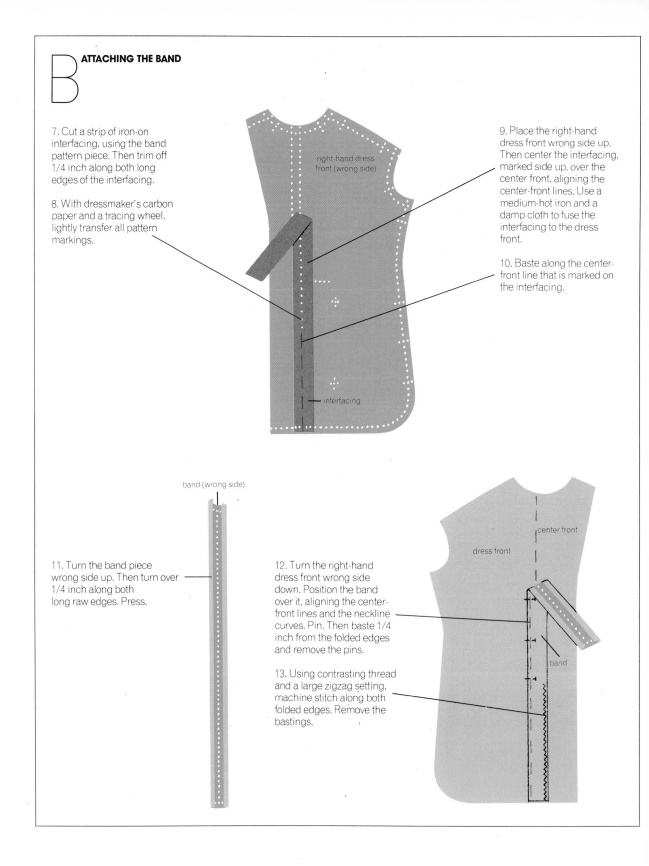

right-hand dress front (wrong side)

interfacing

band (wrong side)

center front

dress front

band

C LINING THE POCKETS

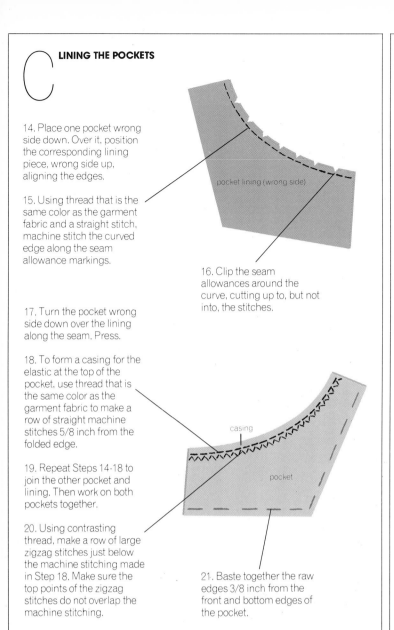

14. Place one pocket wrong side down. Over it, position the corresponding lining piece, wrong side up, aligning the edges.

15. Using thread that is the same color as the garment fabric and a straight stitch, machine stitch the curved edge along the seam allowance markings.

16. Clip the seam allowances around the curve, cutting up to, but not into, the stitches.

17. Turn the pocket wrong side down over the lining along the seam. Press.

18. To form a casing for the elastic at the top of the pocket, use thread that is the same color as the garment fabric to make a row of straight machine stitches 5/8 inch from the folded edge.

19. Repeat Steps 14-18 to join the other pocket and lining. Then work on both pockets together.

20. Using contrasting thread, make a row of large zigzag stitches just below the machine stitching made in Step 18. Make sure the top points of the zigzag stitches do not overlap the machine stitching.

21. Baste together the raw edges 3/8 inch from the front and bottom edges of the pocket.

22. Cut a length of 1/2-inch-wide elastic that is 2 1/2 inches shorter than the casing.

23. Attach a safety pin to one end of the elastic. Then insert the safety pin into one end of the casing. Work the pin through until it emerges from the other end of the casing.

24. Pin through both ends of the casing to catch the elastic, and remove the safety pin.

25. Machine stitch 1/4 inch from the raw edges across both ends of the casing.

D ASSEMBLING THE POCKET

26. Lay the elasticized pocket so that it is lining side up. Position the matching pocket backing, wrong side up, over it. Match the side seam edges.

27. At the bottom and front of the pocket, align the raw edges of the backing with the bastings on the pocket. Then pin together the pieces around all three sides.

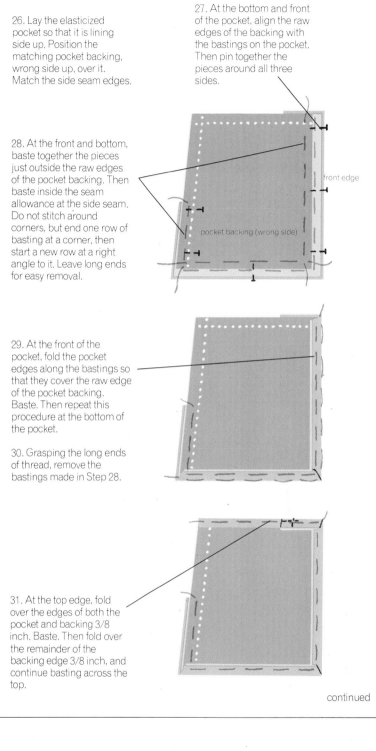

28. At the front and bottom, baste together the pieces just outside the raw edges of the pocket backing. Then baste inside the seam allowance at the side seam. Do not stitch around corners, but end one row of basting at a corner, then start a new row at a right angle to it. Leave long ends for easy removal.

29. At the front of the pocket, fold the pocket edges along the bastings so that they cover the raw edge of the pocket backing. Baste. Then repeat this procedure at the bottom of the pocket.

30. Grasping the long ends of thread, remove the bastings made in Step 28.

31. At the top edge, fold over the edges of both the pocket and backing 3/8 inch. Baste. Then fold over the remainder of the backing edge 3/8 inch, and continue basting across the top.

continued

ATTACHING POCKETS AND FACING TO THE DRESS

32. On the dress front sections, place pins at the cross marks of the pocket placement lines.

33. Turn the dress front wrong side down. Then position the pockets on the dress fronts, aligning the corners of each pocket with the pins. Also align the side seam lines. Pin. Baste 1/4 inch from the folded edges and remove all pins and the other bastings.

34. Using a straight stitch and thread of the same color as the garment fabric, machine stitch 1/8 inch from the folded edges. Then remove the remaining bastings.

35. Using contrasting thread and a large zigzag setting, machine stitch on top of the row of straight stitches.

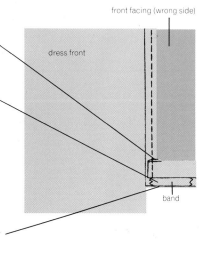

42. Trim the facing seam allowance to 1/4 inch.

43. Fold back the facing and dress seam allowances. Then trim the band to 1/8 inch from the stitching.

44. Clip through the garment hem allowance on a line with the facing hem. Cut to within 1/8 inch of the stitches. Then make another clip, this time cutting from the folded edge and 1/8 inch below the stitching, to create an L-shaped notch in the hem allowance.

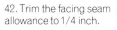

36. Follow your pattern instructions to stitch together the yoke, fronts and back and the collar of the dress.

37. Press the yoke seam allowances toward the dress back. Then, using contrasting thread and a large zigzag setting, machine stitch along the top of the yoke seams.

38. Still following the pattern, stitch and finish the collar and the back neck facing and stitch the front facings to the dress at the neck edge only.

39. Turn the garment wrong side down. Then fold back the front facings wrong sides out along the front fold lines.

40. Baste within the seam allowances the bottom edges of the facing to the hem edge of the dress.

41. Machine stitch along the seam allowance markings. Then remove all the bastings.

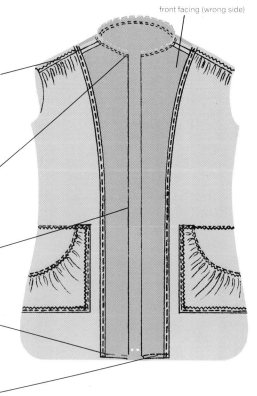

45. Turn the facing to the wrong side of the garment, pushing out the corners with the tips of a pair of scissors.

46. Following your pattern instructions, complete the garment up to the point that the sleeves would normally be sewed into the dress.

47. Using contrasting thread and a large zigzag setting, machine stitch along the edges of the collar as shown.

ATTACHING THE ARMHOLE FACING

48. Turn the armhole facing wrong side up. Then baste the ends together at the underarm seam, forming a circle. Machine stitch and remove the bastings. Press open the seams. Then trim to 1/2 inch.

49. To finish the unnotched edge of the facing, turn the edge over 1/4 inch and press flat. Then machine stitch 1/8 inch from the fold.

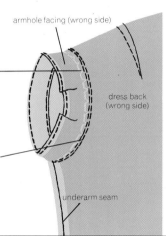

armhole facing (wrong side)

dress front

50. Turn the garment wrong side down. Pin the facing, wrong side up, to it along the armhole seam markings. Pin at the notches and seam intersections, then at 1/2-inch intervals. Baste and remove the pins.

51. Machine stitch along the seam markings, beginning and ending at the intersection between the underarm and armhole seams. Remove the basting.

52. Trim the garment seam allowance to 1/4 inch. Then trim the facing seam allowance to 1/8 inch.

53. Clip into both seam allowances up to, but not into, the stitches.

54. Turn the garment wrong side out. Then turn the facing so that it extends away from the garment. Press the armhole seam allowances toward the facing.

55. Understitch (Glossary) inside to the armhole seam. Begin and end the stitching at the underarm seam. Be sure the understitching catches the seam allowances beneath the facing fabric.

armhole facing (wrong side)

dress back (wrong side)

underarm seam

56. Turn the facing over the wrong side of the dress. Press flat.

57. Pin the facing to the dress at the shoulder and underarm seams as shown. Then attach the facing with a slip stitch (Appendix). Remove the pins.

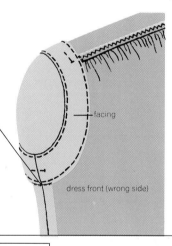

facing

dress front (wrong side)

FINISHING THE TENNIS DRESS

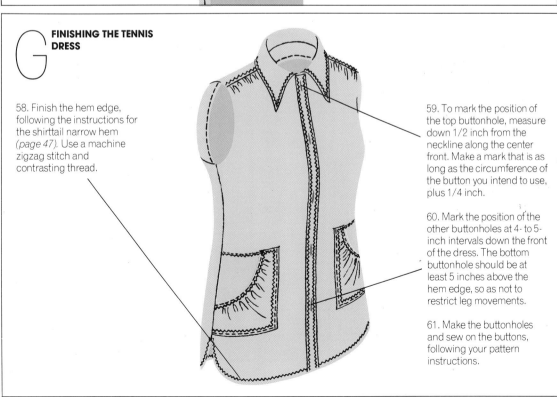

58. Finish the hem edge, following the instructions for the shirttail narrow hem (page 47). Use a machine zigzag stitch and contrasting thread.

59. To mark the position of the top buttonhole, measure down 1/2 inch from the neckline along the center front. Make a mark that is as long as the circumference of the button you intend to use, plus 1/4 inch.

60. Mark the position of the other buttonholes at 4- to 5-inch intervals down the front of the dress. The bottom buttonhole should be at least 5 inches above the hem edge, so as not to restrict leg movements.

61. Make the buttonholes and sew on the buttons, following your pattern instructions.

Geared up for the great outdoors

With warm wool on one side and rain-shedding poplin on the other, these reversible jackets can take in stride the fast-changing weather of any autumn or spring day. The duffel bags shown with them are ideal lightweight carryalls that fold up for easy storage. Both the jackets and the bags are home-sewing projects, explained in detail starting overleaf.

Each jacket comes from a standard shirt-style jacket pattern—purchased one size larger than your normal size to accommodate the bulk of two fabrics and then modified to achieve reversibility. In this design, even the closures reverse. One set of doubled-up shank buttons works for both sides.

The duffel bags need no commercial pattern; they can be made from scratch out of simple rectangles and circles of fabric, plus cotton webbing for the tote straps. For bulky loads, the large bag includes a detachable shoulder strap of adjustable length. Materials required for both the jackets and the bags are specified on the following pages.

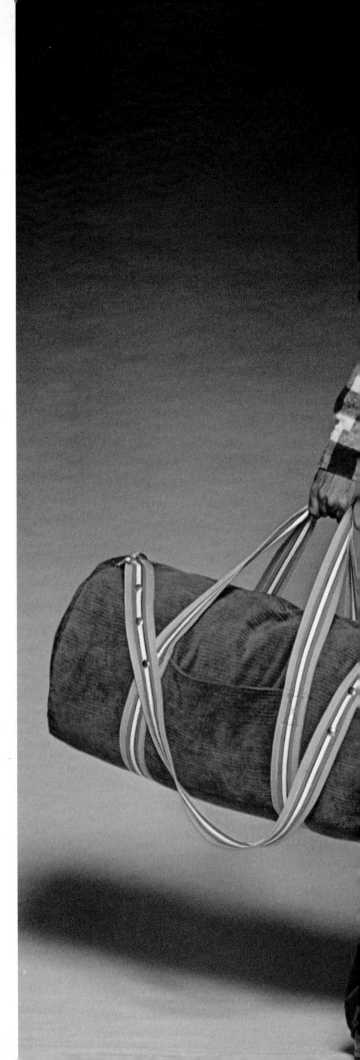

PREPARING THE PATTERN PIECES FOR THE REVERSIBLE JACKET

A MODIFYING THE COMMERCIAL PATTERN

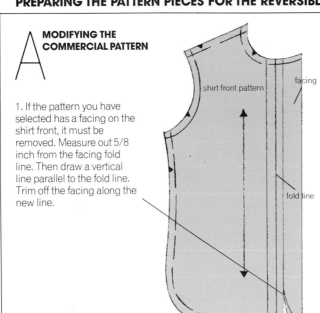

1. If the pattern you have selected has a facing on the shirt front, it must be removed. Measure out 5/8 inch from the facing fold line. Then draw a vertical line parallel to the fold line. Trim off the facing along the new line.

2. If the pattern has a one-piece cuff, you must modify the pattern in order to make a two-piece cuff. Measure out 5/8 inch from the fold line at the center of the pattern into the unnotched half of the cuff. Draw a line across the pattern parallel to the fold line. Cut the pattern piece along the new line.

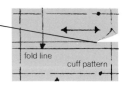

B MAKING THE NEW POCKET PATTERN PIECES

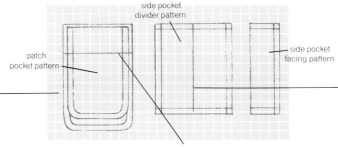

3. Cut out a piece of paper approximately 14 inches long and 26 inches wide. Mark it with a grid of 1-inch squares.

4. Transfer to your grid the shapes of the new pocket pattern pieces, as diagramed here. The pockets will be slightly different sizes for a man's or woman's jacket. Follow the instructions in Steps 5-9 for precise measurements.

5. Make the man's patch pocket pattern 10 3/4 inches long and 7 1/4 inches wide. Make the woman's patch pocket —superimposed on the man's in the diagram— 9 1/2 inches long and 6 3/4 inches wide.

6. Mark the fold lines for the patch pockets—2 3/4 inches down from the top edge on the man's pocket, 2 1/2 inches down from the top edge for the woman's. Then mark the seam lines 5/8 inch in from the side and bottom edges.

7. Make the man's side pocket divider pattern 9 inches long and 8 inches wide; make the woman's divider 8 inches square.

8. Mark the fold line at the center of the pocket divider, then mark seam lines 5/8 inch in from the side edges.

9. Make the man's side pocket facing pattern 9 inches long and 3 inches wide; make the woman's pattern 8 by 3 inches. Mark a seam line 5/8 inch in from one long edge.

10. Cut out the pattern pieces.

C MARKING THE POCKET PLACEMENT POINTS

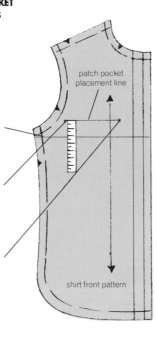

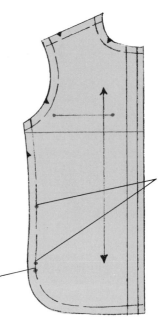

11. Place the shirt front pattern on a flat surface. Draw a straight line across the pattern from the intersection of the underarm seams to the opposite edge.

12. Using a ruler, measure up 2 inches from the line drawn in Step 11, and make a mark 1/2 inch in from the armhole seam line.

13. Measure the width of the patch pocket pattern piece at the top edge between the seam lines. Make another mark equal to this distance directly opposite the first mark. Then connect the two marks.

14. If on the pattern there is no marking for the beginning of the shirttail curve, make a mark on the seam line at the point where the side seam line stops curving and becomes vertical.

15. Measure up 1 inch from the mark made in the previous step. Make another mark to indicate the bottom point of the side pocket. Then measure up 6 inches for the woman's shirt—as in this example—and make a mark to indicate the top pocket point. Measure up 6 1/2 inches for a man's shirt.

16. Repeat Steps 14-15 to mark the side pocket points on the shirt back patterns.

A LAYING OUT THE PATTERN PIECES ON THE POPLIN FABRIC

1. For the cotton poplin shirt, you will need 1/4 yard more fabric than is recommended on the pattern envelope. Fold the fabric in half lengthwise, wrong side out.

2. Lay out the pattern pieces as indicated here if you are using 45-inch-wide fabric. If your fabric is of a different width, use the suggested layout included with your commercial pattern.

3. Place the center-back fold line and the collar—with the edges extending as shown —on the fabric fold. Then arrange the pattern pieces for the shirt front, sleeve, cuff, patch pocket, side pocket facing and side pocket divider on the fabric.

4. Pin the pattern pieces to the fabric. Then cut them out—except for the collar.

5. Transfer all seam lines, notches, fold lines and any other pattern markings onto the fabric, using a tracing wheel and dressmaker's carbon paper. Mark the shirttail curve and the side pocket points carefully, using chalk. Remove the pattern pieces.

6. Flip over the pattern piece for the side pocket facing —as indicated by the dash lines. Pin the pattern to the fabric again. Cut it out, so that you have four pocket facing pieces in all.

7. Cut out the collar, opening out the fabric at the fold so that it is a single layer, making only one collar section. Mark, as in Step 5.

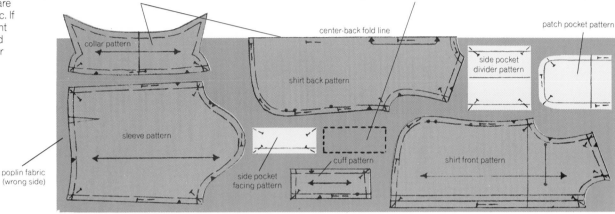

B LAYING OUT THE PATTERN PIECES ON THE WOOL FABRIC

8. For the wool shirt, buy the amount of fabric recommended on your pattern envelope. If you are making the shirt with a regular plaid fabric—as in the photograph on pages 112-113—buy an additional 1/4 yard for matching the plaid. Fold the fabric in half lengthwise, wrong side out.

9. If your fabric is a solid color, or if it is not 54 inches wide, follow the layout included with your pattern.

10. Determine which stripe in the plaid will be the main stripe in your design.

11. If you are working with a 54-inch-wide plaid fabric, begin to lay out the pattern pieces, making sure the notches on all corresponding pattern pieces—for example, the front and back shirt sections —are located in the same position on the main stripe of the plaid.

12. Make sure the center-front line on the shirt front pattern piece is located at the exact center of one of the main plaid stripes, so that the plaid will match at the center front when the garment is completed.

13. Place the patch pocket pattern on the fabric. The main plaid stripe should cross the fold line at the same point that it crosses the patch pocket placement line on the shirt front.

14. Locate the sleeve pattern on the fabric so that the main plaid stripe runs vertically down the center of the sleeve.

15. Position the cuff pattern piece so that the main plaid stripe runs horizontally around the center of the cuff.

16. Place the collar pattern on the fabric fold.

17. Pin the pattern pieces to the fabric and cut them out. Follow the instructions in Box A, Step 7, to cut out the collar.

18. Transfer all pattern markings as in Box A, Step 5. Use a contrasting color chalk to emphasize the markings on the wool fabric if the tracing wheel markings are not clearly visible.

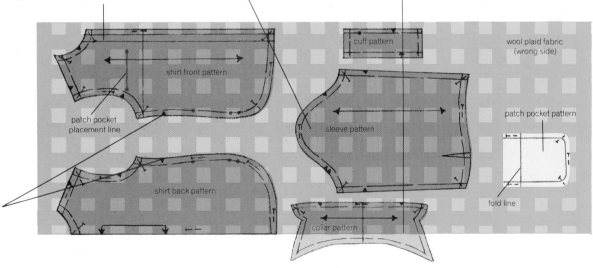

MAKING THE PATCH POCKET

A PREPARING THE POCKET

1. Place a patch pocket section wrong side up. Turn down the top edge 1/4 inch and press. Machine stitch close to the folded edge.

2. Machine stitch around the other three sides, sewing on the seam line.

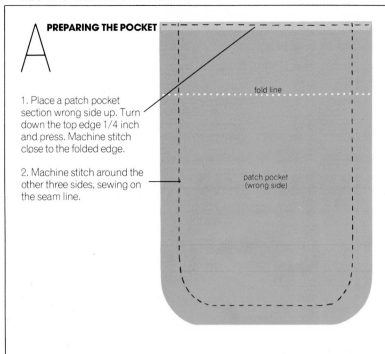

fold line

patch pocket (wrong side)

3. Turn the pocket section wrong side down. Fold down the top edge on the fold line.

4. Pin, then machine stitch each side hem edge, removing the pins as you sew.

5. Trim the two top corners diagonally. Trim the hem seam allowances to 1/4 inch. Then trim the pocket seam allowances to 1/4 inch, starting at the top of the fold, as shown.

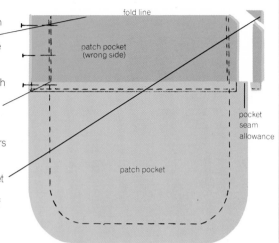

fold line

patch pocket (wrong side)

patch pocket

pocket seam allowance

6. Place the pocket wrong side up. Turn over the hem on the fold line. Gently push out the corners.

7. On each side of the pocket at the bottom, notch the curves at 1/2-inch intervals.

8. Fold in the seam allowances just beyond the line of machine stitching made in Step 2. Press.

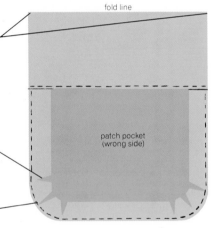

fold line

patch pocket (wrong side)

9. Turn the pocket wrong side down. Set your machine at 6 to 8 stitches to the inch. Topstitch the pocket, sewing 1/4 inch from the top edge, and 1/4 inch in from the sides.

10. Make two more rows of topstitching across the pocket. Stitch the first row 1 1/4 inches down from the fold line for the woman's shirt, and 2 inches down for the man's; then stitch the second row 1/4 inch below the first.

11. Repeat Steps 1-10 on the remaining patch pocket sections.

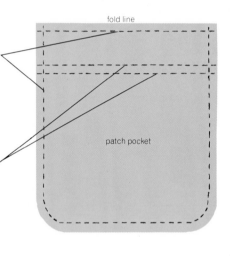

fold line

patch pocket

B ATTACHING THE POCKET

12. Place a shirt front section wrong side down. Align the fold line on the pocket to the placement line on the shirt front—visible on the wrong side.

13. Pin and baste the pocket to the shirt front, then remove the pins.

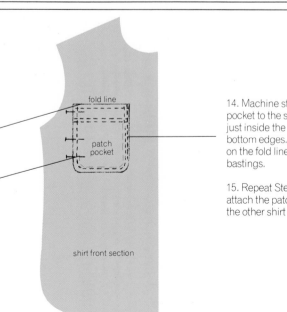

fold line

patch pocket

shirt front section

14. Machine stitch the pocket to the shirt, sewing just inside the side and bottom edges. Do not stitch on the fold line. Remove the bastings.

15. Repeat Steps 12-14 to attach the patch pockets to the other shirt front sections.

FACING THE SIDE POCKETS

A MARKING THE SHIRT FRONTS

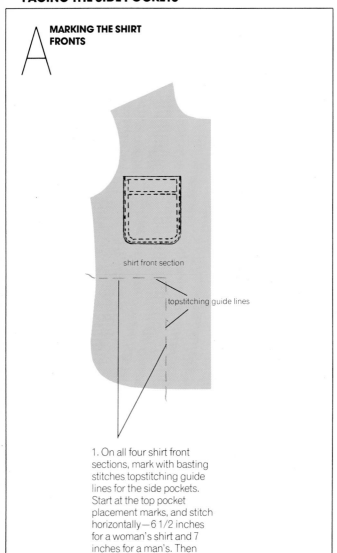

shirt front section

topstitching guide lines

1. On all four shirt front sections, mark with basting stitches topstitching guide lines for the side pockets. Start at the top pocket placement marks, and stitch horizontally—6 1/2 inches for a woman's shirt and 7 inches for a man's. Then stitch vertically to the bottom of the shirt.

B PREPARING THE FACING

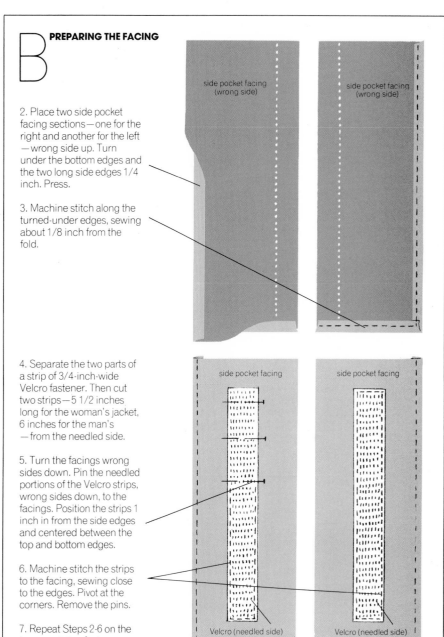

side pocket facing (wrong side)

side pocket facing (wrong side)

2. Place two side pocket facing sections—one for the right and another for the left—wrong side up. Turn under the bottom edges and the two long side edges 1/4 inch. Press.

3. Machine stitch along the turned-under edges, sewing about 1/8 inch from the fold.

side pocket facing

side pocket facing

4. Separate the two parts of a strip of 3/4-inch-wide Velcro fastener. Then cut two strips—5 1/2 inches long for the woman's jacket, 6 inches for the man's —from the needled side.

5. Turn the facings wrong sides down. Pin the needled portions of the Velcro strips, wrong sides down, to the facings. Position the strips 1 inch in from the side edges and centered between the top and bottom edges.

6. Machine stitch the strips to the facing, sewing close to the edges. Pivot at the corners. Remove the pins.

7. Repeat Steps 2-6 on the two remaining facings.

Velcro (needled side)

Velcro (needled side)

C ATTACHING THE SIDE POCKET FACINGS

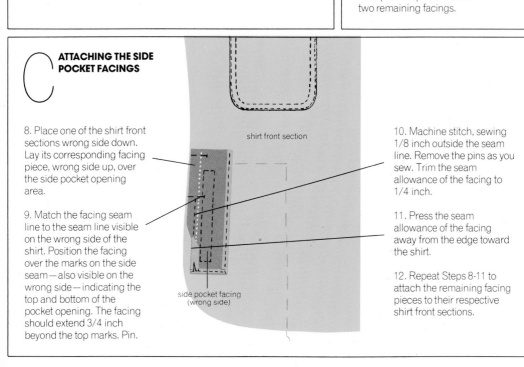

shirt front section

side pocket facing (wrong side)

8. Place one of the shirt front sections wrong side down. Lay its corresponding facing piece, wrong side up, over the side pocket opening area.

9. Match the facing seam line to the seam line visible on the wrong side of the shirt. Position the facing over the marks on the side seam—also visible on the wrong side—indicating the top and bottom of the pocket opening. The facing should extend 3/4 inch beyond the top marks. Pin.

10. Machine stitch, sewing 1/8 inch outside the seam line. Remove the pins as you sew. Trim the seam allowance of the facing to 1/4 inch.

11. Press the seam allowance of the facing away from the edge toward the shirt.

12. Repeat Steps 8-11 to attach the remaining facing pieces to their respective shirt front sections.

ASSEMBLING THE SHIRTS

A — STITCHING THE SHIRT SEAMS

1. Place the wool shirt fronts wrong sides up.

2. Cut two 2-inch-wide strips of iron-on interfacing. The strips should be long enough to extend 1/4 inch into the seam allowances at the top and bottom of the shirt fronts.

3. Position the strips so that they extend 1/4 inch into the top, bottom and center-front seam allowance.

4. Follow the instructions that come with the interfacing to fuse the pieces to the fabric.

5. Place the wool shirt back wrong side down. Over it, lay the two wool shirt fronts, wrong side up. Turn the facings away from the shirt fronts, as shown. Match and pin the shoulder seam lines.

6. Machine stitch the shoulder seams, removing the pins as you sew.

7. Match the side seam lines, and pin the sections together, making sure to align the plaid stripes.

8. Machine stitch the side seams, beginning at the underarm and continuing down to the marks for the top of the pocket opening. Remove the pins as you sew.

9. Match the marks indicating the beginning of the shirttail curve at each side seam. Then match the marks indicating the bottom of the pocket opening.

10. Pin and machine stitch between the two marks on each side. The distance of the stitching should be 1 inch.

11. Repeat Steps 5-10 on the poplin shirt.

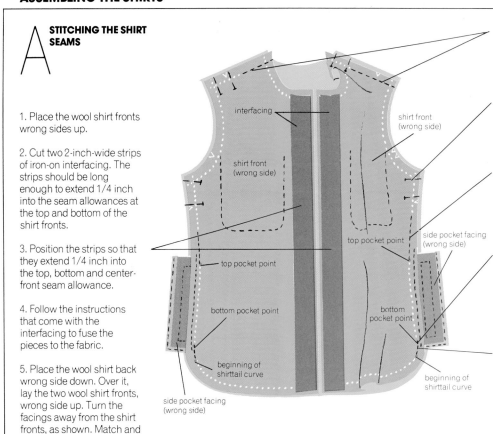

interfacing

shirt front (wrong side)

shirt front (wrong side)

top pocket point

top pocket point

bottom pocket point

bottom pocket point

side pocket facing (wrong side)

beginning of shirttail curve

beginning of shirttail curve

side pocket facing (wrong side)

B — STITCHING THE SLEEVES

12. Place one of the wool sleeves together, wrong side out. Match the plaid stripes and the seam lines. Pin the sleeve seam along the underarm seam line.

13. Machine stitch, beginning at the armhole and continuing down about 12 inches. Leave the rest of the sleeve seam open. Remove the pins.

14. Repeat Steps 12 and 13 on the other sleeves. Follow the pattern directions to set in the sleeves.

end of sleeve stitching

sleeve (wrong side)

C — JOINING THE TWO SHIRTS AT THE FRONT

15. Place the wool and poplin shirts together, wrong sides out.

16. Match the shoulder seams, and pin at the neck edges.

17. Slip the poplin sleeves into the wool sleeves. Then position the sleeves so that they are on the outside of the garment and extend away from the shirts, as shown.

18. Pin the two shirts together down both front seams. Then pin across both bottom-front sections until you reach the marks indicating the beginning of the shirttail curve.

19. Turn the pocket facings toward the shirt backs. Then machine stitch down both center fronts and around to the marks at the shirttail curves. Remove the pins as you sew.

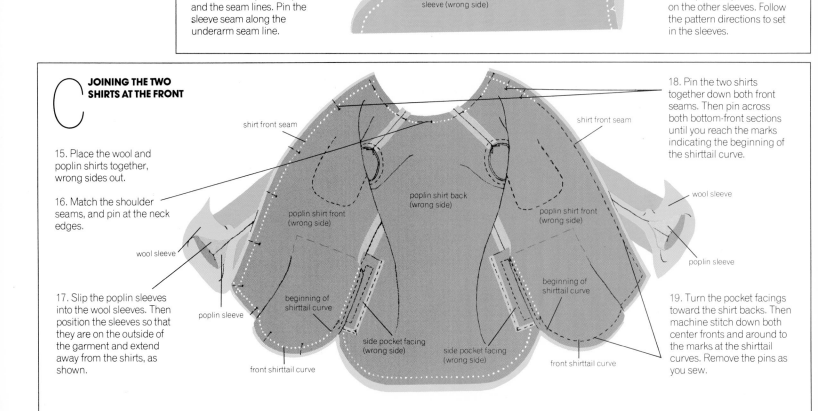

shirt front seam

shirt front seam

poplin shirt back (wrong side)

poplin shirt front (wrong side)

poplin shirt front (wrong side)

wool sleeve

wool sleeve

poplin sleeve

poplin sleeve

beginning of shirttail curve

beginning of shirttail curve

poplin sleeve

side pocket facing (wrong side)

side pocket facing (wrong side)

front shirttail curve

front shirttail curve

JOINING THE TWO SHIRTS AT THE BACK

20. Turn the facings toward the shirt fronts, as shown.

21. Pin the two shirts together around the back shirttail curve, making sure to match the points for the beginning of the shirttail curve on both sides.

22. Machine stitch the shirts together around the back curve, removing the pins as you sew.

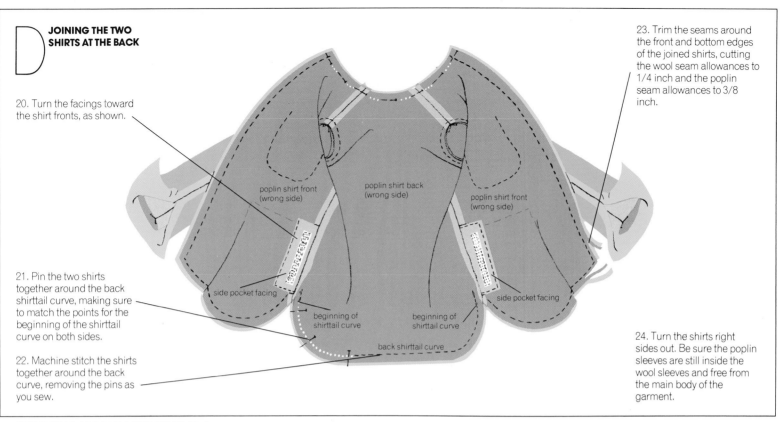

poplin shirt front (wrong side)

poplin shirt back (wrong side)

poplin shirt front (wrong side)

side pocket facing

beginning of shirttail curve

beginning of shirttail curve

side pocket facing

back shirttail curve

23. Trim the seams around the front and bottom edges of the joined shirts, cutting the wool seam allowances to 1/4 inch and the poplin seam allowances to 3/8 inch.

24. Turn the shirts right sides out. Be sure the poplin sleeves are still inside the wool sleeves and free from the main body of the garment.

INSERTING THE POCKET DIVIDERS

A
PREPARING THE POCKET DIVIDERS

1. Turn the bottom edge of one of the two side pocket dividers under 1/4 inch. Press. Then machine stitch just inside the fold.

2. Cut out two strips of the fuzzy side of the Velcro— 5 1/2 inches long for the woman's jacket, 6 inches long for the man's.

3. Place the strips on the right side of the side pocket divider. Position the strips 2 inches from the fold line, and center them between the top raw edge and the bottom hem of the divider.

4. Pin the strips to the divider, then machine stitch around all four sides of the strips, pivoting at the corners and removing the pins as you sew.

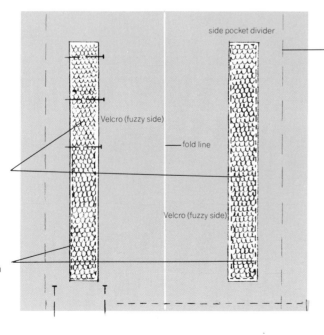

side pocket divider

Velcro (fuzzy side)

fold line

Velcro (fuzzy side)

5. Baste along the seam-line marks—5/8 inch in from each long side edge of the divider—so that the stitching lines will be visible on both sides of the piece.

6. Repeat Steps 1-5 on the other side pocket divider.

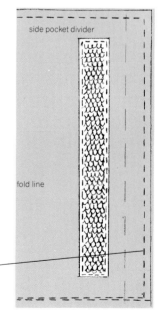

side pocket divider

fold line

7. Fold the divider in half along the fold line, wrong sides together. Then machine stitch around the top, bottom and side edges. Repeat on the other pocket divider.

continued

B INSTALLING THE POCKET DIVIDERS

8. Place the assembled jacket poplin side out. Flatten out the garment at the side, with one of the pocket openings spread apart.

9. Working through a pocket opening on the poplin side, fold the side pocket facing pieces at the opening toward the shirt fronts on the inside of the garment.

10. At the pocket opening, fold the back seams of the wool and poplin shirts toward the back—inside the shirts. Press the facings and the seams in place.

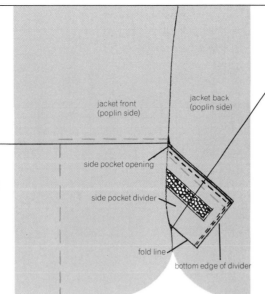

jacket front (poplin side)
jacket back (poplin side)
side pocket opening
side pocket divider
fold line
bottom edge of divider

11. Slip a side pocket divider, with the fold-line facing toward the fronts of the shirts, into the pocket opening. Sandwich the long side edge of the divider between the back seams.

12. Slide the bottom of the pocket divider down toward the shirttail. Align the Velcro strips on the two side pocket facings with those on the divider. Seal the Velcro strips shut.

13. Match the basted seam lines on the pocket divider with the folded edge of the wool back seam.

14. Pin and baste the pocket divider—uppermost in the drawing—to the wool shirt back seam, sewing on the seam line. Remove the pins.

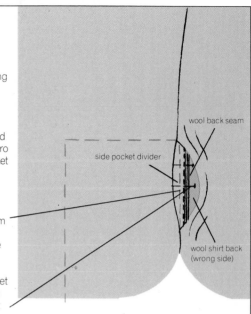

wool back seam
side pocket divider
wool shirt back (wrong side)

15. Place the folded-under back seam allowance of the poplin shirt over the basted seam line—and the extended seam allowance—of the pocket divider. Match the folded poplin edge to the basted seam line on the divider.

16. Pin and baste, sewing through all six thicknesses of fabric. These are: the folded-over wool back seam allowance; two layers of the pocket divider; and the folded-under poplin back seam allowance. Remove the pins.

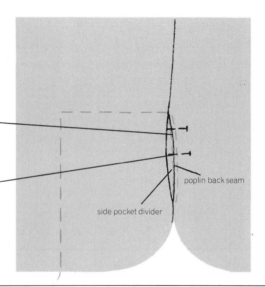

poplin back seam
side pocket divider

17. Turn the garment over to check if the wool shirt back seam allowance is aligned evenly and is caught by the bastings. (You will see both rows of bastings on this side.) Also check to see that the front pocket opening on this side is free and not caught by the basting stitches.

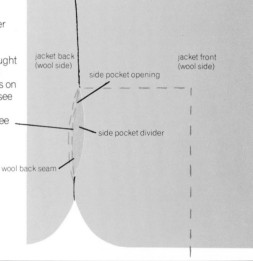

jacket back (wool side)
jacket front (wool side)
side pocket opening
side pocket divider
wool back seam

C STITCHING THE SIDE POCKET DIVIDER

18. Turn the jacket poplin side up. Machine stitch the divider to the backs of the shirts, sewing from the top pocket point to the bottom pocket point. Sew 1/4 inch toward the back from the basted edge of the pocket opening, again stitching through all six fabric thicknesses.

19. Remove the two rows of bastings made in Box B, Steps 14 and 16.

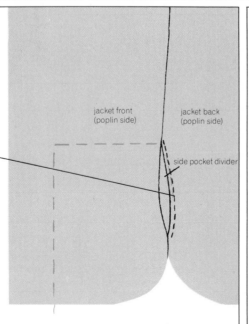

jacket front (poplin side)
jacket back (poplin side)
side pocket divider

D TOPSTITCHING THE SIDE POCKET

20. With the poplin side of the jacket still facing up, make a row of topstitching, following the guide bastings made in Box A (page 117). Set the machine at 6 to 8 stitches to the inch.

21. Make another row of topstitching 1/4 inch outside the row made in the previous step. Remove the bastings.

22. Repeat Steps 8-21 to complete the other side pocket.

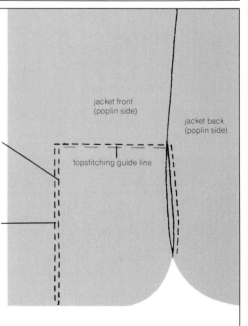

jacket front (poplin side)
jacket back (poplin side)
topstitching guide line

FINISHING THE SLEEVES

A. PREPARING THE PLACKET

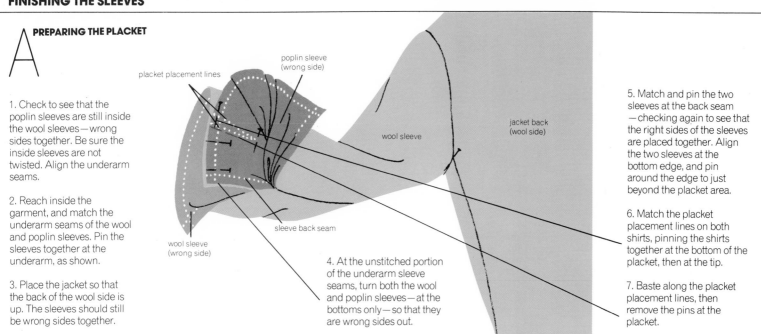

1. Check to see that the poplin sleeves are still inside the wool sleeves—wrong sides together. Be sure the inside sleeves are not twisted. Align the underarm seams.

2. Reach inside the garment, and match the underarm seams of the wool and poplin sleeves. Pin the sleeves together at the underarm, as shown.

3. Place the jacket so that the back of the wool side is up. The sleeves should still be wrong sides together.

4. At the unstitched portion of the underarm sleeve seams, turn both the wool and poplin sleeves—at the bottoms only—so that they are wrong sides out.

5. Match and pin the two sleeves at the back seam—checking again to see that the right sides of the sleeves are placed together. Align the two sleeves at the bottom edge, and pin around the edge to just beyond the placket area.

6. Match the placket placement lines on both shirts, pinning the shirts together at the bottom of the placket, then at the tip.

7. Baste along the placket placement lines, then remove the pins at the placket.

B. STITCHING THE PLACKET

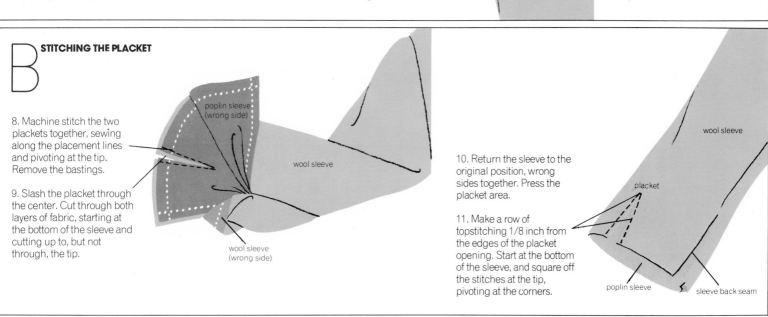

8. Machine stitch the two plackets together, sewing along the placement lines and pivoting at the tip. Remove the bastings.

9. Slash the placket through the center. Cut through both layers of fabric, starting at the bottom of the sleeve and cutting up to, but not through, the tip.

10. Return the sleeve to the original position, wrong sides together. Press the placket area.

11. Make a row of topstitching 1/8 inch from the edges of the placket opening. Start at the bottom of the sleeve, and square off the stitches at the tip, pivoting at the corners.

C. STITCHING THE UNDERARM SEAMS

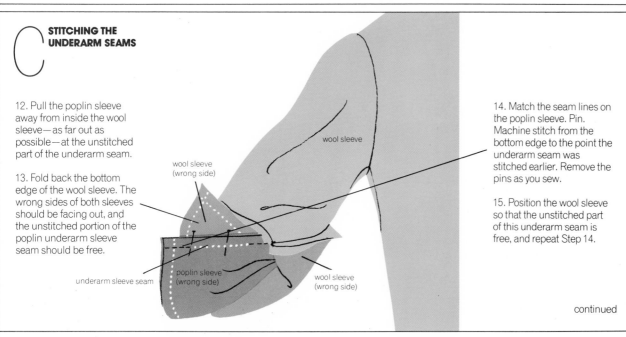

12. Pull the poplin sleeve away from inside the wool sleeve—as far out as possible—at the unstitched part of the underarm seam.

13. Fold back the bottom edge of the wool sleeve. The wrong sides of both sleeves should be facing out, and the unstitched portion of the poplin underarm sleeve seam should be free.

14. Match the seam lines on the poplin sleeve. Pin. Machine stitch from the bottom edge to the point the underarm seam was stitched earlier. Remove the pins as you sew.

15. Position the wool sleeve so that the unstitched part of this underarm seam is free, and repeat Step 14.

continued

D MAKING THE PLEATS

16. With the right side of the wool sleeve facing up, position the bottom of the sleeve so that the placket is facing toward the back, as shown.

17. Fold in two 1/2-inch pleats, approximately 3/4 inch in front of the placket opening. Make sure the pleats open and are smoothed toward the back of the sleeve—in this case, toward the placket opening. Pin the pleats in place.

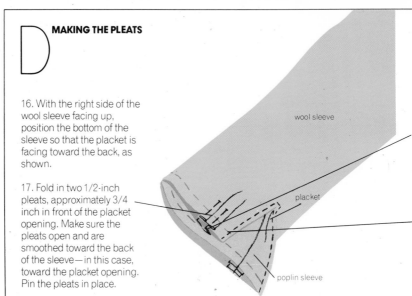

18. Turn the bottom of the sleeve up so that the poplin side is facing out. Then fold and pin in two pleats on this side of the sleeve, as in Steps 16 and 17. Make sure these pleats also open toward the back of the sleeve, that is, in the opposite direction from the pleats on the wool sleeve.

19. Turn the sleeve, wool side up. Baste around the bottom of the sleeve, sewing through both sleeves and through all layers of fabric at the two pairs of pleats. Remove the pins.

20. Repeat Steps 2-19 on the other sleeve.

E PREPARING THE CUFFS

21. Using the pattern piece for the cuff, cut out two pieces of iron-on interfacing. Mark the seam lines, then trim the seam allowances to 1/4 inch.

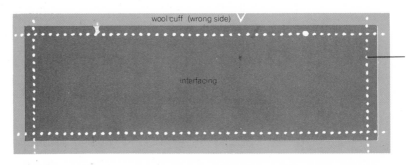

22. Place the wool section of one of the cuffs wrong side up. Cover the cuff with one of the interfacing pieces, matching the seam lines. Follow the instructions that come with the interfacing to fuse the two pieces together.

23. Place a poplin cuff section wrong side up. Fold down the seam allowance on the notched edge. Press flat.

24. Turn the wool cuff section interfaced side down. Lay the poplin section, wrong side up, over it, matching the seam lines. Then pin them together at the sides and along the unnotched edge.

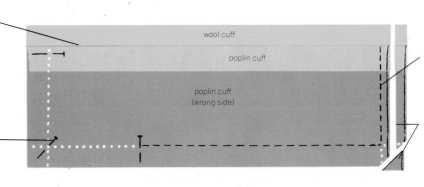

25. Machine stitch around the pinned edges, sewing on the seam lines and removing the pins as you go.

26. Trim the corners diagonally. Then trim off the seam allowances to 1/4 inch beyond the machine stitching.

27. Turn the cuff so that both right sides are facing out. Gently poke out the corners. At the cuff opening, the wrong side of the wool seam allowance will extend away from the cuff.

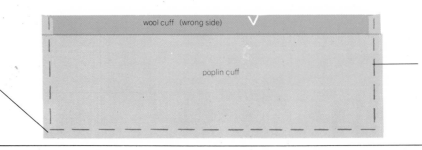

28. Roll out the machine-stitched edges of the cuff with your fingers so the seams are even. Baste around the edges. Press.

F ATTACHING THE CUFFS

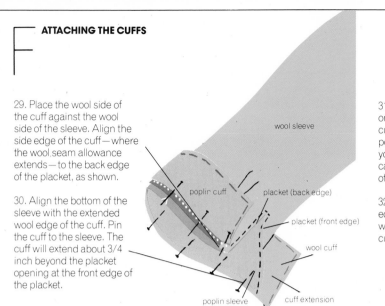

29. Place the wool side of the cuff against the wool side of the sleeve. Align the side edge of the cuff—where the wool seam allowance extends—to the back edge of the placket, as shown.

30. Align the bottom of the sleeve with the extended wool edge of the cuff. Pin the cuff to the sleeve. The cuff will extend about 3/4 inch beyond the placket opening at the front edge of the placket.

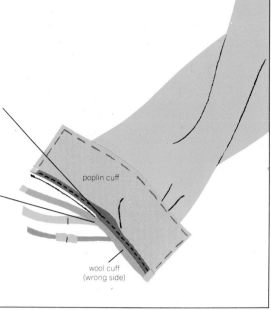

31. Machine stitch, sewing on the seam line of the wool cuff and over the extended portion of the interfacing. As you stitch, be careful not to catch the folded-under edge of the poplin cuff.

32. Trim the poplin sleeve edge to 3/8 inch, and the wool sleeve edge and wool cuff edge to 1/4 inch.

G FINISHING THE CUFF

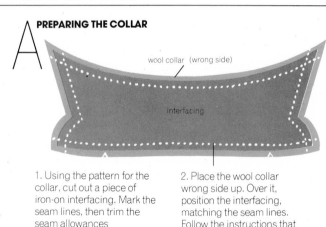

33. Turn the sleeve so that the placket is visible. Pull the cuff away from the sleeve so that the poplin side is facing up.

34. Pull the free poplin edge of the cuff away from the cuff itself. Press the trimmed seam allowances of the cuff and sleeves toward the cuff.

35. Lap the folded edge of the poplin cuff over the row of machine stitching. Pin.

36. To enclose the cuff extension—beyond the placket—fold the wool seam allowance into the cuff along the seam allowance, so that the folded edges of both cuff sections are aligned. Pin.

37. Slip stitch (Appendix) the folded edges of the cuff extension together. Then continue to slip stitch along the folded edge of the poplin cuff to attach it to the poplin sleeve. Remove the pins and the bastings around the sides of the cuff.

38. Repeat Steps 22-37 to prepare and attach the other cuff.

MAKING THE COLLAR

A PREPARING THE COLLAR

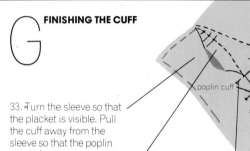

1. Using the pattern for the collar, cut out a piece of iron-on interfacing. Mark the seam lines, then trim the seam allowances to 1/4 inch.

2. Place the wool collar wrong side up. Over it, position the interfacing, matching the seam lines. Follow the instructions that come with the interfacing to fuse the two pieces together.

3. Place the poplin collar section wrong side up. Fold down the seam allowance at the notched edge. Press flat.

4. Turn the wool collar interfacing side down. Lay the poplin collar, wrong side up, over it.

5. Match the seam lines and center-front edges on both collars. Pin the collars together at the sides and along the unnotched edge.

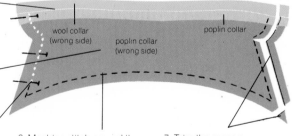

6. Machine stitch around the three pinned edges, sewing on the seam line and removing the pins as you go.

7. Trim the corners diagonally. Then trim the seam allowances to 1/4 inch beyond the machine stitching.

8. Clip both sides of the collar at the curves, cutting up to, but not through, the machine stitching.

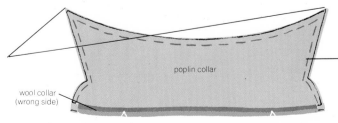

9. Turn the collar so that the right sides are facing out. Gently poke out the corners.

10. Roll the edges of the collar out with your fingers so the seams are even. Baste around the machine-stitched edges. Press.

continued

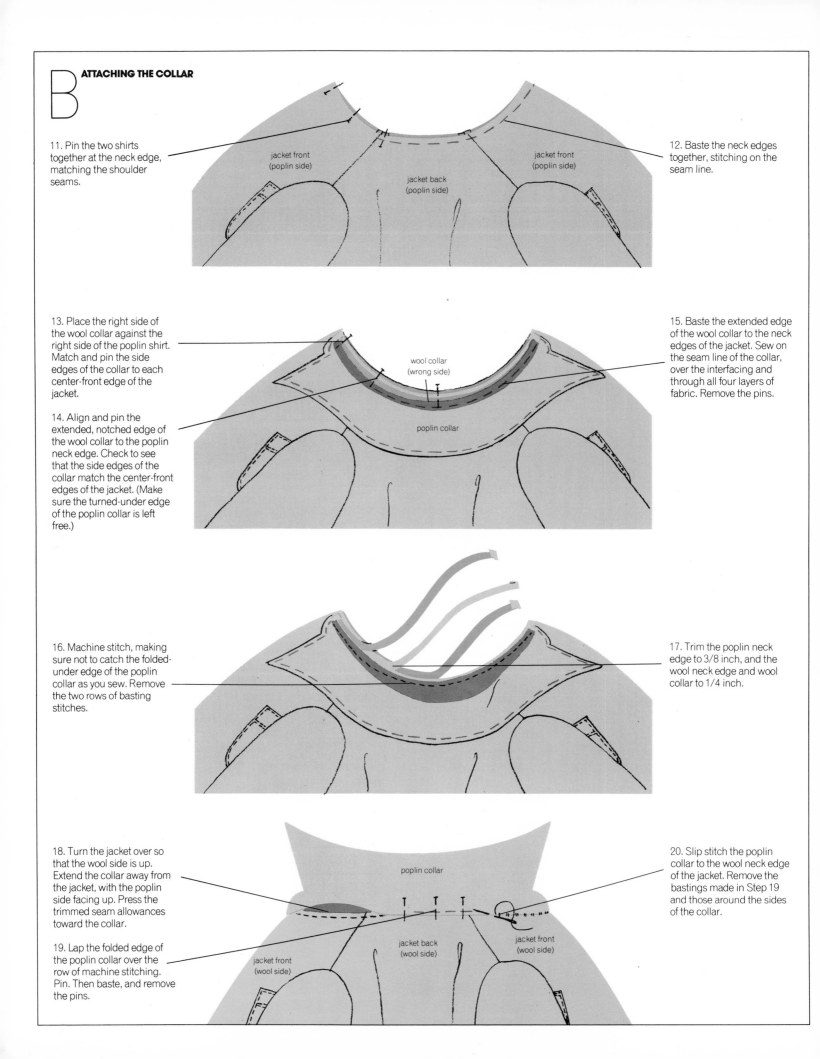

11. Pin the two shirts together at the neck edge, matching the shoulder seams.

jacket front (poplin side)

jacket back (poplin side)

jacket front (poplin side)

12. Baste the neck edges together, stitching on the seam line.

13. Place the right side of the wool collar against the right side of the poplin shirt. Match and pin the side edges of the collar to each center-front edge of the jacket.

14. Align and pin the extended, notched edge of the wool collar to the poplin neck edge. Check to see that the side edges of the collar match the center-front edges of the jacket. (Make sure the turned-under edge of the poplin collar is left free.)

wool collar (wrong side)

poplin collar

15. Baste the extended edge of the wool collar to the neck edges of the jacket. Sew on the seam line of the collar, over the interfacing and through all four layers of fabric. Remove the pins.

16. Machine stitch, making sure not to catch the folded-under edge of the poplin collar as you sew. Remove the two rows of basting stitches.

17. Trim the poplin neck edge to 3/8 inch, and the wool neck edge and wool collar to 1/4 inch.

18. Turn the jacket over so that the wool side is up. Extend the collar away from the jacket, with the poplin side facing up. Press the trimmed seam allowances toward the collar.

19. Lap the folded edge of the poplin collar over the row of machine stitching. Pin. Then baste, and remove the pins.

poplin collar

jacket front (wool side)

jacket back (wool side)

jacket front (wool side)

20. Slip stitch the poplin collar to the wool neck edge of the jacket. Remove the bastings made in Step 19 and those around the sides of the collar.

FINISHING THE JACKET

A MAKING THE TOPSTITCHING

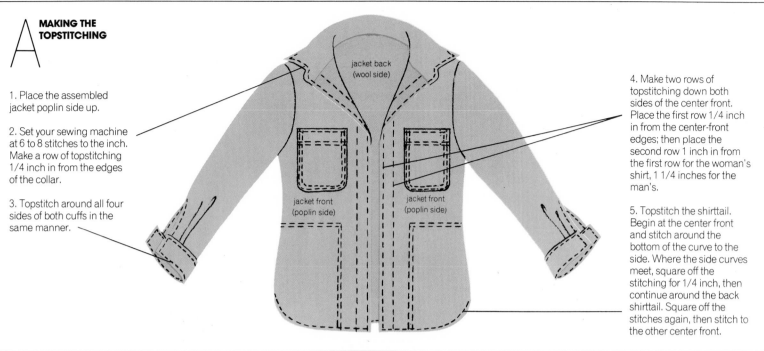

1. Place the assembled jacket poplin side up.

2. Set your sewing machine at 6 to 8 stitches to the inch. Make a row of topstitching 1/4 inch in from the edges of the collar.

3. Topstitch around all four sides of both cuffs in the same manner.

4. Make two rows of topstitching down both sides of the center front. Place the first row 1/4 inch in from the center-front edges; then place the second row 1 inch in from the first row for the woman's shirt, 1 1/4 inches for the man's.

5. Topstitch the shirttail. Begin at the center front and stitch around the bottom of the curve to the side. Where the side curves meet, square off the stitching for 1/4 inch, then continue around the back shirttail. Square off the stitches again, then stitch to the other center front.

B MAKING THE BUTTONHOLES AND THE BUTTON SHANKS

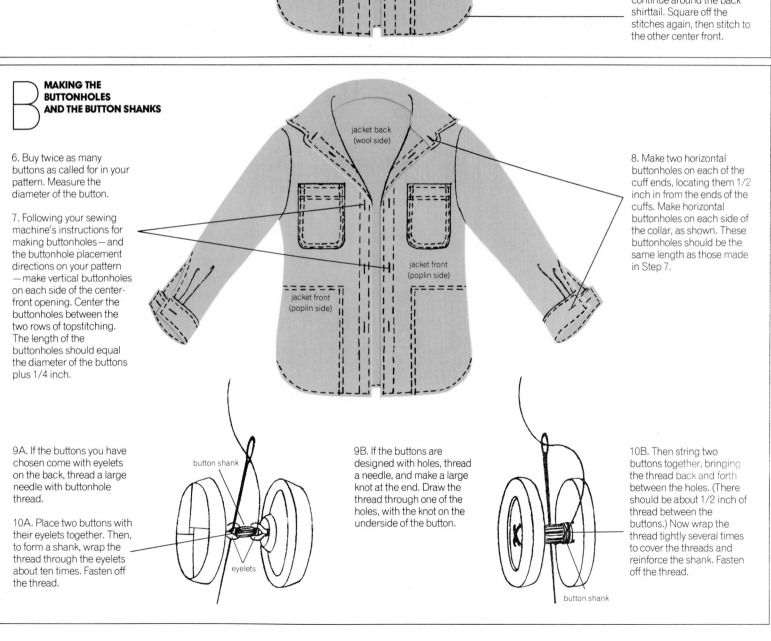

6. Buy twice as many buttons as called for in your pattern. Measure the diameter of the button.

7. Following your sewing machine's instructions for making buttonholes—and the buttonhole placement directions on your pattern—make vertical buttonholes on each side of the center-front opening. Center the buttonholes between the two rows of topstitching. The length of the buttonholes should equal the diameter of the buttons plus 1/4 inch.

8. Make two horizontal buttonholes on each of the cuff ends, locating them 1/2 inch in from the ends of the cuffs. Make horizontal buttonholes on each side of the collar, as shown. These buttonholes should be the same length as those made in Step 7.

9A. If the buttons you have chosen come with eyelets on the back, thread a large needle with buttonhole thread.

10A. Place two buttons with their eyelets together. Then, to form a shank, wrap the thread through the eyelets about ten times. Fasten off the thread.

9B. If the buttons are designed with holes, thread a needle, and make a large knot at the end. Draw the thread through one of the holes, with the knot on the underside of the button.

10B. Then string two buttons together, bringing the thread back and forth between the holes. (There should be about 1/2 inch of thread between the buttons.) Now wrap the thread tightly several times to cover the threads and reinforce the shank. Fasten off the thread.

MAKING THE PATTERNS FOR THE DUFFEL BAGS

1. To make the bag pattern for the small—11 inches by 19 inches—duffel bag shown on page 113, first cut out a large piece of paper that measures at least 20 inches by 23 inches. If you are making the large—13 1/2 inches by 26 inches —bag, the paper should measure 22 inches by 29 inches. (In the instructions that follow, dimensions for the large bag are given in parentheses.)

2. On it, draw a rectangle that measures 17 1/8 inches by 19 inches (21 inches by 27 inches). Use the straight edge of the paper for one of the longer sides of the rectangle, as shown.

3. At the mid-point on each vertical line make a dot.

paper

bag pattern

fold

4. Draw cutting lines 5/8 inch outside of, and parallel to, the three drawn sides of the rectangle.

5. Make notch marks on the seam allowances opposite the dots made in Step 3.

6. Make another pair of notch marks on the seam allowances at the lower corners, just above the edge of the paper.

7. Draw a grain-line arrow. Then label the pattern as indicated.

8. Cut out the pattern along the cutting lines.

9. To make the pocket pattern, draw a rectangle that measures 8 inches by 10 inches (10 inches by 12 1/2 inches). This time one of the shorter sides of the rectangle should be one straight edge of the paper.

paper

pocket pattern

fold

10. Complete the pattern following Steps 4 and 6-8.

11. To make the pattern for the round ends, first draw 15-inch-long horizontal and vertical lines in the center of a piece of paper. The lines should bisect each other at a right angle, forming a cross.

12. Using a compass and swinging from the intersection of the two lines, draw a circle that measures 11 (13 1/2) inches in diameter.

13. Adjust the compass, and draw a cutting line 5/8 inch outside of the circle.

14. Draw a grain-line arrow on the vertical line.

paper

bag end pattern

15. Make double notch marks on the seam allowance at both ends of the grain line.

16. Make single notch marks on the seam allowance at the ends of the horizontal line.

17. Cut out the pattern along the outer circle.

LAYING OUT, CUTTING AND MARKING

1. To make the duffel bag, you will need 1 1/8 (1 5/8) yards of 45-inch-wide fabric; 2 3/4 (3 1/8) yards of 2-inch-wide strapping; a 19-inch (27-inch) heavy-duty metal zipper; and heavy-duty thread. To make the detachable shoulder strap for the large bag, you will also need 2 yards of strapping; four 2-inch-wide D rings; and six 1/2-inch heavy-duty snap fasteners.

2. Fold the fabric in half crosswise, wrong side out, aligning edges.

selvage

fabric (wrong side)

bag pattern

pocket pattern

bag end pattern

fold

fold

fold

3. Pin the pattern pieces on the fabric. Make sure the grain lines are parallel to the selvages, and the two rectangular patterns are on the fold of the fabric as indicated.

4. Cut out the pattern pieces, cutting notch marks outward as you go.

5. Using a tracing wheel and dressmaker's carbon paper, mark the seam lines on the wrong sides of the fabric pieces. Remove the patterns.

MAKING THE DUFFEL BAGS

A HEMMING AND ATTACHING THE POCKET PIECE

1. Place the pocket piece, wrong side up, on an ironing board.

2. Turn in the edges 1/4 inch on the narrow sides of the piece. Press.

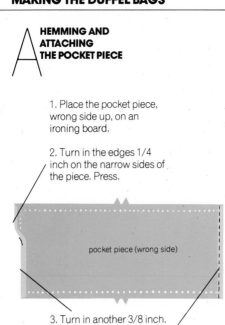

pocket piece (wrong side)

3. Turn in another 3/8 inch. Press.

4. Machine stitch along the hems.

5. Place the bag piece, wrong side down, on a flat surface.

6. Center the pocket piece, also wrong side down, over it so that the double notch marks of the pocket piece line up with those of the bag piece. Pin.

7. Baste 1/2 inch in from the long edges of the pocket piece. Remove the pins.

8. To delineate the center bottom of the bag, make two rows of machine stitching, 1/8 inch apart, through the center of the pocket piece between the notches.

9. To outline the bottoms of the pockets, make two rows of stitching—1/8 inch apart—on both sides of the stitchings made in Step 8. The distance from the center bottom to the pocket bottoms should be 3 (4) inches.

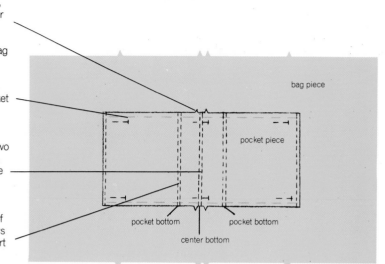

bag piece

pocket piece

pocket bottom   pocket bottom

center bottom

B MAKING AND ATTACHING THE STRAP HANDLES

10. Cut the strapping to a length of 2 yards and 23 inches (3 yards and 4 inches).

11. Fold the strapping in half. Mark the mid-point with a pin.

14. With the raw ends of the strap facing down, match the strap seam with the center bottom of the bag. Then cover 5/8 inch of the raw pocket edge with the long side of the strap. Pin.

15. Pin the strap to the pocket and the bag pieces up to the hemmed edges of the pockets. Conceal 5/8 inch of the basted edge of the pocket piece as you pin.

16. Attach the strap to the other side in the same way, this time aligning the pin mark made on the strap in Step 11 to the center bottom. Make sure the strap handles are not twisted.

12. Machine stitch the cut ends together, 1/2 inch from the edge.

13. Trim the corners diagonally. Press open the seam.

17. Machine stitch 1/8 inch in from the outside edge of the strap, removing the pins as you sew. At the point where the pocket piece ends, pivot, then stitch across the strap.

18. Repeat Step 17 on the inside edge and other side. Then remove the bastings made in Step 7.

19. Reinforce the base of the strap handles by stitching a 2-inch-long boxed X, 1/4 inch inside the stitchings made in Steps 17 and 18. Repeat on the other three corners.

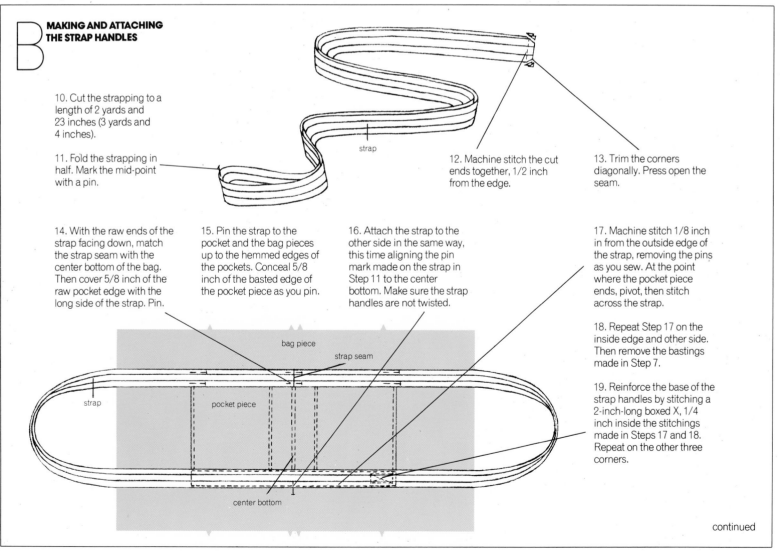

strap

bag piece

strap seam

strap   pocket piece

center bottom

continued

C ATTACHING THE ZIPPER

20. Turn the seam allowance under along the narrow sides of the bag piece. Press. If the fabric frays, finish the raw edges with zigzag stitches, or sew on a strip of seam binding.

21. Place the zipper, face up, under one folded edge. Keep the fabric 1/4 inch from the zipper teeth to prevent snagging. Pin.

22. Baste 1/8 inch from the folded edge. Remove the pins.

23. Machine stitch close to the folded edge. Reinforce by stitching another row 1/8 inch away. Remove the basting.

24. Bring the other folded edge around and over to the zipper, forming a tubular bag body behind. Attach the zipper to the edge, following Steps 21-23. If necessary, slide open the zipper to avoid catching the excess fabric behind.

25. If you are making the detachable shoulder strap for the large bag, skip to Box E.

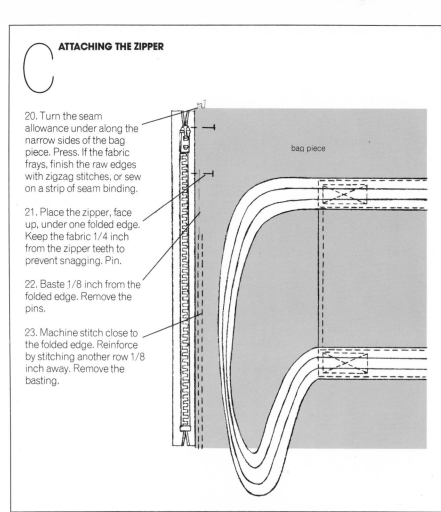

bag piece

D ATTACHING THE ROUND ENDS

26. Turn the bag body wrong side out.

27. Position the round end pieces, wrong sides out, to the openings of the bag body. Match the notches and pin.

28. Baste just outside the seam-line markings. Remove the pins.

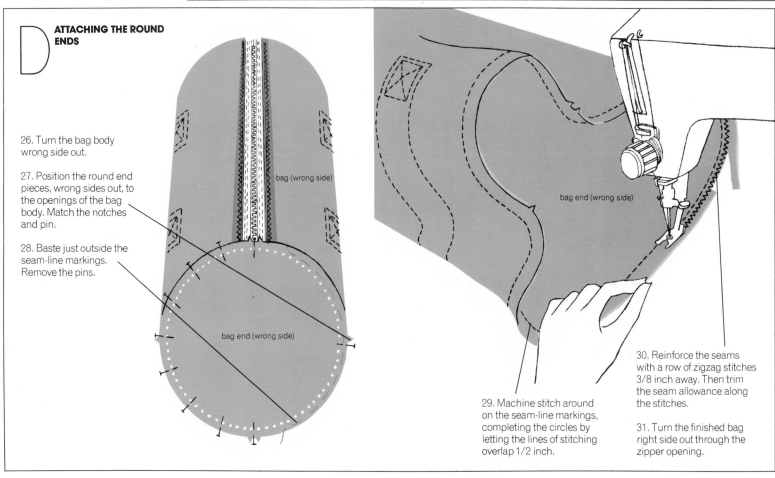

bag (wrong side)

bag end (wrong side)

bag end (wrong side)

29. Machine stitch around on the seam-line markings, completing the circles by letting the lines of stitching overlap 1/2 inch.

30. Reinforce the seams with a row of zigzag stitches 3/8 inch away. Then trim the seam allowance along the stitches.

31. Turn the finished bag right side out through the zipper opening.

32. First make the shoulder strap carriers by cutting two lengths of the strapping 3 inches long.

33. Slide two D rings on each piece. Then fold the strap pieces in half and machine stitch 1/4 inch from the cut ends.

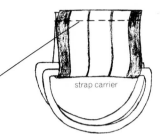

strap carrier

34. Position the carriers on the bag body over the zippered ends, aligning the raw edges and centering the pieces. Pin.

35. Machine baste 1/2 inch from the raw edges, removing the pins as you sew.

36. Attach the round ends to the bag body, following the instructions in Box D.

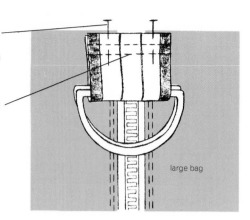

large bag

37. Cut a 1 3/4-yard-long strip of strapping. Finish the raw ends with hand overcast or machine zigzag stitches.

38. Turn in the ends 1/2 inch. Press.

39. Machine stitch 1/4 inch in from the folded ends.

40. Mark the positions for the snaps on the strap. Place the first marks 1 inch from each end. Then make five more marks at 3-inch intervals along each end.

41. Punch holes through the strap over the markings.

42. Install the snaps, following the instructions that come with the kit. On each end of the strap, place the bottom parts of the snaps in the three holes closest to the ends and the top parts in the remaining three holes.

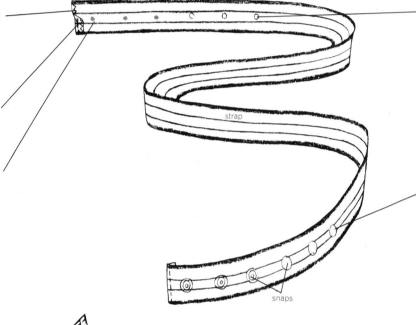

strap

snaps

43. Feed the finished shoulder strap through the D rings as illustrated. Snap the strap in place to the desired length.

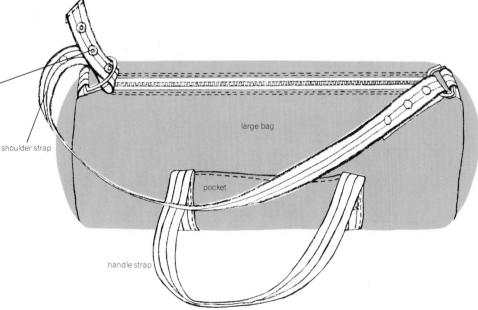

shoulder strap

large bag

pocket

handle strap

A bright idea in overalls

When a clever seamstress elevates the lowly overall design into a pattern for a ski suit like the one at left, she not only sets a new height in winter fashion, but can save herself two thirds of the cost of a comparable outfit bought in a shop. In addition, ski overalls offer functional advantages over pants. Their high front and back bibs help keep the skier warm and dry. And the elasticized straps that rest lightly on the shoulders are far more comfortable than the tight waistband on ski pants.

Both the overalls and form-fitted jacket start with standard patterns. The overalls pattern must be one size larger than your normal size, and the jacket two sizes larger, to allow for padding and other thermal underpinnings. In its metamorphosis to ski wear, the overalls pattern gets welt pockets, and snow cuffs inside the bottoms of the pants legs. The jacket is then padded, quilted, pocketed, zippered—and finished with ready-made wrist cuffs. Detailed directions for both the overalls and jacket begin overleaf.

TAKING MEASUREMENTS

1. Put on the sweater and undergarments you would normally wear under a ski outfit.

2. Measure your bustline around the fullest part of the bust, loosely draping the tape.

3. Measure your waistline around the narrowest part of the waist.

4. Measure down from your waist to the fullest part of your hips.

5. Measure the circumference of your hips around the fullest part.

6. Measure across the widest part of the back, from the center of one armhole to the center of the other.

7. Measure the circumference of your upper arm, placing the tape 1 inch below the underarm.

8. To determine the proper sleeve length, slightly bend your elbow. Then measure along the outside of the arm, from the shoulder bone to the wristbone.

9. Measure the circumference of your wrist at the wristbone.

10. To establish the desired length of the finished jacket, measure from the top of your spine to the point where you want the hem to fall—about 10 to 12 inches below the waistline.

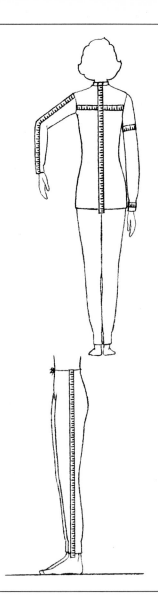

11. Tie a cord around your waist. To determine your crotch length, sit on a hard surface and measure from the cord to that surface.

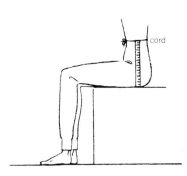

12. Measure along the side seam from the cord to the desired finished length of the pants—usually the ankle.

PREPARING THE JACKET PATTERN

A ADJUSTING THE LENGTH OF THE PATTERN

1. To adjust the hem on the jacket back pattern, measure down the center-back seam line from the neck seam line a distance equal to the desired length of the jacket. Make a mark.

2. Measure the distance between the mark and the bottom edge of the pattern. Then take that measurement and make a series of marks across the pattern, following the curve at the bottom edge of the pattern. Connect the marks to create a new hemline.

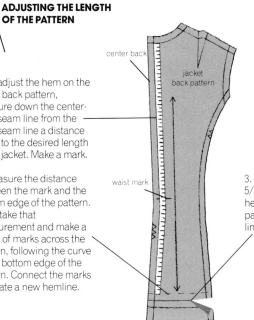

center back

jacket back pattern

waist mark

3. Draw a new cutting line 5/8 inch below the new hemline. Then trim the pattern along the cutting line.

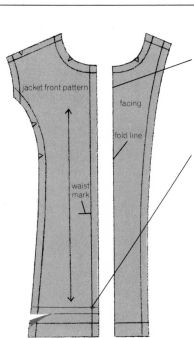

jacket front pattern

facing

fold line

waist mark

4. If your jacket front pattern has an all-in-one facing, cut it off along the fold line.

5. On the back pattern, measure the center-back line from the adjusted hemline to the waist mark. Then, on the front pattern, measure that distance from the waist on the center-front line. Make a mark.

6. Repeat Steps 2 and 3 to finish the hemline adjustment on the front pattern.

7. To adjust the hemline on the side-front and side-back jacket patterns, repeat Steps 5 and 6.

ADJUSTING THE PATTERNS AT THE CROSS BACK, BUST, WAIST AND HIP

8. Pin together the back and the side-back patterns, aligning the side-back seam lines.

9. Measure across the pattern pieces from the middle of the armhole seam line to the center-back seam line. Double the measurement.

10. Add 2 1/2 inches for ease to your cross back measurement.

11. Subtract the measurement found in Step 10 from the measurement determined in Step 9. Then divide the difference by two.

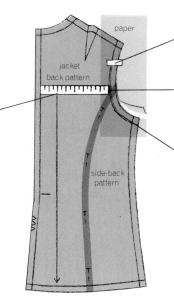

12. Tape a piece of paper under the joined pieces at the armhole.

13. At the center of the armhole, measure out from the original seam line a distance equal to the figure determined in Step 11. Make a mark.

14. From the mark, draw a new seam line that blends into the original seam line above and below the mark.

15. Draw a new cutting line 5/8 inch outside the new seam line. Then trim off the excess paper. Do not unpin the pattern pieces.

16. Pin together the front and the side-front patterns, aligning the side-front seam lines.

17. Add 4 inches for ease to your bust measurement.

18. Add 5 to 6 inches for ease to your waist and hip measurements.

19. At the level of the bust, waist and hiplines, measure across the pattern pieces between the center-front and side seam lines. Then measure across the combined back pattern pieces at the same levels, this time between the center-back and side seam lines.

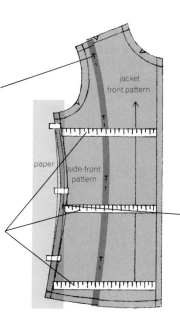

20. Add together the front and back measurements for the bust, waist and hips.

21. Compare the measurements determined in Step 20 with the bust, waist and hip figures found in Steps 17 and 18. Divide the differences by four.

22. Using the figures determined in Step 21, repeat Steps 12-15 to take in or let out the back pattern. Make the adjustments at the side seam—the waist in this example. Adjust the front pattern in the same manner. Then unpin the pattern pieces.

ADJUSTING THE PRINCESS SEAM LINE ON THE JACKET FRONT

23A. If your pattern was designed with a princess seam line starting at the shoulder, skip to Box E.

23B. If the princess seam line starts at the armhole, you will have to modify the pattern. Working on the jacket front pattern, measure along the shoulder seam line 1 1/2 inches from the armhole seam line. Mark.

24. Starting at the mark made in Step 23, draw a slightly curved line that blends into the side-front seam line at the bust level —about 1 inch below the underarm seam line.

25. Draw a line from the end of the one drawn in Step 24 to the edge of the pattern. Then transfer the notches to the new seam line.

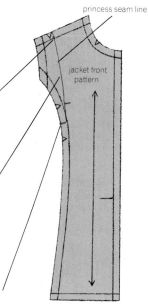

26. Cut the pattern apart along the lines drawn in Steps 24 and 25.

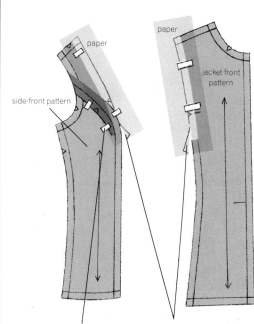

27. Tape the piece cut off the jacket front pattern to the side-front pattern, aligning the armhole and princess seam lines.

28. Tape paper under both patterns at the top of the princess seam lines. Draw a new cutting line 5/8 inch outside each seam line. Transfer the notches. Then trim the paper along the new cutting lines.

continued

D ADJUSTING THE PRINCESS SEAM LINE ON THE JACKET BACK

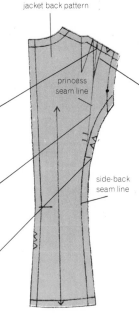

jacket back pattern

princess seam line

side-back seam line

29. On the jacket back pattern, measure half the width of the dart at the shoulder seam line.

30. Starting at the armhole seam line, measure along the shoulder seam line 1 1/2 inches plus the measurement found in Step 29. Make a mark.

31. Draw a slightly curved line from the mark made in Step 30, blending it into the side-back seam line.

32. Draw a line from the end of the one drawn in Step 31 to the edge of the pattern.

33. Draw a new shoulder dart, equal in width to the original. Start at the shoulder cutting line, and make slightly curved lines at equal distances from the adjusted princess seam line. Blend the two lines into the new seam line at a point level with the tip of the original dart. Transfer the notches.

34. Pin the dart closed. Redraw the shoulder seam and cutting lines so that they are straight.

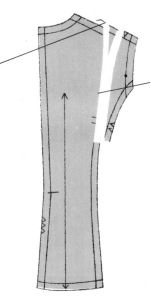

35. Trim the shoulder edge along the adjusted cutting line. Then unpin the dart.

36. Cut apart the pattern along the princess seam line, cutting out the dart as you do so.

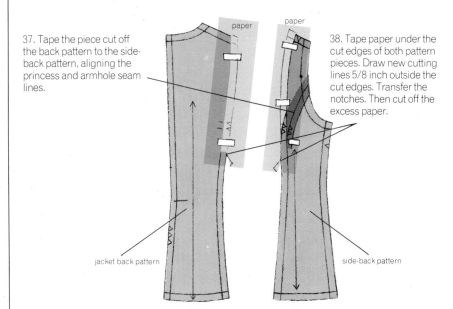

paper   paper

jacket back pattern   side-back pattern

37. Tape the piece cut off the back pattern to the side-back pattern, aligning the princess and armhole seam lines.

38. Tape paper under the cut edges of both pattern pieces. Draw new cutting lines 5/8 inch outside the cut edges. Transfer the notches. Then cut off the excess paper.

E MAKING THE POCKET PATTERNS

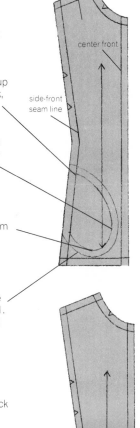

jacket front pattern

center front

side-front seam line

39. To indicate the pocket opening on the jacket front pattern, measure up 3 inches from the hemline along the side-front seam line. Mark. Then measure up 6 1/4 inches from the mark, and make a second mark.

40. Make a mark 1 inch in from the center-front seam line at a point 1 inch below the center of the pocket opening.

41. Measure up 3/4 inch from the hemline, halfway between the side-front seam line and the mark made in Step 40. Mark.

42. Draw in the pocket outline with a smooth curved line connecting the marks made in Steps 39-41. Then draw another curved line 5/8 inch beyond the outline.

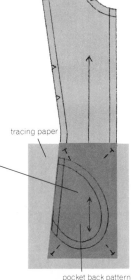

tracing paper

pocket back pattern

43. To make the pocket back pattern, first pin a piece of tracing paper over the pocket outline and trace around it. Be sure to trace the side-front seam and cutting lines and the pocket opening marks. Draw a grain-line arrow parallel to the center front. Then remove the tracing paper and cut out the pattern.

44. Pin another piece of tracing paper over the pocket outline.

45. To make the pocket front pattern, first draw a line —parallel to the center front —that touches the front edge of the pocket outline. Then draw lines perpendicular to that line. These lines should touch the top and bottom of the pocket outline, as shown.

46. Trace the side-front seam and cutting lines of the pattern. These lines should meet the horizontal lines made in Step 45.

47. Draw a grain-line arrow parallel to the center front. Then remove the tracing paper and cut out the pattern.

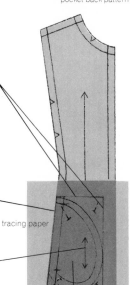

tracing paper

pocket front pattern

48. Measure the sleeve pattern from the shoulder dot to the hemline. Then compare the measurement with your sleeve length. Shorten or lengthen the pattern, as necessary, on the pattern adjustment line.

49. Draw a cutting line 5/8 inch below the hemline. Trim off the excess paper.

50. Draw a line across the pattern at the base of the sleeve cap—1 inch below the armhole seam line. Then measure the line between the underarm seam lines.

51. Add 2 1/2 inches for ease to your upper arm measurement. Then subtract that amount from the measurement made in Step 50. Divide by two.

52. Make a mark at the midpoint of the sleeve hemline. Then divide each half in half again. If you have a two-piece sleeve, divide each piece in half.

53. Draw a line from the shoulder dot to the quarter mark below it, as shown. Then draw a line from the underarm dot to the other quarter mark.

54. Measure the sleeve hemline between the vertical seam lines. If you have a two-piece sleeve, add the measurements together.

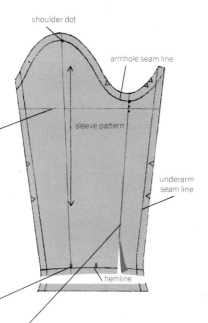

shoulder dot

armhole seam line

sleeve pattern

underarm seam line

hemline

55. Add 6 inches to your wrist measurement. Then subtract that amount from the measurement found in Step 54; divide by two.

56. Cut the pattern along the lines drawn in Step 53, cutting through the shoulder edge.

57. Lay the pattern on a piece of paper. Then, at the line drawn in Step 50, spread apart the cut edges by the amount determined in Step 51.

58. Spread apart the cut edges at the hemline by the amount determined in Step 55. Then tape the cut edges to the paper.

59. Measure down 3/8 inch from the shoulder dart. Mark, then redraw the sleeve cap seam line from that mark, blending the new line into the original at the notches.

60. Draw a new cutting line 5/8 inch outside the adjusted seam line.

61. Join the hemline and cutting line across the attached paper. Then trim the excess paper.

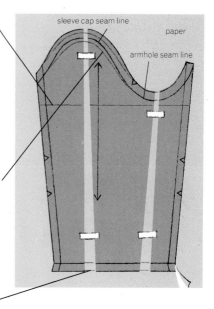

sleeve cap seam line

paper

armhole seam line

62. Make a duplicate of the sleeve pattern. Draw the grain-line arrow so that it extends to the bottom of the pattern.

63. Measure the length of the knitted cuff. Then, on the duplicate pattern, measure that distance along the underarm seam lines from the hemline. Draw a line parallel to the hemline and cut off the pattern along the line to form top and bottom sleeve sections.

64. Tape paper to the cut edges of both pattern sections. Add new cutting lines 3/8 inch from the edges. Trim off the excess paper.

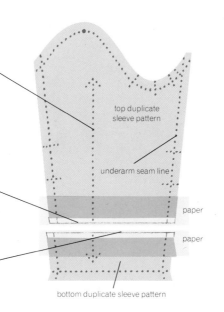

top duplicate sleeve pattern

underarm seam line

paper

paper

bottom duplicate sleeve pattern

65. On the original sleeve pattern, measure the distance between the cut edges at the sleeve cap and armhole seam lines.

66. On the side-front pattern, measure down from the armhole seam line along the side-front seam line the amount determined in Step 65. Mark.

67. Taper a line from that mark into the original armhole seam line at the notches. Then add a cutting line 5/8 inch outside the adjusted seam line and trim the pattern along the new cutting line.

68. Repeat Steps 66 and 67 on the side-back pattern.

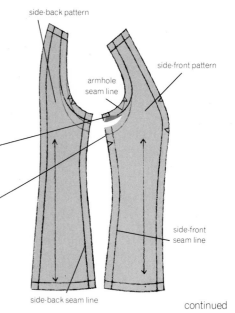

side-back pattern

side-front pattern

armhole seam line

side-front seam line

side-back seam line

continued

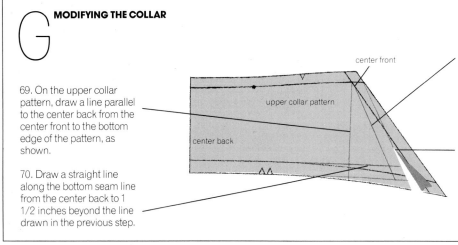

G MODIFYING THE COLLAR

69. On the upper collar pattern, draw a line parallel to the center back from the center front to the bottom edge of the pattern, as shown.

70. Draw a straight line along the bottom seam line from the center back to 1 1/2 inches beyond the line drawn in the previous step.

71. Draw a diagonal line from the center front to the end of the line drawn in Step 70.

72. Draw new cutting lines 5/8 inch outside the lines drawn in Steps 70 and 71 and extend the center-front seam line to the bottom cutting line. Then trim the pattern along the new cutting lines.

73. Repeat Steps 69-72 on the undercollar pattern.

MAKING QUILTING DESIGN LINES ON THE JACKET PATTERN

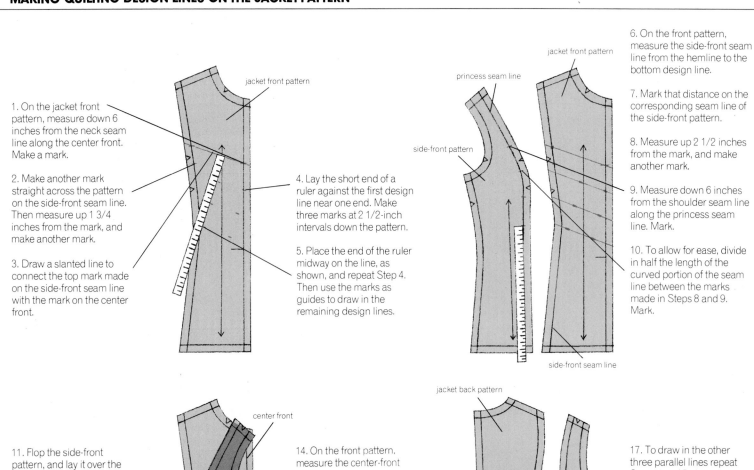

1. On the jacket front pattern, measure down 6 inches from the neck seam line along the center front. Make a mark.

2. Make another mark straight across the pattern on the side-front seam line. Then measure up 1 3/4 inches from the mark, and make another mark.

3. Draw a slanted line to connect the top mark made on the side-front seam line with the mark on the center front.

4. Lay the short end of a ruler against the first design line near one end. Make three marks at 2 1/2-inch intervals down the pattern.

5. Place the end of the ruler midway on the line, as shown, and repeat Step 4. Then use the marks as guides to draw in the remaining design lines.

6. On the front pattern, measure the side-front seam line from the hemline to the bottom design line.

7. Mark that distance on the corresponding seam line of the side-front pattern.

8. Measure up 2 1/2 inches from the mark, and make another mark.

9. Measure down 6 inches from the shoulder seam line along the princess seam line. Mark.

10. To allow for ease, divide in half the length of the curved portion of the seam line between the marks made in Steps 8 and 9. Mark.

11. Flop the side-front pattern, and lay it over the front pattern, aligning the bottom marks on the side-front seam lines. Make sure the grain-line arrows are parallel.

12. Carefully transfer the position of the design lines on the center front of the front pattern to the side seam line of the side-front pattern.

13. Turn the side-front pattern over. Connect the corresponding marks with four slanted lines.

14. On the front pattern, measure the center-front seam line from the hemline to the bottom design line.

15. Mark that distance on the center-back seam line of the back pattern.

16. Repeat Steps 2 and 3 to draw in the bottom design line.

17. To draw in the other three parallel lines repeat Steps 4 and 5, this time working toward the top of the pattern.

18. Using the back pattern as a guide, repeat Steps 6-13 to draw design lines on the side-back pattern.

PREPARING THE PANTS PATTERN

A ADJUSTING THE CROTCH AND THE HIPLINE

1. Draw a line across the pants front pattern, from the top of the crotch seam line to the side seam line. The line should be perpendicular to the grain-line arrow.

2. Measure from the waist seam line to the line drawn in Step 1.

3. Add 2 inches for ease to your crotch length measurement. Compare that measurement to the one determined in Step 2. Adjust the pattern on the pattern adjustment line.

4. Mark the position of your hipline. Then measure across the pattern at that level, from the crotch to the side seam line. Repeat on the back pattern. Add the two measurements together and double the sum.

5. Add 3 inches for ease to your hip measurement, then subtract the figure found in Step 4 from that measurement. If the difference is more than 2 inches, buy a larger pattern.

6. If the difference is 2 inches or less, divide it by four, and make the adjustment at the side seam line as shown.

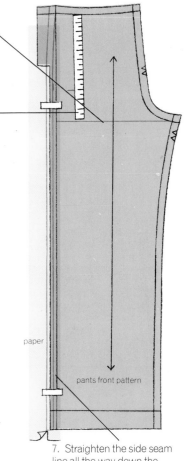

7. Straighten the side seam line all the way down the leg. Then add a cutting line 5/8 inch outside the seam line. Trim the excess paper.

B MODIFYING THE BIB PATTERN

8. If your pattern is designed with an all-in-one facing at the top of the bib, it should be removed, since the bib will be lined. Draw a line 5/8 inch above the fold line on the bib. Then trim the pattern along the line.

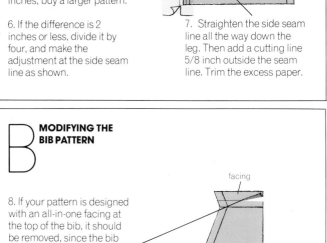

C MAKING A SEPARATE STRAP PATTERN

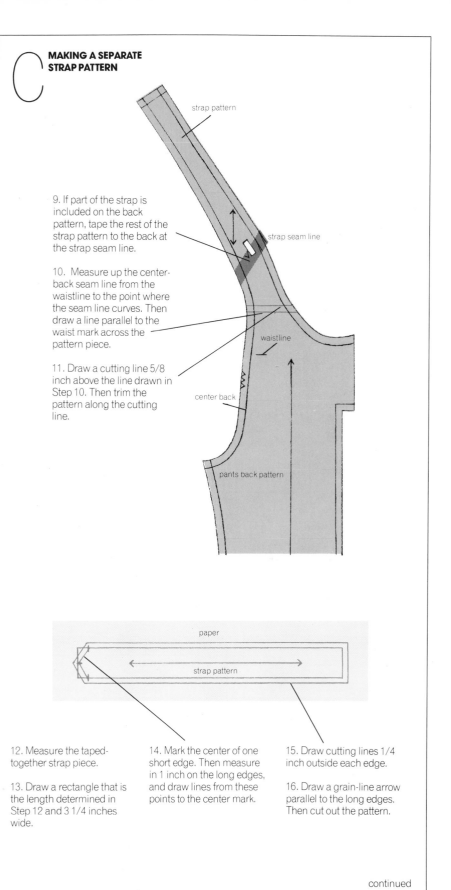

9. If part of the strap is included on the back pattern, tape the rest of the strap pattern to the back at the strap seam line.

10. Measure up the center-back seam line from the waistline to the point where the seam line curves. Then draw a line parallel to the waist mark across the pattern piece.

11. Draw a cutting line 5/8 inch above the line drawn in Step 10. Then trim the pattern along the cutting line.

12. Measure the taped-together strap piece.

13. Draw a rectangle that is the length determined in Step 12 and 3 1/4 inches wide.

14. Mark the center of one short edge. Then measure in 1 inch on the long edges, and draw lines from these points to the center mark.

15. Draw cutting lines 1/4 inch outside each edge.

16. Draw a grain-line arrow parallel to the long edges. Then cut out the pattern.

continued

137

D ▷ MAKING THE BACK FACING

17. If your pattern does not have a back facing, fold under the pants front pattern along the side seam line. Then lay the folded edge against the side seam line of the back pattern. Line up the dots indicating the bottom of the side opening. Pin.

18. Extend the waist seam line at the top of the front pattern across the back pattern. Make sure the line is at a right angle to the grain line.

19. Unpin the two pattern pieces.

20. Pin tracing paper over the top of the back pattern. Then trace the outline of the facing and draw a cutting line 5/8 inch below the bottom seam line.

21. Draw a grain line parallel to the center back. Then remove the tracing paper and cut out the facing pattern.

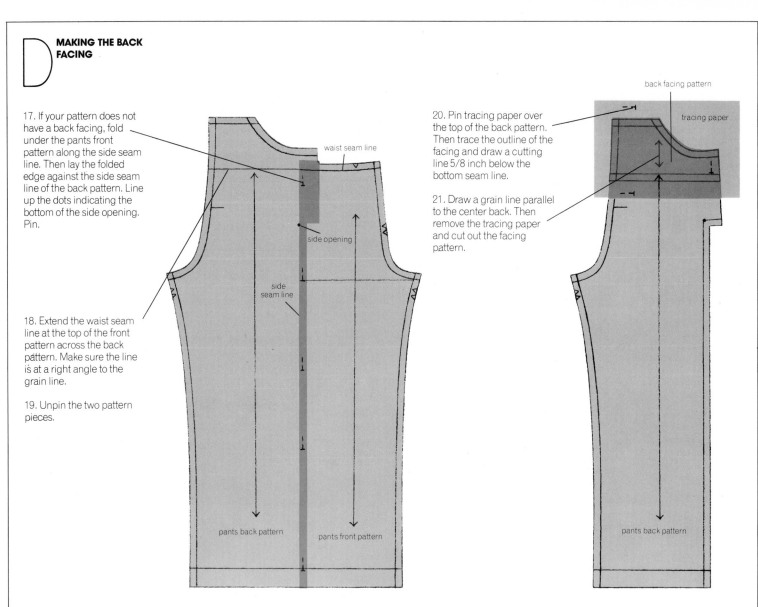

E ▷ MAKING THE SNOW CUFF PATTERN

22. Adjust the hem length on the front and back pants patterns at the pattern adjustment lines. Add a cutting line 2 inches below the hemline.

23. Measure the hemline on both patterns from the inseam to the side seam lines.

24. Draw a rectangle that is the length determined in Step 23, and 6 inches wide.

25. Draw cutting lines 5/8 inch outside the short ends and one long side of the rectangle. Draw a cutting line 3/4 inch from the other long side.

26. Draw a grain-line arrow parallel to the short edges.

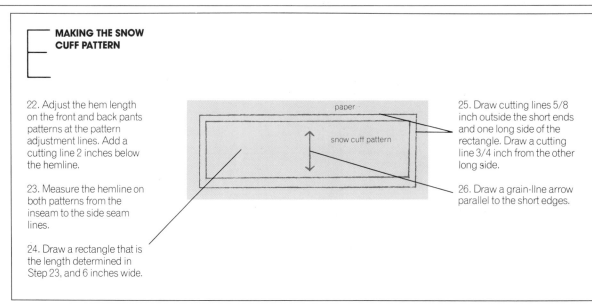

LAYING OUT, CUTTING AND MARKING

1. To make the ski suit, you will need water repellent, lightweight coated fabric; nylon lining; batting and backing fabric for the jacket quilting; prequilted fabric for the pants; one pair of knitted cuffs; 1/4 yard of nonwoven interfacing; 1 1/2-inch-wide elastic and 3/8- inch-wide nonroll elastic; two 1 1/2-inch-wide overall hooks and six snaps for the pants; two 6-inch lightweight metal zippers for the jacket pockets; two 8- . inch lightweight metal zippers for the pants pockets; and a lightweight metal separating zipper for the jacket front.

2. To determine the length of zipper for the jacket front, measure the front pattern along the center-front seam line to within 1 1/2 inches of the hemline. Add to this figure 1/2 the width of the upper collar.

3. To estimate the amount of garment, backing and batting fabric you will need for the jacket, use string to form a rectangle that is half the width of the fabric you plan to use and several yards long.

4. Arrange the jacket pattern pieces within the rectangle, as shown, keeping the grain-line arrows parallel to the lengthwise strings. Do not use the duplicate sleeve pattern or the pocket patterns.

5. Adjust the length of the rectangle so that it just accommodates the pattern pieces. Then measure the length.

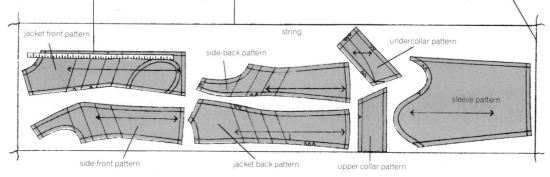

6. Repeat Steps 3-5 to determine the amount of garment and prequilted fabric you will need for the pants.

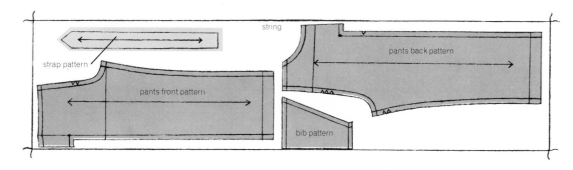

7. Arrange the jacket pattern pieces on folded garment fabric, following the layout determined in Step 4. Then pin the pattern pieces to the fabric. Insert the pins within the seam allowance to prevent marking the fabric. Cut around the pattern pieces.

8. Repeat Step 7 to cut out the backing pieces, only this time do not use the upper or undercollar patterns. Then use dressmaker's carbon and a tracing wheel to transfer all pattern markings.

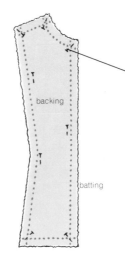

9. Lay the batting out flat. On it, arrange the backing pieces — rather than the pattern pieces — marked side up. Pin. Then cut out the batting and, without unpinning the backing, set the pieces aside. They will be joined with quilting.

10. Following the layout determined in Step 6, pin and cut out the pants pieces as you did the jacket.

11. Repeat Step 10 to cut out the prequilted pieces, but do not cut out a strap piece. Then transfer all pattern markings.

12. Use a string rectangle to determine the amount of lining fabric needed. Within the rectangle, arrange all of the jacket patterns — except the upper and undercollar. Use the duplicate patterns for the sleeve and the pocket patterns. Also include the bib pattern, the back facing and snow cuff patterns for the pants.

13. Fold the lining fabric in half lengthwise, with the selvage edges together and the wrong sides facing out.

14. Arrange the pattern pieces on the fabric, following the layout determined in Step 12.

15. Cut out the lining pieces. Put aside two scraps at least 8 inches by 10 inches for the pants pockets. Then mark the pieces with dressmaker's carbon and a tracing wheel.

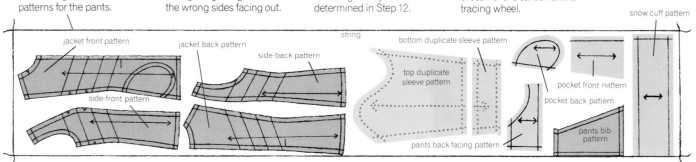

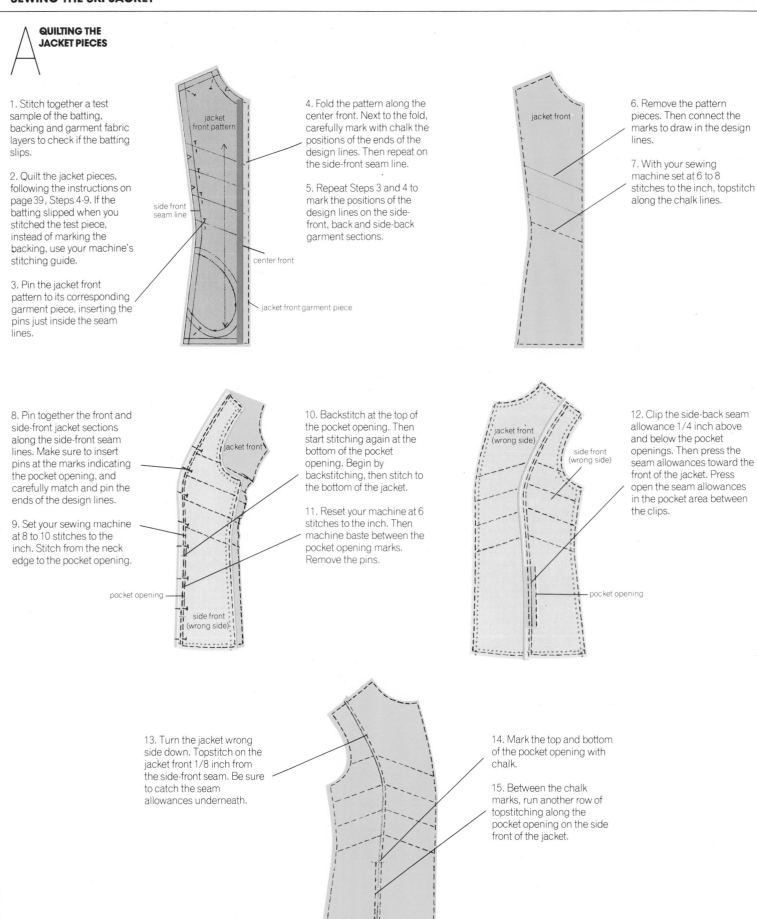

A QUILTING THE JACKET PIECES

1. Stitch together a test sample of the batting, backing and garment fabric layers to check if the batting slips.

2. Quilt the jacket pieces, following the instructions on page 39, Steps 4-9. If the batting slipped when you stitched the test piece, instead of marking the backing, use your machine's stitching guide.

3. Pin the jacket front pattern to its corresponding garment piece, inserting the pins just inside the seam lines.

jacket front pattern

side front seam line

center front

jacket front garment piece

4. Fold the pattern along the center front. Next to the fold, carefully mark with chalk the positions of the ends of the design lines. Then repeat on the side-front seam line.

5. Repeat Steps 3 and 4 to mark the positions of the design lines on the side-front, back and side-back garment sections.

jacket front

6. Remove the pattern pieces. Then connect the marks to draw in the design lines.

7. With your sewing machine set at 6 to 8 stitches to the inch, topstitch along the chalk lines.

8. Pin together the front and side-front jacket sections along the side-front seam lines. Make sure to insert pins at the marks indicating the pocket opening, and carefully match and pin the ends of the design lines.

9. Set your sewing machine at 8 to 10 stitches to the inch. Stitch from the neck edge to the pocket opening.

jacket front

pocket opening

side front (wrong side)

10. Backstitch at the top of the pocket opening. Then start stitching again at the bottom of the pocket opening. Begin by backstitching, then stitch to the bottom of the jacket.

11. Reset your machine at 6 stitches to the inch. Then machine baste between the pocket opening marks. Remove the pins.

jacket front (wrong side)

side front (wrong side)

pocket opening

12. Clip the side-back seam allowance 1/4 inch above and below the pocket openings. Then press the seam allowances toward the front of the jacket. Press open the seam allowances in the pocket area between the clips.

13. Turn the jacket wrong side down. Topstitch on the jacket front 1/8 inch from the side-front seam. Be sure to catch the seam allowances underneath.

14. Mark the top and bottom of the pocket opening with chalk.

15. Between the chalk marks, run another row of topstitching along the pocket opening on the side front of the jacket.

16. Lay the pocket back section wrong side down.

17. Open the zipper, and place it face up along the side seam edge of the pocket section. Align the bottom of the zipper tape with the raw edge at the top of the pocket section. Pin.

18. Machine baste down the center of the zipper tape, removing pins as you go.

19. Turn the pocket front section wrong side down. Align the other zipper tape with the side seam edge. Also align the bottom of the tape with the raw edge at the top of the pocket section. Pin.

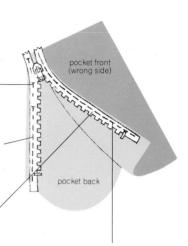

pocket front (wrong side)

pocket back

20. Machine baste down the center of the zipper tape, removing pins as you go.

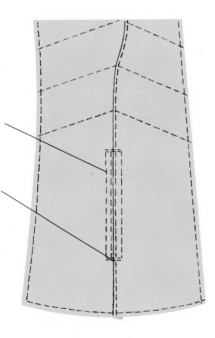

jacket front (wrong side)

pocket back (wrong side)

side-front seam allowance

21. Fold the jacket front section, wrong side out, along the side-front seam with the front piece on top. Extend the side-front seam allowance. Lay the pocket back section, wrong side up, on the extended seam allowance.

22. Align the bottom stop of the zipper with the mark indicating the top of the pocket opening and the top stop with the bottom mark. Also align the zipper teeth with the seam. Pin.

23. Machine stitch just inside the line of machine basting between the pocket opening marks. Remove the pins as you stitch.

24. Close the zipper. Flop the jacket front so that the side front is on top. Then pin the pocket front section to the front seam allowance. Machine stitch between the pocket opening marks, removing the pins as you stitch.

25. Unfold the jacket, keeping it wrong side up. Smooth both halves of the pocket away from the zipper, and pin them flat on the jacket. Press.

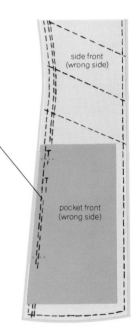

side front (wrong side)

pocket front (wrong side)

26. Turn the jacket wrong side down.

27. Topstitch 3/8 inch from each long pocket edge and across the pocket opening marks.

28. Reinforce the pocket opening with a second row of stitching on top of the first.

continued

C FINISHING THE POCKET

29. Turn the jacket front wrong side up. Turn both pocket pieces toward the front of the jacket. Then trim the pocket front section around the raw edges of the pocket back section.

30. Pin the raw edges together. Machine stitch across the top of the pocket, 5/8 inch from the edge. Make sure you catch the zipper tape in the stitching. Then stitch around the rest of the pocket, 5/8 inch from the edge.

31. Finish the raw edges with zigzag stitches. Then remove the machine basting to open the pocket.

32. Repeat Steps 8-31 to assemble the other jacket front.

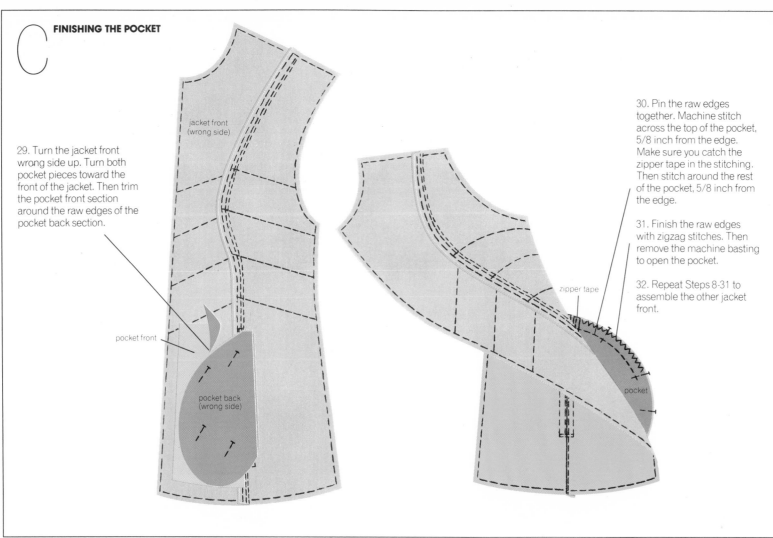

jacket front
(wrong side)

pocket front

pocket back
(wrong side)

zipper tape

pocket

D ASSEMBLING THE BODY OF THE JACKET

33. Stitch the jacket backs together at the center back, carefully matching the design quilting lines. Then open out the center-back seam allowance, and run rows of topstitching 1/8 inch from each side of the seam.

34. Stitch the side backs to the jacket back, again matching the design quilting lines. Then press the side-back seam allowance toward the center back, and topstitch 1/8 inch from the seam, making sure to catch the seam allowances underneath.

35. Stitch together the jacket fronts and jacket back at the side and shoulder seam lines.

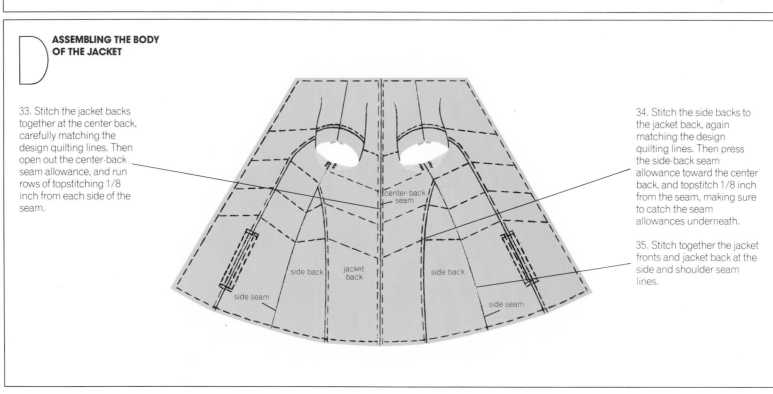

center-back seam

side back

jacket back

side back

side seam

side seam

ATTACHING THE
UNDERCOLLAR

36. Use the upper collar pattern piece to cut a piece of prequilted fabric. Then, with dressmaker's carbon and a tracing wheel, transfer all pattern markings to the quilting.

37. Pin the quilting to the wrong side of the upper collar. Stitch around the piece, 1/4 inch from the edges. Remove the pins.

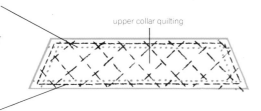

upper collar quilting

38. Use one undercollar pattern piece to cut two pieces of nonwoven interfacing. Transfer all the pattern markings.

39. Repeat Step 37 to attach the interfacing to the two undercollar pieces. Also stitch along the roll line.

40. Stitch the undercollar pieces together along the center-back seam line.

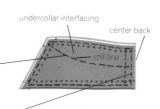

undercollar interfacing

center back

roll line

41. Stay stitch (*Glossary*) around the neck edge of the jacket, 1/2 inch from the edge. Then clip the neck edge up to, but not into, the stay stitching.

42. Pin the neck edge of the undercollar to the neck edge of the jacket with the wrong sides facing out.

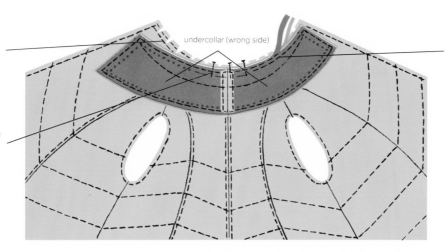

undercollar (wrong side)

43. Baste and remove the pins. Then machine stitch and remove the bastings.

44. Trim the collar seam allowance to 1/4 inch and the jacket seam allowance to 3/8 inch. Then press the seam allowances toward the collar.

45. Divide the front edges of the undercollar in half along the seam line. Mark with chalk.

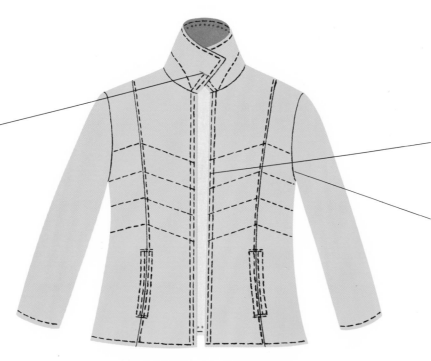

46. Machine stitch down the center front of both jacket fronts. Stitch from the chalk mark on the undercollar to the hem.

47. Stitch together the underarm seam of the sleeves and attach the sleeves to the jacket, following your pattern instructions.

continued

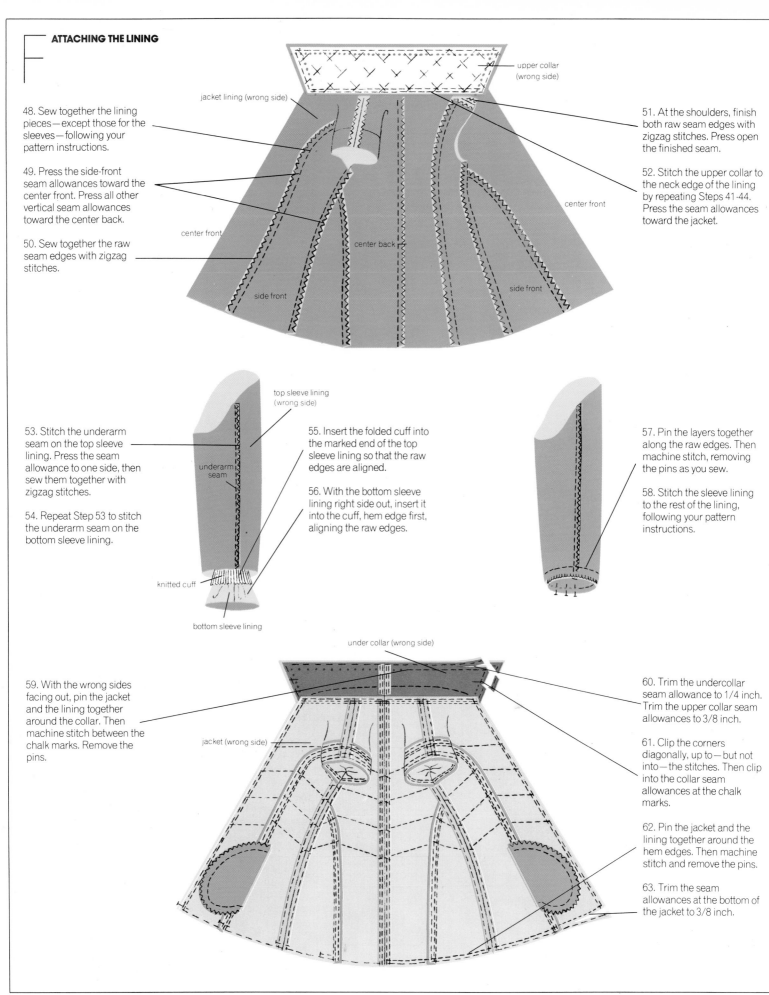

upper collar (wrong side)

jacket lining (wrong side)

48. Sew together the lining pieces—except those for the sleeves—following your pattern instructions.

49. Press the side-front seam allowances toward the center front. Press all other vertical seam allowances toward the center back.

50. Sew together the raw seam edges with zigzag stitches.

center front

center front

center back

side front

side front

51. At the shoulders, finish both raw seam edges with zigzag stitches. Press open the finished seam.

52. Stitch the upper collar to the neck edge of the lining by repeating Steps 41-44. Press the seam allowances toward the jacket.

top sleeve lining (wrong side)

underarm seam

knitted cuff

bottom sleeve lining

53. Stitch the underarm seam on the top sleeve lining. Press the seam allowance to one side, then sew them together with zigzag stitches.

54. Repeat Step 53 to stitch the underarm seam on the bottom sleeve lining.

55. Insert the folded cuff into the marked end of the top sleeve lining so that the raw edges are aligned.

56. With the bottom sleeve lining right side out, insert it into the cuff, hem edge first, aligning the raw edges.

57. Pin the layers together along the raw edges. Then machine stitch, removing the pins as you sew.

58. Stitch the sleeve lining to the rest of the lining, following your pattern instructions.

under collar (wrong side)

jacket (wrong side)

59. With the wrong sides facing out, pin the jacket and the lining together around the collar. Then machine stitch between the chalk marks. Remove the pins.

60. Trim the undercollar seam allowance to 1/4 inch. Trim the upper collar seam allowances to 3/8 inch.

61. Clip the corners diagonally, up to—but not into—the stitches. Then clip into the collar seam allowances at the chalk marks.

62. Pin the jacket and the lining together around the hem edges. Then machine stitch and remove the pins.

63. Trim the seam allowances at the bottom of the jacket to 3/8 inch.

G INSERTING THE ZIPPER

64. Turn the jacket to the outside, making sure to insert the sleeve lining into the sleeves. Then, on both jacket fronts, turn under the raw edges along the center front, inside the lines of machine stitching.

65. Topstitch next to the folded edge, from the opening in the collar to the hem.

66. With the lining side up, turn under the front lining edges toward the wrong side along the center-front seam line. Press flat.

67. Topstitch the lining next to the folded edge, from the opening in the collar to the hem.

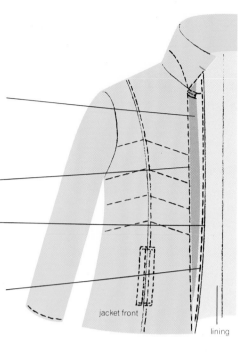

jacket front

lining

68. Turn the jacket wrong side down. Working on the right-hand jacket front, separate the zipper, and insert the top end of the tape into the stitched portion of the collar.

69. Align the top stop with the collar opening and the folded edges of the jacket and lining so that the folds just cover the zipper teeth. Pin.

70. Pin the zipper into the jacket down the front edge. The bottom stop should end 1 to 2 inches from the hemline. Make sure the front folds conceal the zipper teeth.

71. Baste the zipper in place and remove the pins. Then topstitch from the hem to the collar opening. Backstitch at the beginning and end of the row of stitching. Remove the basting.

72. Repeat Steps 68-71 on the left-hand jacket front. Close the zipper after it is basted in to check the alignment of the two sides.

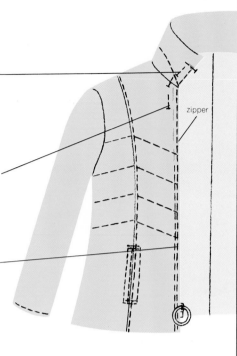

zipper

H FINISHING THE BOTTOM OF THE SLEEVES

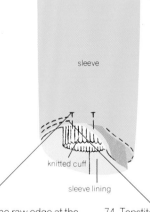

sleeve

knitted cuff

sleeve lining

73. Turn the raw edge at the bottom of the sleeve lining under 1/4 inch. Press. Then turn up the bottom of the sleeve 5/8 inch. Align the folded edges. Pin.

74. Topstitch around the folded edges and remove the pins.

75. Run another row of topstitching 3/8 inch from the edge.

I FINISHING THE JACKET

76. Topstitch around the upper collar, next to the outside edge. Stitch over several stitches at the end of the center-front topstitching. Then run another line of topstitching 3/8 inch from the edge.

77. Machine stitch the upper and undercollars together along the neck seam between the shoulder seams.

78. Topstitch around the hem, next to the fold. Then run another line of topstitching 3/8 inch from the edge.

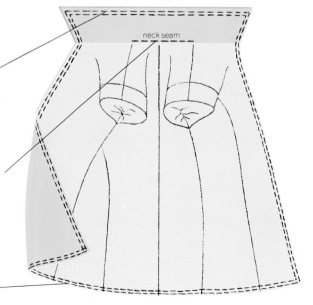

neck seam

A STITCHING THE PANTS LEGS

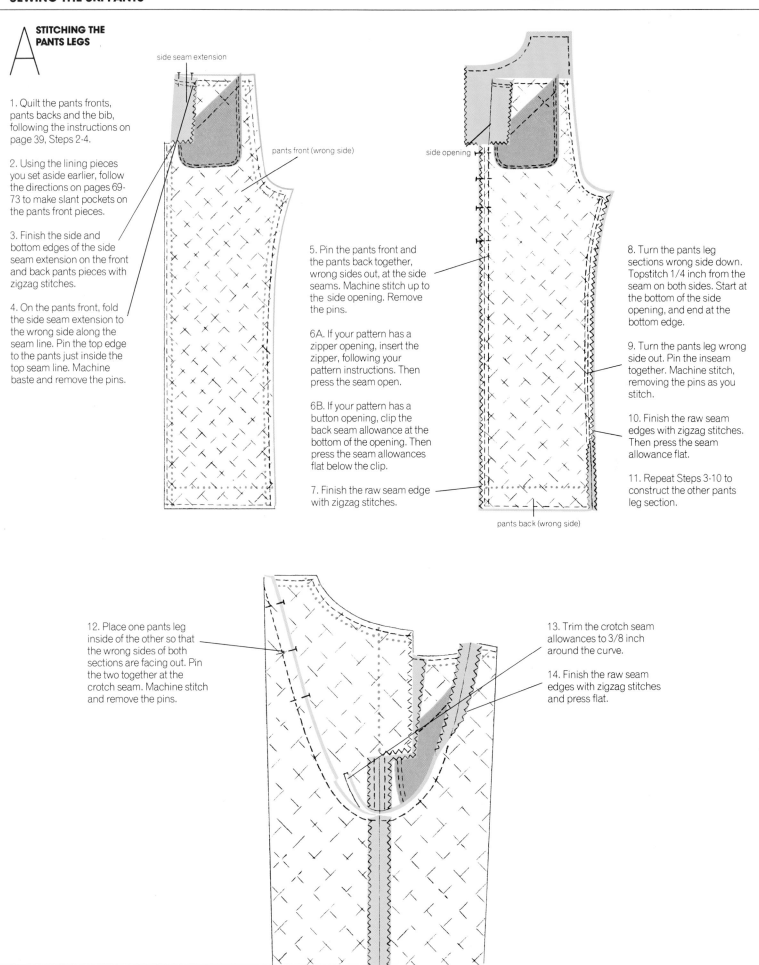

side seam extension

pants front (wrong side)

1. Quilt the pants fronts, pants backs and the bib, following the instructions on page 39, Steps 2-4.

2. Using the lining pieces you set aside earlier, follow the directions on pages 69-73 to make slant pockets on the pants front pieces.

3. Finish the side and bottom edges of the side seam extension on the front and back pants pieces with zigzag stitches.

4. On the pants front, fold the side seam extension to the wrong side along the seam line. Pin the top edge to the pants just inside the top seam line. Machine baste and remove the pins.

5. Pin the pants front and the pants back together, wrong sides out, at the side seams. Machine stitch up to the side opening. Remove the pins.

6A. If your pattern has a zipper opening, insert the zipper, following your pattern instructions. Then press the seam open.

6B. If your pattern has a button opening, clip the back seam allowance at the bottom of the opening. Then press the seam allowances flat below the clip.

7. Finish the raw seam edge with zigzag stitches.

side opening

8. Turn the pants leg sections wrong side down. Topstitch 1/4 inch from the seam on both sides. Start at the bottom of the side opening, and end at the bottom edge.

9. Turn the pants leg wrong side out. Pin the inseam together. Machine stitch, removing the pins as you stitch.

10. Finish the raw seam edges with zigzag stitches. Then press the seam allowance flat.

11. Repeat Steps 3-10 to construct the other pants leg section.

pants back (wrong side)

12. Place one pants leg inside of the other so that the wrong sides of both sections are facing out. Pin the two together at the crotch seam. Machine stitch and remove the pins.

13. Trim the crotch seam allowances to 3/8 inch around the curve.

14. Finish the raw seam edges with zigzag stitches and press flat.

B ATTACHING THE BIB

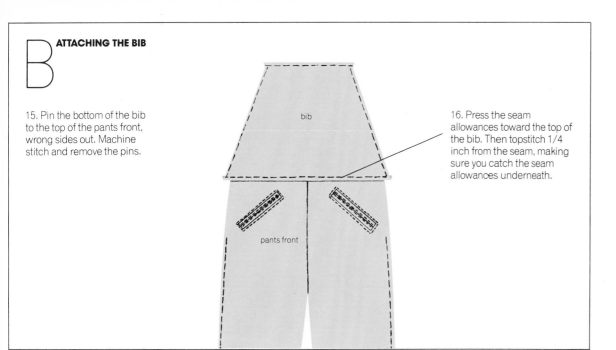

15. Pin the bottom of the bib to the top of the pants front, wrong sides out. Machine stitch and remove the pins.

16. Press the seam allowances toward the top of the bib. Then topstitch 1/4 inch from the seam, making sure you catch the seam allowances underneath.

C STITCHING THE STRAPS

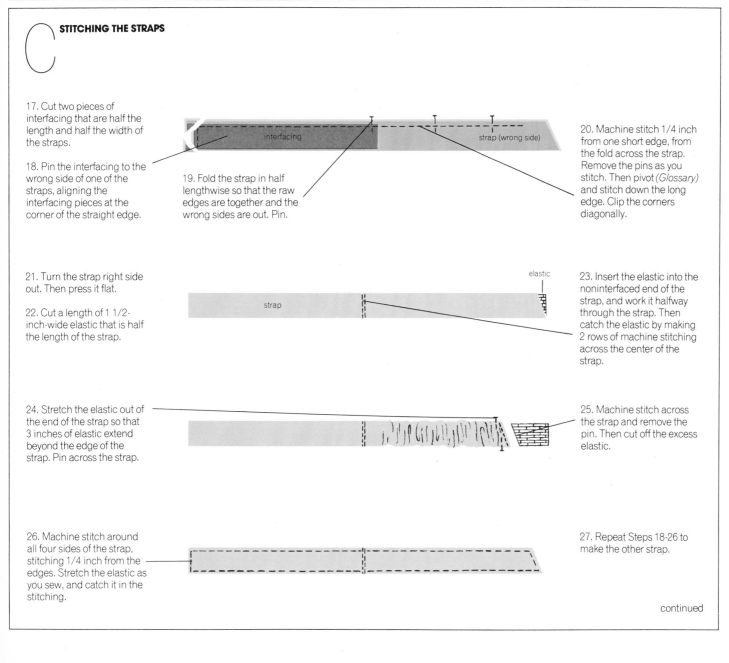

17. Cut two pieces of interfacing that are half the length and half the width of the straps.

18. Pin the interfacing to the wrong side of one of the straps, aligning the interfacing pieces at the corner of the straight edge.

19. Fold the strap in half lengthwise so that the raw edges are together and the wrong sides are out. Pin.

20. Machine stitch 1/4 inch from one short edge, from the fold across the strap. Remove the pins as you stitch. Then pivot (Glossary) and stitch down the long edge. Clip the corners diagonally.

21. Turn the strap right side out. Then press it flat.

22. Cut a length of 1 1/2-inch-wide elastic that is half the length of the strap.

23. Insert the elastic into the noninterfaced end of the strap, and work it halfway through the strap. Then catch the elastic by making 2 rows of machine stitching across the center of the strap.

24. Stretch the elastic out of the end of the strap so that 3 inches of elastic extend beyond the edge of the strap. Pin across the strap.

25. Machine stitch across the strap and remove the pin. Then cut off the excess elastic.

26. Machine stitch around all four sides of the strap, stitching 1/4 inch from the edges. Stretch the elastic as you sew, and catch it in the stitching.

27. Repeat Steps 18-26 to make the other strap.

continued

D ATTACHING THE STRAPS

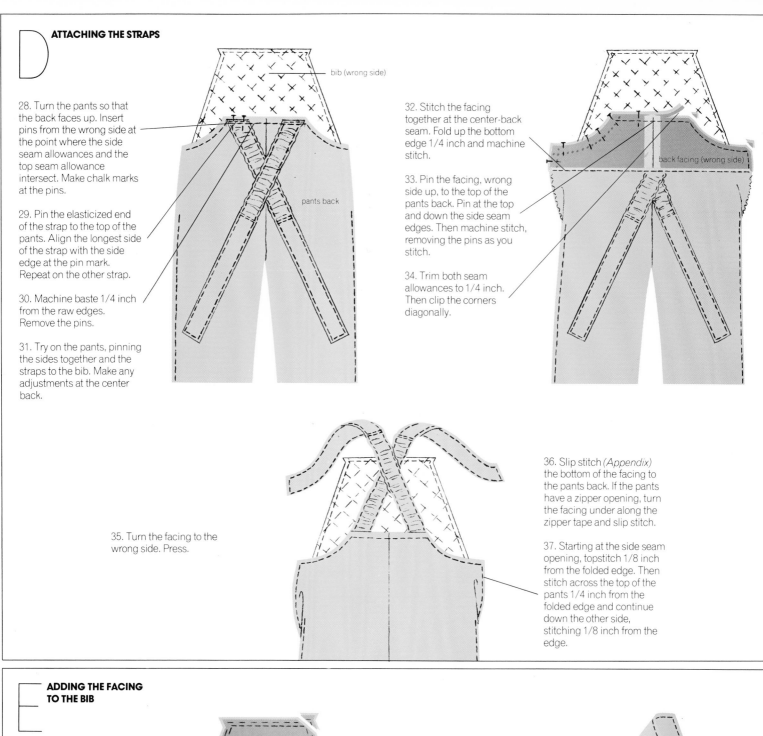

bib (wrong side)

28. Turn the pants so that the back faces up. Insert pins from the wrong side at the point where the side seam allowances and the top seam allowance intersect. Make chalk marks at the pins.

29. Pin the elasticized end of the strap to the top of the pants. Align the longest side of the strap with the side edge at the pin mark. Repeat on the other strap.

30. Machine baste 1/4 inch from the raw edges. Remove the pins.

31. Try on the pants, pinning the sides together and the straps to the bib. Make any adjustments at the center back.

pants back

32. Stitch the facing together at the center-back seam. Fold up the bottom edge 1/4 inch and machine stitch.

33. Pin the facing, wrong side up, to the top of the pants back. Pin at the top and down the side seam edges. Then machine stitch, removing the pins as you stitch.

34. Trim both seam allowances to 1/4 inch. Then clip the corners diagonally.

back facing (wrong side)

35. Turn the facing to the wrong side. Press.

36. Slip stitch (*Appendix*) the bottom of the facing to the pants back. If the pants have a zipper opening, turn the facing under along the zipper tape and slip stitch.

37. Starting at the side seam opening, topstitch 1/8 inch from the folded edge. Then stitch across the top of the pants 1/4 inch from the folded edge and continue down the other side, stitching 1/8 inch from the edge.

E ADDING THE FACING TO THE BIB

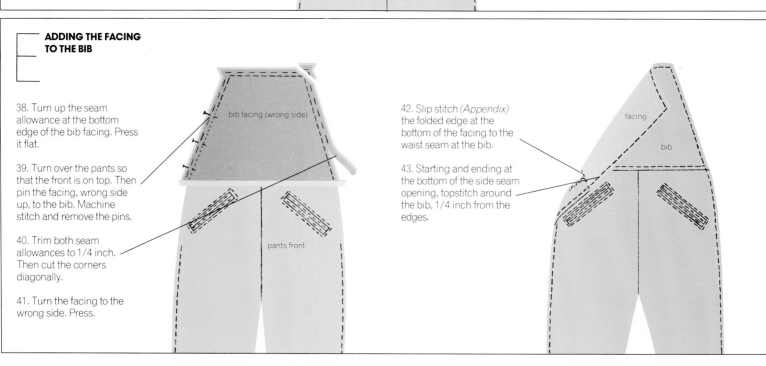

38. Turn up the seam allowance at the bottom edge of the bib facing. Press it flat.

39. Turn over the pants so that the front is on top. Then pin the facing, wrong side up, to the bib. Machine stitch and remove the pins.

40. Trim both seam allowances to 1/4 inch. Then cut the corners diagonally.

41. Turn the facing to the wrong side. Press.

bib facing (wrong side)

pants front

42. Slip stitch (*Appendix*) the folded edge at the bottom of the facing to the waist seam at the bib.

43. Starting and ending at the bottom of the side seam opening, topstitch around the bib, 1/4 inch from the edges.

facing

bib

F MAKING THE SNOW CUFF

44. Stitch together the snow cuff at the seam. Use a French seam *(page 43)*.

45. To make a casing, first press up one raw edge 1/4 inch. Next, turn up another 1/2 inch and pin. Then machine stitch along the inside edge, leaving a 1-inch opening at the seam. Remove the pins as you stitch.

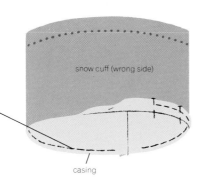

snow cuff (wrong side)

casing

46. Measure the casing. Then cut a length of 3/8-inch-wide elastic two thirds that measurement.

47. Thread the elastic through the casing. Then overlap the edges 1 inch and stitch. First make a rectangle, then stitch an X inside it. Finish stitching the casing.

casing

48. Slip the elasticized cuff, wrong side out, over the leg. Pin along the raw edges. Then machine stitch, removing the pins as you stitch.

49. Stitch the raw edges of the seam allowances together with zigzag stitches.

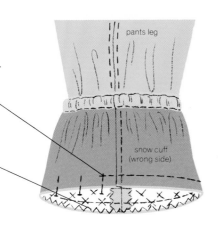

pants leg

snow cuff (wrong side)

50. Push the snow cuff inside the pants leg until you have a 1 1/2-inch hem. Pin around the leg. Then topstitch 1 1/2 inch from the fold, removing the pins as you stitch.

51. Repeat Steps 44-50 to attach the other snow cuff.

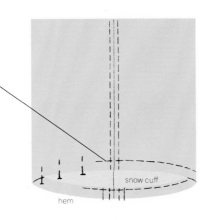

snow cuff

hem

G FINISHING THE PANTS

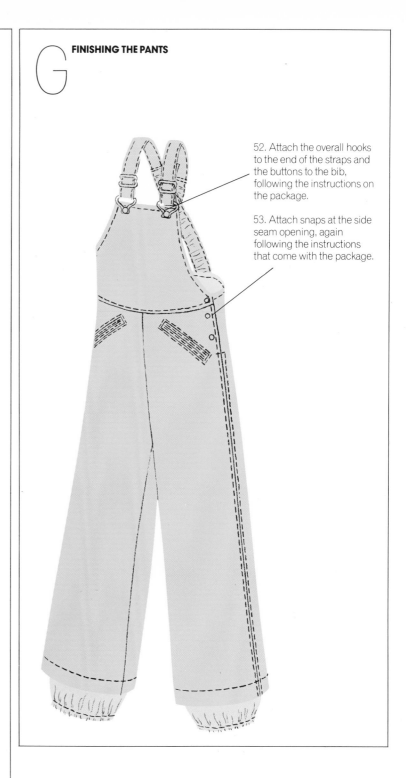

52. Attach the overall hooks to the end of the straps and the buttons to the bib, following the instructions on the package.

53. Attach snaps at the side seam opening, again following the instructions that come with the package.

5
A FAST RUN ON CABLES

Whether it is a nubbly undyed-wool pullover like that worn by the equestrian on the preceding pages, a downy cashmere vest or a silky alpaca cardigan, a sweater is perhaps the most universally prized of all sports apparel. Every sports enthusiast has his favorite; most have a drawerful. And little wonder, too, for there is hardly a sport in which some kind of sweater is not either useful or essential.

AN ODDS-ON FAVORITE — THE SWEATER

Some sweater styles—the white tennis pullover with bands of color trim is one example—may get so closely identified with a sport that they become uniforms of the game. But most can go jauntily from the riding ring to the dock to the golf links.

Among these all-purpose designs, cable knits such as those on pages 160-161 rank among the highest in handsomeness and versatility. Cables can be incorporated into a pullover or cardigan of any weight, and they have the added appeal of being literally threaded with history. As far back as the 15th Century, they were prized by English Channel fishermen, whose wives knitted into garments symbolic designs of the cables, chains and ropes that were part of their husbands' livelihood. In time the various family and village motifs became so highly individualized—and identifiable—that they were like the English port version of the Scottish Highland tartan.

Today the knitter can choose from more than a hundred cable patterns, from simple twists to exotic plaits. And just as British fishing folk combined patterns when their families intermarried, so the home knitter can make a one-of-a-kind sweater by wedding two or more different cables.

While cables have been around for some 500 years, the word sweater was not applied to a garment until 1828 when Englishmen began using the term for both the woolen blankets worn by horses and the pullovers worn by their riders. And it was not until almost the end of the 19th Century that the garment became widely worn. Even then, the popularity of the sweater was due to, of all things, a quixotic German zoologist and physiologist named Gustav Jaeger.

Professor Jaeger published a treatise called *Health-Culture* in 1880 that sent ripples of consternation through the sedate European fashion world. Jaeger insisted that man, being an animal, must wear clothes made of animal fibers: namely, wool. Vegetable fibers (cotton and linen) were *verboten,* said Jaeger, who believed wool would promote cleanliness, prevent rheumatism and gout, and keep down excess fat.

To people choked by celluloid collars and crunched by whalebone corsets, any apparel that promised comfort along with better health was welcome. So smitten was an Englishman named Lewis Tomalin by these ideas that he burned all his household linens, secured a license to sell Jaeger's woolens in England and in 1884 launched the Jaeger Company—a dry goods emporium that became a worldwide business.

Wool had become firmly entrenched in England by 1887. A tricycling brochure reflected the prevailing mood when it noted that cyclists had determined that the "only truly hygienic system of dress is the 'all woollen.'" The system included tweed jackets and knickerbockers—and heavy gray sweaters.

In America, the newfangled sweaters were first adopted on a large scale for playing football. Drab as those early football sweaters usually were, in some shade of navy, maroon or black, they were utilitarian. And worn around town after the game, they became distinctive symbols of prowess. Other athletes, notably crewmen, began to wear them for both the sport and afterward.

For a long time the ladies only admired —or knitted—such garments; they rarely wore them, even for sports, until the Roaring Twenties, when sweaters at last broke out in a rainbow of colors. Then women caught on to the fact that men had discovered decades earlier: It may not prevent obesity, but indoors and out, in sports arenas and beyond, nothing beats a sweater for comfort, practicality and good looks.

Fresh twists for cables

These knits, with additional bulk lent by cabling, are perfectly suited for outdoor wear in winter. Whether they are worked in simple or intricate designs, all cables are made in basically the same way. During the course of knitting, a few stitches are slipped off the regular pair of working needles onto a third needle, bypassed for a time and then picked up again and knitted. This sidetracking, done in a predetermined sequence, creates the raised stitches. The patterns thus formed vary, as these swatches do, according to the number of stitches employed and the ways in which the stitches are twisted—as explained overleaf.

Thick wool yarns, worked with large needles, emphasize the sturdy, three-dimensional qualities of cable stitching. From left to right are plaited, cactus, uneven twist, pretzel, wedding ring and wishbone cable patterns.

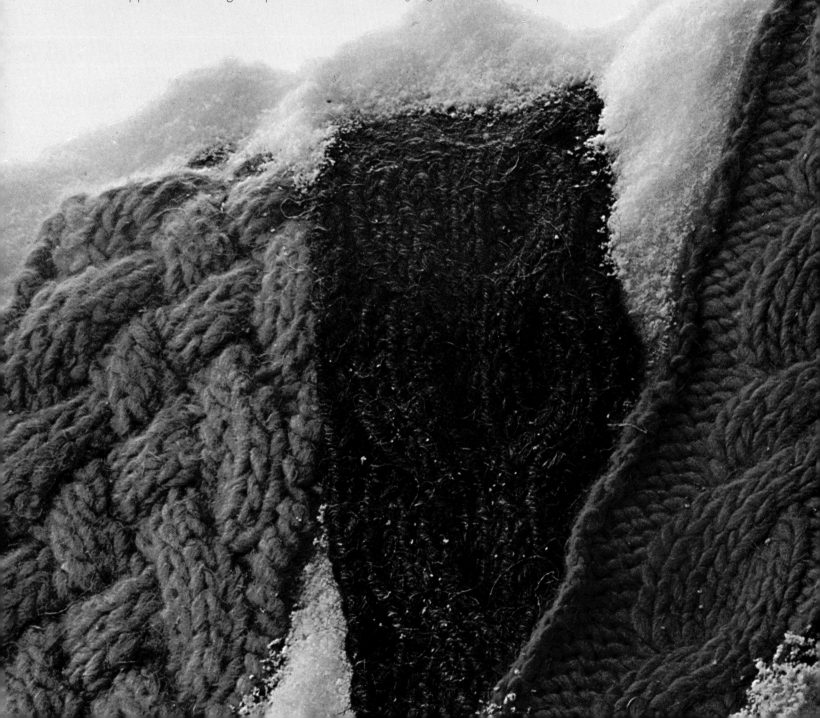

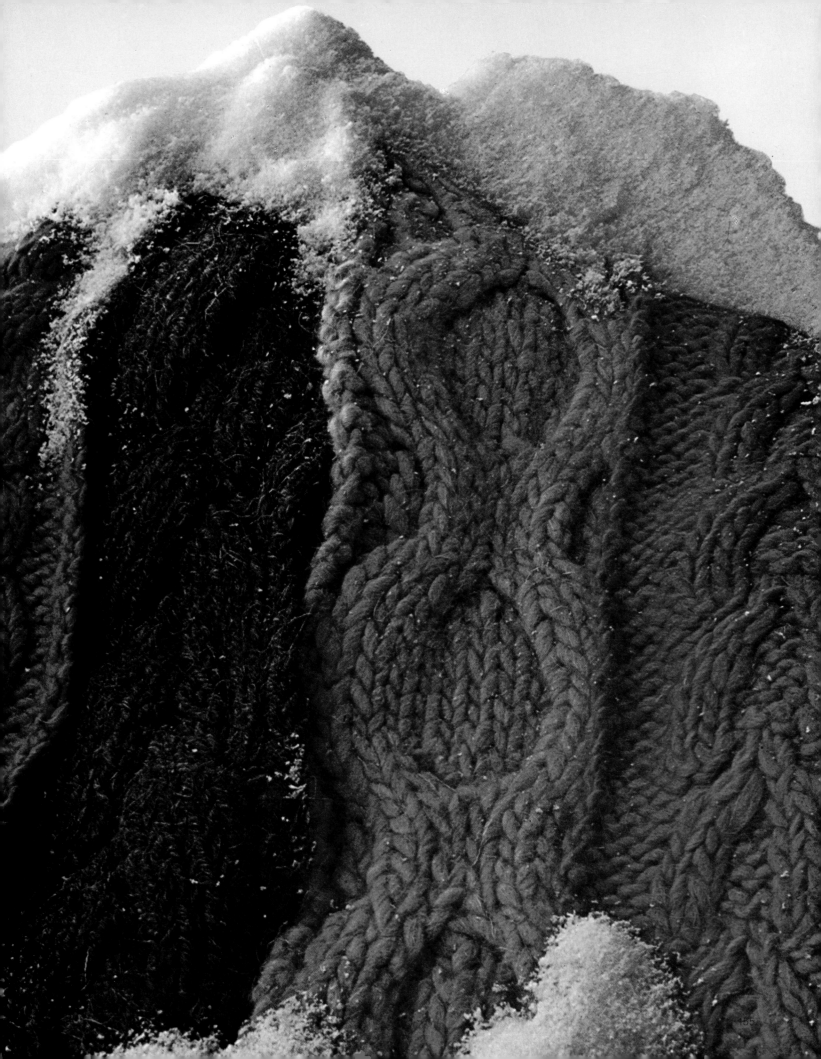

Instructions for knitting the cable stitch patterns

To knit the cable stitch patterns pictured on the preceding pages, in addition to a standard pair of straight needles you will need a third implement: a short, double-pointed needle. In making the cables, you slip some stitches from the working needles onto the double-pointed needle. After you knit a few stitches on the working needles, you then work the stitches from the double-pointed needle back onto the working needles.

The illustrations that accompany the instructions show how to use the double-pointed needle to make front cables, which twist to the left, and back cables, which twist to the right. The basic knitting stitches and the elementary techniques involved are explained in the Appendix.

For these patterns, use a pair of Size 13 straight knitting needles, a fairly large double-pointed needle and bulky yarn. Work in a relatively heavy gauge—5 stitches for every 2 inches.

THE UNEVEN TWIST CABLE PATTERN
Cast on any multiple of 8 stitches that measures the desired width of your work.

Row 1: Purl the first stitch. Then knit each of the next 6 stitches. Purl the next stitch. Repeat this sequence of 8 stitches across the row.

Row 2: Knit the first stitch. Then purl each of the next 6 stitches. Knit the next stitch.
Repeat this sequence of 8 stitches across the row.

Row 3: Repeat row 1.

Row 4: Repeat row 2.

Row 5: Purl the first stitch. Then slip the next 3 stitches onto a double-pointed needle and hold the stitches at the back of the work (drawing 1). Bring the yarn under the right-hand needle in the correct position for knitting, and knit

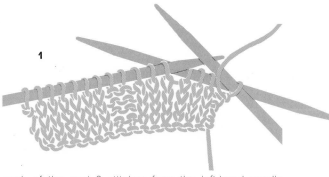

each of the next 3 stitches from the left-hand needle (drawing 2).

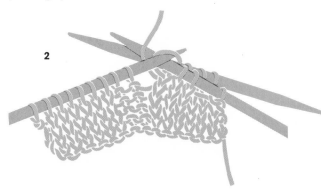

Now slide the 3 stitches on the double-pointed needle to the right-hand end of that needle and knit the stitches to form a back cable (drawing 3). Purl the next stitch.

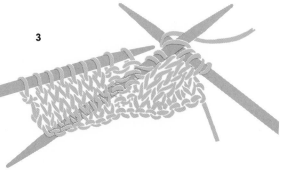

Repeat this sequence of 8 stitches across the row.

Row 6: Repeat row 2.

Row 7: Repeat row 1.

Row 8: Repeat row 2.

Row 9: Repeat row 1.

Row 10: Repeat row 2.

Row 11: Repeat row 1.

Row 12: Repeat row 2.

Row 13: Repeat row 1.

Row 14: Repeat row 2.

Row 15: Repeat row 5, following the sequence of purling the first stitch, slipping the next 3 stitches onto the double-pointed needle and holding them in back of the work; knitting the next 3 stitches, knitting the 3 stitches from the double-pointed needle and purling the next stitch (*drawings 1, 2 and 3, left*). Again, repeat this sequence of 8 stitches across the row.

Row 16: Repeat row 2.

Repeat the preceding 16 rows for the desired length. Then bind off.

THE WEDDING RING CABLE PATTERN

Cast on any multiple of 14 stitches plus 2 stitches that measures the desired width of your work.

Row 1: Purl the first 2 stitches. Then slip the next 3 stitches onto a double-pointed needle and hold the stitches at the back of the work (*drawing 1, left*). Bring the yarn under the right-hand needle in the correct position for knitting, then knit each of the next 3 stitches on the left-hand needle (*drawing 2, left*). Now slide the 3 stitches on the double-pointed needle to the right-hand end of that needle, and knit the stitches to form a back cable (*drawing 3, left*). Now slip the next 3 stitches onto the double-pointed needle and hold the stitches at the front of the work (*drawing 4, arrow*).

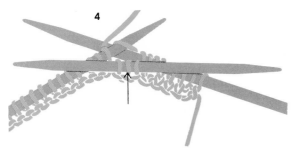

Knit each of the next 3 stitches on the left-hand needle (*drawing 4*). Slide the 3 stitches on the double-pointed needle to the right-hand end, and knit them (*drawing 5*)

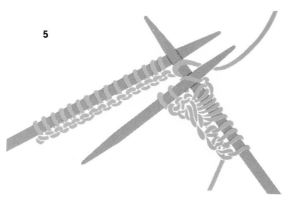

to form a front cable. Repeat this sequence of 14 stitches —purl 2 stitches, make one back cable, then one front cable, across the row. End the row by purling the remaining 2 stitches.

Row 2: Knit the first 2 stitches. Then purl each of the next 12 stitches. Repeat this sequence of 14 stitches across the row. End the row by knitting the last 2 stitches.

Row 3: Purl the first 2 stitches. Then knit each of the next 12

stitches. Repeat this sequence of 14 stitches across the row. End the row by purling the last 2 stitches.

Row 4: Repeat row 2.
Row 5: Repeat row 3.
Row 6: Repeat row 2.
Row 7: Repeat row 3.
Row 8: Repeat row 2.
Row 9: Repeat row 3.
Row 10: Repeat row 2.
Row 11: Purl the first 2 stitches. Then follow the instructions in row 1 for making the back and front cables, but this time reverse the order, first working the 6 stitches of the front cable (*drawings 4 and 5, near left*), then working the 6 stitches of the back cable (*drawings 1, 2 and 3, far left*). Repeat this sequence of 14 stitches—purl 2 stitches, make one front cable, then one back cable—across the row. End the row by purling the last 2 stitches.

Row 12: Repeat row 2.
Row 13: Repeat row 3.
Row 14: Repeat row 2.
Row 15: Repeat row 3.
Row 16: Repeat row 2.

Repeat the preceding 16 rows for the desired length. Then bind off.

THE PLAITED CABLE PATTERN

Cast on any multiple of 17 stitches plus 2 stitches that measures the desired width of your work.

Row 1: Purl the first 2 stitches. Then knit each of the next 15 stitches. Repeat this sequence of 17 stitches across the row. End the row by purling the last 2 stitches.

Row 2: Knit the first 2 stitches. Then purl each of the next 15 stitches. Repeat this sequence of 17 stitches across the row. End the row by knitting the last 2 stitches.

Row 3: Purl the first 2 stitches. Then make a front cable. To begin, slip the next 3 stitches onto a double-pointed needle and hold the stitches at the front of the work. Knit each of the next 3 stitches on the left-hand needle (*drawing 4, near left*). Now slide the 3 stitches on the double-pointed needle to the right-hand end of that needle and knit them (*drawing 5, near left*). Work one more front cable—beginning with slipping the first 3 stitches onto the double-pointed needle—on the next 6 stitches. Knit the next 3 stitches. Repeat the sequence of 17 stitches—purl 2 stitches, work 2 front cables, knit 3 stitches—across the row. End the row by purling the last 2 stitches.

Row 4: Repeat row 2.
Row 5: Repeat row 1.
Row 6: Repeat row 2.
Row 7: Purl the first 2 stitches. Knit each of the next 3 stitches. Now make a back cable as follows: slip the next 3 stitches onto a double-pointed needle and hold the stitches at the back of the work (*drawing 1, far left*); bring the yarn under the right-hand needle in the correct position for knitting, and knit each of the next 3 stitches on the left-hand needle (*drawing 2, far left*), then knit the 3 stitches from the double-pointed needle (*drawing 3, far left*). Work one more back cable on the next 6 stitches. Repeat the sequence of

17 stitches—purl 2, knit 3, work 2 back cables—across the row. End by purling the last 2 stitches.

Row 8: Repeat row 2.

Repeat the preceding 8 rows for the desired length. Then bind off.

THE WISHBONE CABLE PATTERN

Cast on any multiple of 12 stitches plus 4 stitches that measures the desired width of your work.

Row 1: Purl the first 4 stitches. Knit the next 2 stitches. Purl the next 4 stitches. Repeat this sequence—knit 2 stitches, purl 4 stitches—across the row.

Row 2: Knit the first 4 stitches. Purl the next 2 stitches. Knit the next 4 stitches. Repeat this sequence—purl 2 stitches, knit 4 stitches—across the row.

Row 3: Repeat row 1.

Row 4: Repeat row 2.

Row 5: Repeat row 1.

Row 6: Knit the first 4 stitches. Bring the yarn in front of the work as if to purl. Insert the tip of the right-hand needle in the next stitch from the back to front, as if to purl, and slip the stitch onto the needle (*drawing 6, arrow*). Slip the next

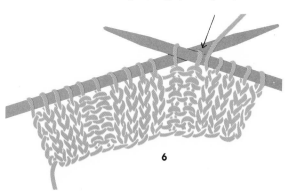

6

stitch in the same manner (*drawing 6*). Bring the yarn to the back of the work in the correct position for knitting, and knit each of the next 4 stitches. Repeat this sequence—slip 2 stitches as if to purl, knit 4 stitches—across the row.

Row 7: Purl the first 4 stitches. Slip 2 stitches onto a double-pointed needle; hold the stitches at the front of the work, then purl the next 2 stitches (*drawing 7*). Keeping the yarn

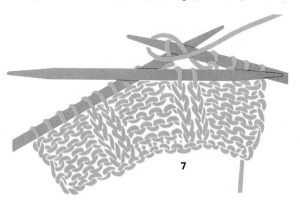

7

in the purl position at the front of the work, place the yarn over the needle to make a new stitch (*drawing 8, arrow*).

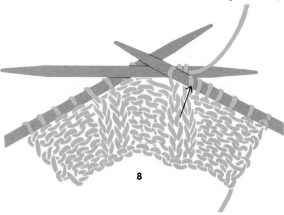

8

Now slide the 2 stitches on the double-pointed needle to the right-hand end of that needle. Insert the tip of the working needle through both of the stitches on the double-pointed needle, then knit the stitches together to decrease 1 stitch (*drawing 8*). Slip the next 2 stitches onto the double-pointed needle; hold the stitches at the back of the work, and knit the next 2 stitches together to decrease 1 stitch (*drawing 9*). Now bring the yarn forward as if to purl,

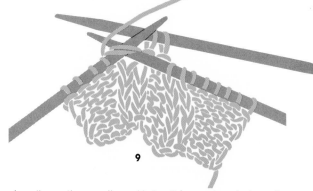

9

place it over the needle and bring it forward again to make 1 stitch (*drawing 10, arrow*), and purl the 2 stitches from

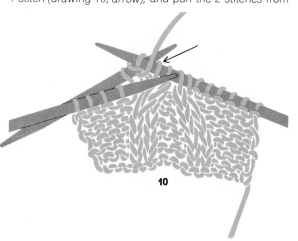

10

the double-pointed needle (*drawing 10*). Purl each of the next 4 stitches.

Repeat the sequence of 12 stitches—slip 2 stitches onto the double-pointed needle and hold them in front of the work, purl 2 stitches, yarn over to increase 1 stitch, knit the 2 stitches from the double-pointed needle together to decrease 1 stitch, slip 2 stitches onto the double-pointed needle, holding them at the back of the work, knit 2 stitches together to decrease 1 stitch, yarn forward and over to increase 1 stitch, purl the 2 stitches from the double-pointed needle, purl 4—across the row.

Row 8: Knit the first 4 stitches. Purl the next 2 stitches. Knit the next stitch. Purl the next 2 stitches. Knit the next stitch. Purl the next 2 stitches. Repeat this sequence of 12 stitches across the row. Then end the row by knitting the last 4 stitches.

Repeat the preceding 8 rows for the desired length of the pattern. Then bind off.

THE CACTUS CABLE PATTERN

Cast on any multiple of 14 stitches plus 2 stitches that measures the desired width of your work.

Row 1: Purl the first 2 stitches. Make a back cable following this sequence: slip the next 3 stitches onto the double-pointed needle and hold the stitches at the back of the work (*drawing 1, page 156*). Bring the yarn under the right-hand needle in the correct position for knitting and knit each of the next 3 stitches on the left-hand needle (*drawing 2, page 156*). Then slide the 3 stitches on the double-pointed needle to the right-hand end of that needle, and knit the stitches (*drawing 3, page 156*). Now make a front cable following this sequence: slip the next 3 stitches onto the double-pointed needle and hold the stitches at the front of the work; knit each of the next 3 stitches on the left-hand needle (*drawing 4, page 157*). Slide the 3 stitches on the double-pointed needle to the right-hand end of that needle, and knit them (*drawing 5, page 157*) to complete the front cable. Purl the next 2 stitches. Slip the next 3 stitches onto the double-pointed needle and work another back cable. Then work another front cable. Repeat this sequence of 14 stitches—purl 2 stitches, make one back cable, then one front cable—across the row. Then end the row by purling the last 2 stitches.

Row 2: Knit the first 2 stitches. Purl each of the next 12 stitches. Repeat this sequence of 14 stitches across the row. End the row by knitting the last 2 stitches.

Row 3: Purl the first 2 stitches. Then knit each of the next 12 stitches. Repeat this sequence of 14 stitches across the row. End the row by purling the last 2 stitches.

Row 4: Repeat row 2.
Row 5: Repeat row 3.
Row 6: Repeat row 2.
Row 7: Repeat row 3.
Row 8: Repeat row 2.
Row 9: Repeat row 3.
Row 10: Repeat row 2.

Row 11: Purl the first 2 stitches. Now follow the instructions in row 1 for making a front cable on the next 6 stitches. Then follow the instructions in row 1 for making a back cable on the next 6 stitches. Repeat this sequence of 14 stitches—purl 2 stitches, make one front cable then one back cable—across the row. End the row by purling the last 2 stitches.

Repeat rows 2 through 11 for the desired length. Then bind off.

THE PRETZEL CABLE PATTERN

Cast on any multiple of 18 stitches plus 4 stitches that measures the desired width of your work.

Row 1: Purl the first 2 stitches. Then knit each of the next 18 stitches. Continue to knit each multiple of 18 stitches across the row. End the row by purling the last 2 stitches.

Row 2: Knit the first 2 stitches. Then purl each of the next 18 stitches. Continue to purl each multiple of 18 stitches across the row. End the row by knitting the last 2 stitches.

Row 3: Repeat row 1.
Row 4: Repeat row 2.
Row 5: Repeat row 1.
Row 6: Repeat row 2.

Row 7: Purl the first 2 stitches. Now work a front cable on the next 12 stitches. To make the cable, begin by slipping the next 6 stitches onto a double-pointed needle and hold them in front of the work; then knit each of the next 6 stitches on the left-hand needle, as illustrated in drawing 4 for the Wedding Ring Cable Pattern, page 157. Now slide the 6 stitches on the double-pointed needle to the right-hand end of that needle and knit them, as illustrated in drawing 5, page 157. Knit the next 6 stitches. Repeat this sequence of 18 stitches—making a front cable on the next 12 stitches, then knitting the next 6 stitches—across the row. End the row by purling the last 2 stitches.

Row 8: Repeat row 2.
Row 9: Repeat row 1.
Row 10: Repeat row 2.
Row 11: Repeat row 1.
Row 12: Repeat row 2.

Row 13: Purl the first 2 stitches. Knit the next 6 stitches. Now work a back cable on the next 12 stitches in the following manner: slip the next 6 stitches onto a double-pointed needle, and hold the stitches at the back of the work, as illustrated in drawing 1 for the Uneven Twist Cable Pattern, page 156. Then knit each of the next 6 stitches on the left-hand needle, as illustrated in drawing 2, page 156. Next slide the 6 stitches on the double-pointed needle to the right-hand end of that needle and knit them, as illustrated in drawing 3, page 156. Continue to repeat this sequence of 18 stitches—knit 6 stitches, work a back cable on the next 12 stitches—across the row. Then end the row by purling the last 2 stitches.

Row 14: Repeat row 2.

Repeat the preceding 14 rows for the desired length. Then bind off.

Bundled in bulky knit pullovers

These thick, cozy hand-knit sweaters owe their special style to cable stitches, taken from the variety of swatches shown on pages 154-155. The turtleneck at far left features two different cable designs: plaited cables on the sleeves and down the center of the front and back—where they are flanked by cactus cables. The hooded V-necked sweater combines conventional stockinette and garter stitches with three vertical bands of the uneven twist cable pattern. Complete instructions for both sweaters, in sizes to fit either men or women, start overleaf.

Instructions for making the sweaters

THE TURTLE-NECK SWEATER

The following directions are for making the turtle-neck sweater *(page 160)* in a woman's small size (8-10). Changes for medium (12-14) and large (16-18) sizes follow in parentheses. Changes for a man's small (36-38), medium (40-42) and large (44-46) size follow in double parentheses. You will need 11 (12, 14) ((15, 17, 19)) four-ounce skeins of bulky wool yarn; two pairs of straight knitting needles, in Sizes 8 and 11 for a woman's small and medium sizes or 10 and 13 for a woman's large and all men's sizes; and a large double-pointed needle. With Size 11 needles, work in a gauge of 4 stitches to the inch for the stockinette pattern (alternating rows of knit and purl stitches); with Size 13 needles, the gauge should be 3 stitches to the inch.

THE BACK

Using the smaller size needles—Size 8 or 10—cast on 64 (72, 60) ((57, 63, 69)) stitches. Work a knit 1 stitch, purl 1 stitch ribbing pattern for 2 1/2 ((3)) inches. On the next row—the wrong side of the work—work in the knit stitch and increase 3 ((4)) stitches, evenly spaced, across the row. Change to the larger size needles—Size 11 or 13. Working on 67 (75, 63) ((61, 67, 73)) stitches, purl the first 5 (5, 3) ((3, 5, 4)) stitches. Follow the instructions for row 1 of the cactus cable pattern on page 159—purl 2 stitches, 1 back cable, 1 front cable, purl 2 stitches—on the next 16 stitches. Purl the next 3 (7, 3) ((2, 3, 7)) stitches. Follow the instructions for row 1 of the plaited cable pattern on page 157—purl 2 stitches, knit 15 stitches, purl 2 stitches—on the next 19 stitches. Purl the next 3 (7, 3) ((2, 3, 7)) stitches. Work the next 16 stitches in the cactus cable pattern again. Purl the last 5 (5, 3) ((3, 5, 4)) stitches. On the next row, knit the first 5 (5, 3) ((3, 5, 4)) stitches. Work the next 16 stitches (row 2 of the cactus cable pattern). Knit the next 3 (7, 3) ((2, 3, 7)) stitches. Work the next 19 stitches (row 2 of the plaited cable pattern). Knit the next 3 (7, 3) ((2, 3, 7)) stitches. Work the next 16 stitches, again following row 2 of the cactus cable pattern. Knit the last 5 (5, 3) ((3, 5, 4)) stitches. Repeat the sequence of the last two rows, until the work measures about 16 1/2 (16 1/2, 17) ((17, 18, 19)) inches, or the desired length to the armhole, ending after row 6 of the bands of cactus cables at each side.

Shaping the armholes: Bind off 3 ((3, 3, 4)) stitches at the beginning of the next row. Purl across the next 21 (25, 19) ((18, 21, 23)) stitches. Work the next 19 stitches, continuing in the sequence of rows of the plaited cable pattern. Purl the remaining 24 (28, 22) ((21, 24, 27)) stitches. On the next row, bind off the first 3 ((3, 3, 4)) stitches. Knit each of the

stitches before the 19 stitches of the center cable. Work across these 19 stitches in the plaited cable pattern; then knit the remaining stitches on the row. Continuing to work the center cable and the stitches on each side in the purl row, knit 1 row sequence to completion, decrease 1 stitch at each side edge on the next row. Repeat the decreases on every other row 4 (5, 4) ((3, 3, 4)) times more. Then work even in the sequence on the 51 (57, 47) ((47, 53, 55)) stitches of the row until the piece measures 7 (7 1/2, 8) ((8 1/2, 9, 9 1/2)) inches above the start of the armhole shaping.

Shaping the shoulders: Bind off 8 (9, 8) ((8, 9, 9)) stitches at the beginning of each of the next 2 rows. Bind off 8 (9, 7) ((7, 8, 9)) stitches at the beginning of each of the next 2 rows. Slip the remaining 19 (21, 17) ((17, 19, 19)) stitches onto a holder to be worked later.

THE FRONT

Work as you did on the back until the work measures approximately 5 (5 1/2, 6) ((6 1/2, 7, 7 1/2)) inches above the start of the armhole shaping, ending when you have completed row 6 of the center plaited cable stitch pattern.

Shaping the neck: Work across the first 20 (22, 19) ((19, 21, 22)) stitches. Slip the next 11 (13, 9) ((9, 11, 11)) stitches at the center onto a holder. Join another ball of yarn, and work across the remaining 20 (22, 19) ((19, 21, 22)) stitches. Work one row even on both sides of the center stitches at once. On the next row, work across the first group of stitches, and decrease 1 stitch at the end of this group—this will be the neck edge. Decrease 1 stitch at the beginning of the second group of stitches—also the neck edge—then work the remaining stitches on the row. Continue to make alternating rows of purl and knit stitches, and repeat the decreases at each neck edge every other row 3 times more. Work even now on the 16 (18, 15) ((15, 17, 18)) stitches at each side until the work measures the same as the back to the shoulders. Shape the shoulders as on the back.

THE SLEEVES

Using the smaller size needles indicated for your size, cast on 33 (35, 27) ((27, 29, 31)) stitches. Work a knit 1 stitch, purl 1 stitch ribbing pattern for 5 ((6)) inches. Change to the larger size needles. On the next row, purl the first 7 (8, 4) ((4, 5, 6)) stitches. Work the next 19 stitches as for row 1 of the plaited cable pattern. Purl the remaining 7 (8, 4) ((4, 5, 6)) stitches. On the next row, knit the first 7 (8, 4) ((4, 5, 6)) stitches. Now work the sequence of stitches in row 2 of the plaited cable pattern on the next 19 stitches. Knit the remaining 7 (8, 4) ((4, 5, 6)) stitches. Repeat the sequence of the last 2 rows—continuing to make the subsequent rows of the plaited cable pattern—until the piece measures 1 inch above the ribbing. Now increase 1 stitch at the beginning and the end of the next row. Repeat this increase every 2 (1 1/2, 2) ((1 1/2)) inches 6 (7, 6) ((8, 9, 9)) times, working now on 47 (51, 41) ((45, 49, 51)) stitches. When the sleeve measures about 12 1/2 ((13 1/2)) inches, ending with row 6 of the plaited cable, work in the purl 1 row, knit 1 row sequence across the entire row to completion. Work even until the sleeve measures 20 1/2 ((21 1/2)) inches —or the desired length—to the underarm.

Shaping the cap: Bind off 3 ((3, 3, 4)) stitches at the beginning of each of the next 2 rows. Now decrease 1 stitch at the beginning and end of every other row for 4 (4 1/2, 5) ((5 1/2, 6, 6 1/2)) inches. Bind off 2 stitches at the beginning of each of the next 4 rows. Bind off.

THE FINISHING TOUCHES
Sew the left shoulder seam. Using the smaller needles, and working on the outside of the work, pick up and knit 48 (52, 44) ((44, 48, 48)) stitches around the neck edge—including the stitches left on the holders. Work now in the knit 1, purl 1 ribbing pattern for 5 ((6)) inches to make the collar. Bind off loosely in the knit 1, purl 1 ribbing pattern. Sew the right shoulder seam, the collar seam and the side and sleeve seams. Sew in the sleeves. Block *(Glossary)*.

THE HOODED V-NECK SWEATER

The directions for this sweater *(page 161),* like those for the turtle neck, are for a woman's small size (8-10); any changes for other women's sizes follow in parentheses; changes for men's sizes are in double parentheses. Use 15 (17, 19) ((20, 22, 24)) four-ounce skeins of bulky wool yarn; Size 13 straight knitting needles, and a double-pointed needle. Work in a gauge of 5 stitches to 2 inches for the stockinette pattern (alternate rows of knit and purl stitches).

THE BACK
Cast on 45 (51, 55) ((53, 59, 63)) stitches. Knit for 2 inches. Change to the stockinette pattern and work even until the work measures 19 inches, or 2 inches less than the desired length to the underarm. Then knit for 2 more inches.
Shaping the armholes: Still using only knit stitches, bind off 4 stitches at the beginning of each of the next 2 rows. On the next row, decrease 1 stitch at the beginning and end of the row. Repeat this decrease on every other row 2 (3) ((2, 3, 4)) times more. Work even on 31 (35, 39) ((39, 43, 45)) stitches until the work measures 8 (8 1/2, 9) ((9 1/2, 10, 10 1/2)) inches above the start of the armhole shaping.
Shaping the shoulders: Bind off 5 (6, 7) ((6, 7, 8)) stitches at the beginning of each of the next two rows. Bind off 5 (6) ((6, 7, 7)) stitches at the beginning of each of the next 2 rows. Bind off loosely the remaining 11 (11, 13) ((15)) stitches for the back of the neck.

THE FRONT
Cast on 48 (54, 58) ((56, 62, 66)) stitches. Knit only for 2 inches, ending with a wrong-side row. On the next row, begin working the stockinette pattern on the first 18 (20, 22) ((20, 22, 24)) stitches. Knit the next 2 (3) ((4, 5, 5)) stitches. Now follow the instructions for row 1 of the uneven twist cable pattern *(page 156)* and work the next 8 stitches in the pattern. Knit the next 2 (3) ((4, 5, 5)) stitches. Work the last 18 (20, 22) ((20, 22, 24)) stitches in the stockinette pattern. Continue to work in this stitch and pattern sequence—repeating the 16 rows of the uneven twist cable pattern at the center—until the work measures approximately 8 inches, ending with either row 4 or row 12 of the cable pattern at the center. On the next row, work 2 (2, 4) ((2)) stitches in the stockinette pattern. Knit the next 2 (3) ((4, 5, 5)) stitches. On the next 8 stitches, work the uneven twist cable pattern, beginning with either row 5 or row 13, depending on where you stopped the pattern in the previous row. Knit 2

(3) ((4, 5, 5)) stitches. Work 4 ((2, 2, 4)) stockinette stitches, followed by 2 (3) ((4, 5, 5)) knit stitches. Work the next 8 stitches (row 5 or row 13) of the uneven twist cable pattern. Knit 2 (3) ((4, 5, 5)) stitches; work 4 ((2, 2, 4)) stitches in the stockinette pattern; then knit 2 (3) ((4, 5, 5)) stitches. Work a final band in the uneven twist cable pattern (row 5 or row 13) on the next 8 stitches. Knit 2 (3) ((4, 5, 5)) stitches. At the end of the row, work the final 2 (2, 4) ((2)) stitches in the stockinette pattern. Continue in this stitch number and pattern sequence—completing and repeating the sequence of the uneven twist cable patterns—until the work measures approximately 2 inches less than the desired length to the underarm. End with either row 4 or row 12 of the cable patterns. On the next row, knit the first 20 (23, 25) ((24, 27, 29)) stitches. Work row 5 or row 13 of the uneven twist cable pattern on the next 8 stitches. Knit the remaining 20 (23, 25) ((24, 27, 29)) stitches. Follow this sequence now until the work measures the same as the back to the underarm. Shape the armholes as you did on the back. When the armhole decreases are completed, work until you reach either row 4 or row 12 of the cable at the center.
Shaping the neck: Knit the first 17 (19, 21) ((21, 23, 24)) stitches. Join another ball of yarn. Work across the remaining 17 (19, 21) ((21, 23, 24)) stitches. Working on both sides at once, knit every row until the work measures the same as the back to the shoulders. Bind off as on the back. Knit the remaining 7 (7, 8) ((9, 9, 10)) stitches at each side for 13 ((14)) more inches for the front of the hood. Bind off.

THE SLEEVES
Cast on 39 (41, 44) ((46, 49, 51)) stitches. Knit for 2 inches. Change to the stockinette pattern. Work even until the sleeve measures 6 inches. Decrease 1 stitch at the beginning and end of the next row. Repeat this decrease every 4 inches 2 times. Work even—in the stockinette pattern—on 33 (35, 38) ((40, 43, 45)) stitches, until the sleeve measures 16 ((17)) inches, or 2 inches less than the desired length to the underarm. Knit for 2 more inches.
Shaping the cap: Continuing to knit only, bind off 4 stitches at the beginning of each of the next 2 rows. Decrease 1 stitch at the beginning and end of the next row. Repeat this decrease on every other row for 5 (5 1/2, 6) ((6 1/2, 7, 7 1/2)) more inches. Bind off 2 stitches at the beginning and end of each of the next 4 rows. Bind off.

THE FINISHING TOUCHES
Sew together the ends of the two bands you made to form the front of the hood. Place the front of the sweater so that the outside is facing you. Pick up 72 ((76)) stitches along the back edge of the strip, and knit each of these stitches. Continuing to make only knit stitches, decrease 1 stitch at the beginning and the end of the next row. Repeat this decrease on every other row 6 times. Now decrease at the beginning and end of every row until 20 ((24)) stitches remain. Work even now for 9 ((10)) inches. Bind off. Sew the bound-off row to the neck edge of the back of the sweater. At each side of the hood, join each 9- or 10-inch-long side to the corresponding side where you decreased, by sewing the edges together. Sew the shoulder, side and sleeve seams. Sew in the sleeves. Block *(Glossary)*.

Cool crochet for summer

Worked with fine cotton or blended yarns, the patterns shown in these swatches will produce crochet wear that is strong and supple enough for the most active sports, yet cool enough for the hottest day. The degree of natural air conditioning the crochet will provide changes with the size of hook—specified for it in the instructions that follow. The lacy twist pattern at far left, for example, requires a large hook to produce a loose and open look, while the millefleur pattern at far right employs a small hook and creates a tight weave with little stretchability.

Arrayed on hillocks of sand, from left to right, are swatches of the lacy twist, vertical stripe, post stitch ribbing, tiny sea shells and millefleur crochet patterns.

Instructions for crocheting the swatch patterns

To make the crochet patterns pictured on the preceding pages, you will need a thin, nubby wool-and-rayon-blend yarn—except for the post stitch ribbing pattern, which was crocheted with lightweight pearl cotton yarn. The size of the crochet hook you should use and the gauge of the stitches vary with the individual pattern.

Each set of directions, which begins at right, specifies the appropriate hook and gauge to use for the pattern. Before you make the pattern, check the gauge by crocheting a sample swatch that measures at least 4 inches square. Use the crochet hook and yarn indicated in the pattern instructions. Then lay the swatch on a flat surface, and count the number of stitches to the inch. To ensure accuracy, use a firm ruler rather than a tape measure.

If the gauge requires more stitches to the inch than you have made in the swatch, change to a smaller hook; if the gauge calls for fewer stitches to the inch, use a larger hook. This change of hook size will also alter the row-to-the-inch gauge.

The basic crochet stitches and techniques needed to make the patterns are explained in the Appendix. The illustrations that accompany the instructions on these pages demonstrate how to work any variations on these basic stitches as well as any unusual techniques that are not commonly encountered.

THE LACY TWIST PATTERN

Use a Size K aluminum crochet hook, and work in a gauge of 9 stitches to 2 inches. Begin the pattern by making a foundation chain of any uneven number of stitches that will give you the desired width of your work.

Row 1: Chain 1, then work 1 single crochet stitch in the second chain from the hook. Work 1 double crochet stitch in the next chain stitch. Now work 1 single crochet stitch in the next chain stitch.

Repeat this sequence—1 double crochet stitch, then 1 single crochet stitch—in each chain stitch across the row. At the end of the row, chain 2, and turn.

Row 2: Work 1 double crochet stitch, going through the back loop only of the first single crochet stitch in the previous row (drawing 1, arrow). Then make 1 single crochet stitch, going through the front loop only of the next double cro-

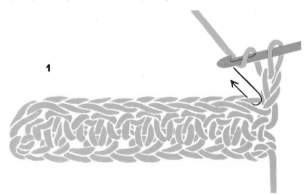

chet stitch (drawing 2, arrow). Work 1 double crochet stitch through the back loop only of the next single crochet stitch.

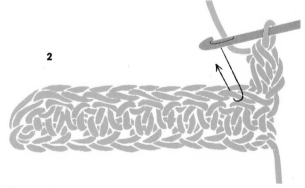

Repeat this sequence—1 single crochet stitch through the front loop only and 1 double crochet stitch through the back loop only—across the row. At the end of the row, chain 1, and turn.

Row 3: Work 1 single crochet stitch through the front loop only of the first double crochet stitch, as illustrated in drawing 2. Now work 1 double crochet stitch through the back loop only of the next single crochet stitch, as illustrated in drawing 1. Work 1 single crochet stitch through the front loop only of the next double crochet stitch. Repeat this sequence of one single crochet stitch through the front loop and 1 double crochet stitch through the back loop—across the row. When you reach the end of the row, chain 2, and turn.

Repeat rows 2 and 3 until the work measures the desired length. Fasten off.

THE VERTICAL STRIPE PATTERN

Use a Size 10 steel crochet hook, and work in a gauge of 8 stitches to the inch. Begin the pattern by making a foundation chain of any multiple of 3 chain stitches plus 2 chain stitches that will give you the desired width of your work. Unlike most crochet patterns, in which even-numbered rows are worked on what will become the wrong side of the finished garment, this pattern calls for odd-numbered rows to be worked on the wrong side.

Row 1: Chain 1, then work 1 single crochet stitch in the second chain from the hook. Continue to make 1 single crochet stitch in each chain stitch across the row. At the end of the row, chain 1, and turn. (Note: Remember that this first row—and all uneven rows thereafter—is the wrong side of the work.)

Row 2: Work 1 single crochet stitch through the back loop only (as illustrated in drawing 1, left) of the first single crochet stitch in the previous row. Then work another single crochet stitch through the back loop only of the next single crochet stitch in the previous row. Now insert the hook from front to back through the next single crochet stitch, then bring the hook out from back to front through the next single crochet stitch (drawing 3, arrow) in the previous row. Place the yarn over the hook, and draw it through to form

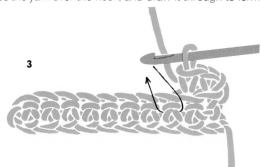

two loops on the hook. Place the yarn over the hook again, and draw it through the two loops on the hook, thus forming the first vertical bar (drawing 4, arrow). Work 1 single crochet stitch through the back loops only of each of the

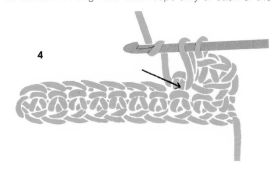

next 2 single crochet stitches, counting the second of the 2 single crochet stitches used to form the previous vertical bar as the first stitch of the next 2 single crochet stitches. Repeat this sequence—1 vertical bar and 1 single crochet stitch through the back loops only of each of the next 2 single crochet stitches—across the row. At the end of the row, chain 1, and turn.

Row 3: Work 1 single crochet stitch in each stitch across the row. At the end of the row, chain 1, and turn.

Row 4: Work 1 single crochet stitch through the back loop only of the first and second stitches on the previous row. Next, insert the hook from front to back, then from back to front, under the threads of the first vertical bar (drawing 5, arrow), and work 1 single crochet stitch through the bar.

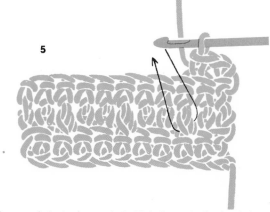

Now work 1 single crochet stitch through the back loop only of each of the next 2 stitches. Repeat this sequence —1 single crochet stitch through the next vertical bar, 1 single crochet stitch through the back loops of each of the next 2 stitches—across the row. At the end of the row, chain 1, and turn.

Repeat rows 3 and 4 until the work measures the desired length. Fasten off.

THE POST STITCH RIBBING PATTERN

Use a Size F aluminum crochet hook, and work in a gauge of 4 stitches to the inch. Begin the pattern by making a foundation chain of any multiple of 17 chain stitches that will give you the desired width of your work.

Row 1: Work 1 half double crochet stitch in the third chain stitch from the hook. Continue to make 1 half double crochet stitch in each chain stitch across the row. At the end of the row, chain 2, and turn. (Note: The chain 2 at the end of the row counts as the first stitch of the following row. This row, and all uneven numbered rows thereafter, is the wrong side of the work.)

Row 2: Work 1 half double crochet stitch in the first stitch of the previous row. Work another half double crochet stitch in the next stitch. Place the yarn over the hook. Now insert the hook from front to back into the space before the next half double crochet stitch in the previous row, and bring the hook out from back to front in the space after the half double crochet stitch *(drawing 6, arrow).* Place the yarn over the hook again, and draw it through the spaces. Place the yarn over the hook once more and draw it through the

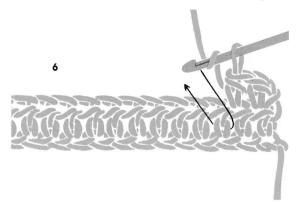

three remaining loops on the hook *(drawing 7).* Make sure you work this stitch—a variation of the regular half double crochet stitch, and known as a long half double crochet stitch—very loosely. Now work 1 half double crochet stitch

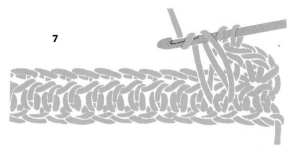

in the next stitch. Make another long half double crochet stitch through the spaces before and after the next half double crochet stitch in the previous row. This sequence of 3 stitches—1 long half double crochet stitch, 1 regular half double crochet stitch and then another long half double crochet stitch—will henceforth be referred to in this pattern as a double long half double crochet rib. Now work 1 half double crochet stitch in each of the next 5 stitches. Make another double long half double crochet rib on the next 3 stitches, and work 1 half double crochet stitch in each of the next 5 stitches.

Continue this sequence—1 double long half double crochet rib, then 5 half double crochet stitches—across the row. After you have made the last long half double crochet stitch, work 1 half double crochet stitch in each of the 3 remaining stitches of the row. When you reach the end of the row, chain 2, and turn.

Row 3: Work 1 half double crochet stitch in each stitch across the row. When you reach the end of the row, chain 2, and turn.

Row 4: Work 1 half double crochet stitch in the first stitch and another half double crochet stitch in the second stitch. Place the yarn over the hook, then insert the hook through

the top threads of the first long half double crochet stitch made in row 2 *(drawing 8, arrow).* Place the yarn over the hook again and draw it through the threads. Place the yarn over the hook once more and draw it through the three remaining loops on the hook (as illustrated in drawing 7,

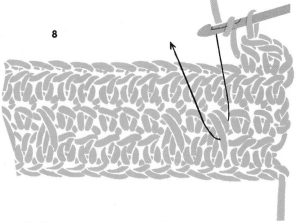

left). This procedure creates 1 long half double crochet stitch, as in row 2; however, in this row, and all subsequent rows of the pattern, the hook is inserted in the front threads of the long half double crochet stitch 2 rows below—as shown in drawing 8—rather than through the spaces of the half double crochet stitch in the previous row—as shown in drawing 6. Again, make sure to work off all long half double crochet stitches very loosely.

Now work 1 half double crochet stitch in the next stitch. Then work another long half double crochet stitch through the top threads of the long half double crochet stitch that you made in row 2—as instructed previously in this row —to complete the first double long half double crochet rib. Then make 1 half double crochet stitch in each of the next 5 stitches.

Continue this sequence—1 double long half double crochet rib, then 5 half double crochet stitches—across the row. After you have made the last long half double crochet stitch, work 1 half double crochet stitch in each of the 3 remaining stitches of the row. When you reach the end of the row, chain 2, and turn.

Repeat rows 3 and 4 until the work measures the desired length. Fasten off.

THE TINY SEA SHELLS PATTERN

Use a Size K aluminum crochet hook, and work in a gauge of 9 stitches to 2 inches. Begin the pattern by making a foundation chain of any even number of stitches that will give you the desired width of your work.

Row 1: Chain 2, then work 1 half double crochet stitch in the third chain stitch from the hook.

Continue to make 1 half double crochet stitch in each chain stitch across the row.

At the end of the row, chain 2, and turn.

Row 2: Work 1 single crochet stitch in the space between the second and third half double crochet stitches of the previous row (drawing 9, arrow), then chain 2 (drawing 9). Skip the next 2 half double crochet stitches. Now work 1

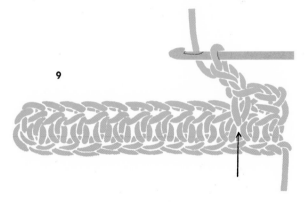

half double crochet stitch in the space before the next half double crochet stitch in the previous row (drawing 10). Chain 2, and skip the next 2 half double crochet stitches.

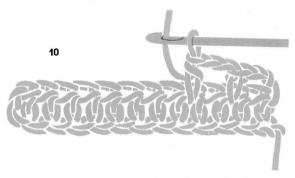

Repeat this sequence—1 single crochet stitch in the space before the next half double crochet stitch, chain 2, skip 2 stitches, 1 half double crochet stitch in the space before the next half double crochet stitch, chain 2, skip 2 stitches —across the row. At the end of the row, work 1 single crochet stitch in the top of the turning chain of the previous row (drawing 11, arrow). Chain 2, and turn.

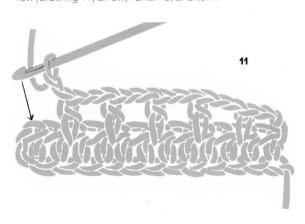

Row 3: Begin by working 2 half double crochet stitches in the first chain-2 space of the previous row (drawing 12, arrow). Continue to work 2 half double crochet stitches in

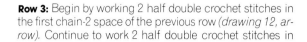
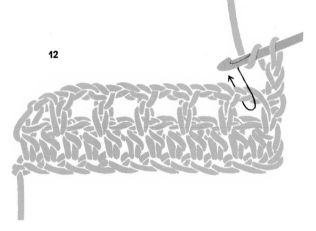

each chain-2 space across the row. At the end of the row, make 2 half double crochet stitches, working them in the top of the turning chain of the previous row (as illustrated in drawing 11, near left). Then chain 2, and turn.
Repeat rows 2 and 3 until the work measures the desired length. Fasten off.

THE MILLEFLEUR PATTERN

Use a Size 10 steel crochet hook, and work in a gauge of 8 stitches to the inch. Begin the pattern by making a foundation chain of any uneven number of stitches that will give you the desired width of your work.

Row 1: Chain 1, then work 1 single crochet stitch and 1 double crochet stitch in the second chain stitch from the hook. Skip 1 chain stitch. Make 1 single crochet stitch and then 1 double crochet stitch in the next chain stitch. Skip 1 chain stitch.
Then repeat this sequence—1 single and 1 double crochet stitch in the next chain stitch, skip 1 chain stitch—across the row. When you reach the end of the row, work 1 single crochet stitch only in the last chain stitch, then chain 1, and turn.

Row 2: Work 1 single crochet stitch and 1 double crochet stitch in the first single crochet stitch of the previous row. Skip 1 double crochet stitch, that is, the next stitch of the previous row. Work 1 single crochet stitch and 1 double crochet stitch in the next single crochet stitch, skip 1 double crochet stitch.
Continue to repeat this sequence across the row. When you reach the end of the row, work 1 single crochet stitch only in the last single crochet stitch of the previous row, then chain 1, and turn.
Repeat row 2 until the work measures the desired length. Fasten off.

A breezy costume for the court

An airy crochet stitch, a naturally absorbent cotton yarn and a breezy style combine to make this tennis dress one of the coolest fashions ever to grace a court. The tank top is sleeveless and V necked, the skirt extra short and flaring. Both owe their porous comfort and sporty look to having been worked in the post stitch ribbing pattern *(pages 167-168)*—a simple variation on the standard half double crochet stitch. Instructions start on page 174.

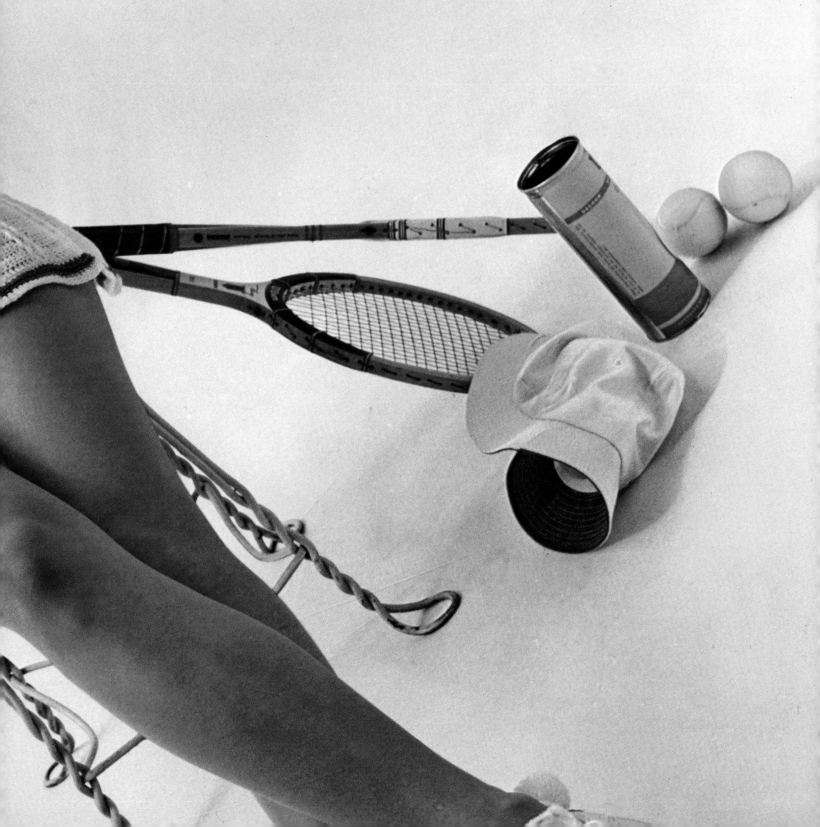

A crochet bikini and its cover-up

Using only one kind of yarn, an adroit crocheter can turn out a close-weave bikini, and a mesh pattern delicate enough to make a see-through cover-up. Crocheting the bikini requires single crochet stitches, worked on a small hook to a tight gauge so that the suit stays in shape when wet. The airy openwork of the cover-up is created by the lacy twist pattern *(page 166),* using a large hook. Instructions for both garments are on pages 175-177.

Instructions for tennis and beach wear

THE TENNIS DRESS

The following instructions are for making the tennis dress pictured on pages 170-171. The directions are written for a petite size (4-6); changes necessary for making a small (8-10), medium (12-14) or large (16-18) size follow in parentheses. To make the garment, you will need 16 ounces of lightweight pearl cotton yarn for the petite and small sizes, 18 ounces for the medium size and 20 ounces for the large size; four ounces of the same yarn in a contrasting color for the trim; and elastic thread. You will also need aluminum crochet hooks in Sizes E and F for a petite size; E, F and G for small; E and F for medium; and F and G for large.

The entire garment was crocheted in the post stitch ribbing pattern (pages 167-168). As you make the top and skirt, work loosely in a gauge of 4 stitches to the inch when using the F hook, and 7 stitches to 2 inches when using the G hook. The skirt is designed to measure about 11 1/2 (12, 12 1/2, 13) inches including 3/4 inch for the waistband and 1/4 inch for the bottom trim. To adjust the length, add or subtract the necessary amount on the front and back pieces before you begin to decrease.

THE TOP

The back: Using the Size F (G, F, G) crochet hook, chain 66 (66, 74, 74) stitches. Do not pull the stitches tight. Turn. On the first row—which will be the wrong side of the work—make 1 half double crochet stitch in the third chain stitch from the hook. Continue to make half double crochet stitches in each of the remaining chain stitches across the row. Chain 2, and turn. (Note: The chain 2 counts as the first stitch of the next row, but should not be worked.)

On the next row—you are now working on the right side of the work—make 1 half double crochet stitch in each of the first 2 half double crochet stitches of the previous row. Following the instructions on page 167 for row 2 of the post stitch ribbing pattern, make 1 double long half double crochet rib on the next 3 stitches. Now work 1 half double crochet stitch in each of the next 4 (4, 5, 5) stitches. Repeat the sequence—1 double long half double crochet rib, then 1 half double crochet stitch in each of the next 4 (4, 5, 5) stitches—across the row. After you complete the final long half double crochet stitch of the last rib, make 3 double crochet stitches in the 3 remaining stitches. Chain 2, and turn.

On the next row, working on 65 (65, 73, 73) stitches, make 1 half double crochet stitch in each stitch across the row. Chain 2 and turn. Now make 1 half double crochet stitch in each of the first 2 stitches of the row. Follow the di-

rections for row 4 of the pattern (page 168) to make the first double long half double crochet rib on this row. Make 1 half double crochet stitch in the next 4 (4, 5, 5) stitches, and continue across the row in the pattern. There should be 9 complete ribs and 8 sections of 4 (4, 5, 5) half double crochet stitches in between, and 3 half double crochet stitches at the end of the row. Now repeat rows 3 and 4 of the pattern for 3 1/2 (3 1/2, 4, 4 1/2) inches, ending on a wrong-side row. Make a decrease as follows: working on the right-side row, decrease 1 stitch at the beginning and end of the row, and decrease 1 stitch at the center of each section of half double crochet stitches across the row. Now work even in the pattern stitch, without decreasing for 4 (4, 4 1/2, 4 1/2) inches more.

Then make an increase. Working on a right-side row, increase 1 stitch at the beginning and end of the row and at the same time, increase 1 stitch at the center of each section of regular half double crochet stitches. Now work even in the pattern stitch without increasing until the work measures 12 (12 1/2, 13, 13 1/2) inches—or the desired length—from the bottom to the underarm.

Shaping the armholes: Slip stitch—by inserting the hook through the stitch, bringing the yarn over the hook, then drawing the yarn through the stitch and the loop on the hook—loosely across the first 5 (5, 6, 6) stitches on the row. Without working these stitches, chain 2, and turn. Continue to work in the pattern stitch—making sure to keep the long half double crochet ribs in line with the ribs on the previous rows—and decrease 1 stitch at the beginning and end of every row for the next 6 (6, 7, 7) rows. Work even in the pattern until the armhole section measures 6 1/2 (6 1/2, 7, 7 1/2) inches from the start of the shaping.

Shaping the back neck and the shoulders: Work in the pattern across the first 12 (12, 13, 13) stitches. Then chain 2, and turn. Working now on these stitches only, decrease 1 stitch at the beginning of the next row—this will be the neck edge. Work across the row in the pattern stitch, without decreasing at the end of the row; this side will be the armhole edge. On the next 4 rows, continue decreasing 1 stitch at the neck edge. The work should measure 7 1/2 (7 1/2, 8, 8 1/2) inches from the beginning of the armhole shaping. Fasten off. Return now to the point at which you began to shape the back neck and shoulders. Skip 19 (19, 21, 21) stitches at the center of the work to allow for the center-back neck edge. Attach yarn. Working on the remaining 12 (12, 13, 13) stitches of the row, decrease 1 stitch at the beginning of the row; this will be the neck edge. Shape the back neck and the shoulders as on the other side, reversing all directions so that the two halves correspond.

The front: Follow the instructions for making the back until the work measures 11 (11 1/2, 12, 12 1/2) inches—or 1 inch less than to the beginning of the back armhole shaping. Working on one side of the front at a time, begin to shape the V neckline. Work across the first 32 (32, 36, 36) stitches of the row. Chain 2 and turn. At the beginning of the next row, decrease 1 stitch. This will be the neck edge. Work across the row, without decreasing at the end of the row—which will be the side, or armhole, edge. Continuing in the pattern, decrease 1 stitch every other row—at the neck edge only—6 (6, 7, 7) more times. Work even now in the pattern stitch until this side of the front measures the same as the back to the armhole. To shape the underarm, begin on a right-side row, and slip stitch across the first 5 (5, 6, 6) stitches. Continue in the pattern across the remaining stitches in the row. Now decrease at the beginning and end of every row 6 (6, 7, 7) times. Then work even until the piece measures the same as the back to the shoulder edge. Fasten off. Return to the point you began the V-neckline shaping—at the center of the work.

Attach yarn. (Note: As opposed to the directions for the back, do not skip any stitches.) Work this side of the front carefully. Follow the instructions for the other side, but reverse all directions so that the two halves correspond.

Finishing the top: Sew the side and shoulder seams. To begin the neck trim, use the Size E (F, E, F) hook and the main color yarn, and attach the yarn at the center back of the neck. Chain 1, and work around the entire neck edge, using single crochet stitches. When you reach the center back again, join the end of the row to the beginning with a slip stitch. Fasten off. Attach yarn in the trim color, and chain 1. Begin to work another row of single crochet stitches around the neck edge. When you reach the center stitch at the center front of the V neck, decrease 1 stitch at each side of the stitch. Continue around the neck edge, using single crochet stitches. If necessary, decrease 2 to 4 evenly spaced stitches across the back neck edge to make the work lie flat and maintain the neckline shaping. When you reach the center back, join the end to the beginning of the row with a slip stitch, then chain 1. Work 1 more row of single crochet stitches in the same manner, but this time decrease 2 or 3 stitches away from the center-front stitch on each side of the V neck. Fasten off.

Attach the main color yarn again, chain 1, and work 1 more row of single crochet stitches in the same manner, again being careful not to decrease at the center front directly over the decrease stitches of the previous row. Decrease at the back again, if necessary. Now work 4 rows of single crochet trim around the armholes as you did around the neck, attaching the yarn at the underarm and decreasing at each side of the shoulder seam and at the underarm, as you did around the neck. Work the armhole trim loosely, to allow for freedom of movement when the garment is worn. Trim the hem similarly, attaching the yarn at one side seam but without decreasing. Now add 1 more row of stitches in the main color so that there are 5 rows in all: 1 row of main color, 2 rows of trim color, then 2 rows of main color.

THE SKIRT

Use the correct hook indicated for your size, and chain 136 (136, 144, 144) stitches loosely. On the next row, make 1 half double crochet stitch in the third chain stitch from the hook, then 1 half double crochet stitch in each remaining stitch. Chain 2 and turn. On the next row—counting the chain 2 of the previous row as the first stitch—make 1 half double crochet stitch in each of the next 5 (5, 5, 5) stitches. Then follow the instructions for row 2 of the post stitch rib-

bing pattern to make 1 double long half double crochet rib in the next 3 stitches. Now make 1 half double crochet stitch in each of the next 12 (12, 13, 13) stitches. Follow this sequence across the row—1 double long half double crochet rib, then 12 (12, 13, 13) half double crochet stitches—until you have made 9 double long half double crochet ribs with 8 sections of 12 (12, 13, 13) half double crochet stitches in between. After the last long half double crochet stitch of the last rib, there should be 6 stitches remaining on the row for all sizes. Make 1 half double crochet stitch in these stitches, then chain 2, and turn.

On the next row (row 3 of the pattern), work 1 half double crochet stitch in each of the stitches across the row. Chain 2, and turn. On the next row, work 1 half double crochet stitch in each of the first 2 stitches of the row. Now follow the instructions for making the double long half double crochet rib in row 4 of the pattern (page 168), but use the number of half double crochet stitches between the ribs—12 (12, 13, 13) stitches—and 6 stitches at the end of the row, as called for in these instructions. Now repeat rows 3 and 4 of the pattern for 6 (8, 10, 12) more rows.

Working on a pattern rib row, begin to decrease as follows. On this row, decrease 1 stitch at the beginning and end of the row, and at the same time decrease 1 stitch at the center of each section of 12 (12, 13, 13) half double crochet stitches. Continue working rows 3 and 4 of the pattern, and repeat the decreases at the beginning and end of the row every fourth row, 2 more times—or until 3 stitches remain beyond the ribs at each end of the row. Continue to decrease at the center of the half double crochet sections every fourth row 7 more times—or until 4 (4, 5, 5) stitches remain in each section. After the decreases, work even in the pattern until the work measures 1 1/2 inches less than the desired length. Fasten off. Repeat the instructions to make the other half of the skirt. Then sew the side seams. Make 5 rows of trim around the hem, following the instructions for trimming the hem of the top.

The waistband: Use a Size E (E, F, F) hook and the main color yarn. Attach the yarn at one side seam, chain 1 and work around the top of the skirt, using single crochet stitches. Join the last stitch to the chain-1 stitch at the beginning with a slip stitch. Cut two strands of elastic thread that measure 2 1/2 to 3 inches less than your waist measurement. Knot the ends of the elastic to form a ring. At the slip stitch, using the yarn again, chain 1 and work 1 row of single crochet stitches over the elastic ring. When you reach the end of the row, join the yarn at the last stitch to the chain 1 with a slip stitch. On the next row, using only the yarn, chain 1 and work another row of single crochet stitches around the top of the skirt, as on the first row. Knot the ends of the second elastic strand. Join the ends of the yarn with a slip stitch, chain 1, then work the next row, as before, to attach the elastic. Fasten off.

THE BIKINI

The basic single crochet stitch (Appendix) was used to make the bikini shown on page 173. The directions that follow are for a small size (10-12); changes for making a medium size (14-16) follow in parentheses. You will need three (four) ounces of thin, nubby rayon and wool yarn, a Size 10 steel crochet hook, elastic thread and four snaps. Work in a gauge of 8 stitches to the inch.

THE BOTTOM

The back: Begin at the crotch, and chain 29 stitches, then turn. On the next row, work 1 single crochet stitch in the second chain from the hook, then 1 single crochet stitch in each chain stitch across the row. Now work 3 rows of single crochet stitches, working even on 28 stitches. On the next row, increase 1 stitch at the beginning and end of the row. Work 39 more rows, increasing 1 stitch at the beginning and end of each row.

When you have 108 stitches on the row, chain 21 (29) stitches at the end of the row. On the next row, work 1 single crochet stitch in the second chain stitch from the hook — made in the previous row — then 1 single crochet stitch in each of the remaining 19 (27) chain stitches. Work 1 single crochet stitch in each of the 108 stitches at the center of the work. At the end of the row, chain 21 (29) stitches and turn. Now work 1 single crochet stitch in the second chain from the hook, then 1 single crochet stitch in each of the remaining 19 (27) chain stitches made in the previous row. Then work 1 single crochet stitch in each of the remaining 128 (136) stitches on the row. There are now 148 (164) stitches on the row. Work even on these stitches for 1 (2) inches. Fasten off.

The front: Begin again at the crotch and chain 29 stitches. Turn. Work 1 single crochet stitch in the second chain stitch from the hook and in each chain stitch across the row. Chain 1 and turn. Work even now in the single crochet stitch on each of the 28 stitches of the row for 1/2 inch. Decrease 1 stitch at the beginning and end of the next row. Work even across the next row. Repeat the decrease row — alternating it with a row of single crochet stitches without decreasing — 3 more times.

Work even now on the 20 stitches, until the work measures 5 inches from the first chain-28 stitches at the bottom of the piece. On the next row, increase 1 stitch at the beginning and end of the row. Repeat this increase for the next 23 rows. There will now be 68 stitches on the row. On the next row, work across the row, then chain 41 (49) stitches, and turn. Now work 1 single crochet stitch in the second chain from the hook and in each of the remaining 39 (47) chain stitches. Work 1 single crochet stitch in each of the 68 stitches at the center of the work. Then chain 41 (49) stitches and turn. On the next row, work 1 single crochet stitch in the second chain stitch from the hook and in each of the remaining 39 (47) chain stitches from the previous row. Work single crochet stitches in the remaining stitches. There are now 148 (164) stitches on the row. Work even now for 1 (2) inches. Fasten off.

The waistband: Chain 12 stitches and turn. Work 1 single crochet stitch in each of the 11 stitches on the first row. On the next row, work single crochet stitches in each stitch across the row, but this time go through only the back loop of the stitch on the previous row (as illustrated in drawing 1, page 166). Repeat the preceding row until the band

measures 16 1/2 (18 1/2) inches. Fasten off. Repeat the preceding steps to make another band that measures exactly the same length.

The leg bands: Chain 7 stitches and turn. Work one row of single crochet stitches in each of the 6 stitches of the row. Now follow the instructions for making the waistband, working single crochet stitches through the back loops only of the stitches in the previous row, for 18 (20) inches. Fasten off. Make the other leg band in the same manner.

Finishing the bottom: Sew the back piece to the front at the crotch and the side seams. Sew the waistband ribbings to the front and the back, and join the two short ends. Sew the leg band ribbings around the leg openings, again joining the short ends. Cut three strands of elastic thread to fit around your hips. Draw the strands, spaced evenly apart, through each ridge of the stitches on the underside of the waistband. Knot the ends. Cut four strands of elastic to fit around the top of your leg. Draw two of these strands through each leg band in the same manner. Knot the ends.

THE TOP

To begin the first cup section, chain 52 (60) stitches and turn. On the next row, work 1 single crochet stitch in the second chain from the hook, then 1 single crochet stitch in each chain stitch across the row. On the next row, work 1 single crochet stitch in each of the 51 (59) stitches. On the next row, continue to work single crochet stitches, but decrease 1 stitch at the beginning and end of the row. Now work 1 row of single crochet stitches without decreasing. Continue to repeat the preceding 2 rows — 1 decrease row, then 1 row of single crochet stitches without decreasing — 13 (15) more times. There will now be 23 (27) stitches on the row. Now begin to decrease at the beginning and end of each of the next 8 (10) rows. There should now be 7 stitches on the row for both sizes. Fasten off. Repeat the preceding steps to form the other cup section.

The ribbing: Follow the instructions for making the waistband, and make another strip of ribbing — working on 11 stitches again — that measures 30 (32) inches, to make the base of the bikini top. Now make two more strips of ribbing — but working on 6 stitches only — that measure 10 (12) inches, to fit around the cups. Finally, make two more strips — again working on 6 inches — that measure 12 (14) inches, to form the straps.

Finishing the top: Sew the 10- or 12-inch-long ribbings around each cup. Place the cups side by side, and overlap for 3/4 inch the ribbings at the bottom of the center front. Then sew the overlap together. Now sew the 30- or 32-inch strip of ribbing to the bottom of the joined cups, centering the ribbing at the center front of the overlap. Attach the two straps, placing one end of each strap at the top center of each cup and the other end of the strap at the top of the base ribbing on the back, and about 2 1/2 inches in from the ends. Now draw three strands of elastic thread through the ridges on the underside of the base ribbing. Draw two strands of elastic thread through each cup ribbing in the same manner, and one strand through each strap. Try on the top, and draw the elastic strands up until the top fits snugly. Knot the ends. Attach four straps to the long strip of ribbing at the back, positioning them where they feel most comfortable for closing.

THE COVER-UP

The cover-up pictured on page 172 was made using the lacy twist pattern (pages 166-167). The garment was designed to measure 46 inches from the hem to the underarm, so that when worn it will stretch to 49 inches. To adjust the length, add or subtract the required amount on the front and back pieces after decreasing and before you begin to shape the armholes. The directions here are for a small size (10-12); changes for a medium size (14-16) follow in parentheses. For the cover-up, you will need 16 (20) ounces of the same yarn used in the bikini and a Size K crochet hook. Work in a gauge of 9 stitches to 2 inches.

THE BACK

Chain 108 (118) stitches and turn. On the next row, work 1 single crochet stitch in the second chain stitch from the hook and in each chain stitch across the row. Work even across the next 3 rows in single crochet stitches on 107 (117) stitches. Now work row 2 of the lacy twist pattern (page 166) on the next row. On the following row, work row 3 of the pattern. Continue to repeat rows 2 and 3 of the pattern, and work even for 2 1/2 inches. On the next row, decrease 1 stitch at the beginning and end of the row. Work the pattern without decreasing for 2 1/2 more inches, then repeat the decrease row. Work the pattern without decreasing for 1 more inch—you will now have worked 6 inches in the pattern stitch. On the next 4 rows, working now on 103 (113) stitches, use only single crochet stitches across the rows.

Begin the pattern stitch again on the next row—repeating rows 2 and 3 and continuing to decrease every 2 1/2 inches. When this band of the pattern measures 5 inches, work another 4 rows of single crochet stitches. Begin the pattern stitch once more, continuing to decrease 1 stitch at each end of the row every 2 1/2 inches. Work in the pattern stitch now for 4 inches. Make another 4-row band of single crochet stitches. Then work the lacy twist pattern stitch for another 3 inches. Make a final 4-row band of single crochet stitches. Start the pattern stitch once more, and working in this stitch to completion, continue to decrease 1 stitch at each end of the row every 2 1/2 inches until there are 77 (87) stitches. Work even until the back measures 46 inches—or the desired length—to the underarm.

Shaping the armholes: Slip stitch across the first 6 stitches. To slip stitch, insert the hook through the stitch on the previous row, bring the yarn over the hook, then draw the yarn through the stitch and the loop on the hook. Then work in the pattern stitch across the row to within the last 6 stitches. Without working these stitches, chain and turn. Work the next row even in the pattern. On the next row, decrease 1 stitch at the beginning and end of the row. Repeat the preceding 2 rows 3 more times. Working on 57 (67) stitches now, work even in the pattern until the back measures 2 1/2 inches from the start of the armhole shaping.

Shaping the neck: Work in the pattern stitch across the first 22 (25) stitches. Chain, and turn. Working now on these stitches only, decrease 1 stitch at the beginning of the next row—this will be the neck edge. Work across the row in the pattern stitch, and do not decrease at the end of the row —which will be the side, or armhole, edge. Continue to work in the pattern stitch, decreasing 1 stitch at the neck edge every 1/2 inch, 7 more times. Work even now on 14 (17) stitches until the piece measures 8 1/4 (8 3/4) inches above the start of the armhole shaping. End the last row at the side edge.

Shaping the shoulder: On the first row, slip stitch across the first 7 (9) stitches. Work across to the end of the row. Chain, and turn. Then slip stitch across the remaining 7 (8) stitches. Fasten off.

Completing the neck and shoulder edges: Return to the point at which you began to shape the neck. Skip 13 (17) stitches at the center of the work. Attach yarn and follow the instructions for shaping the neck and shoulder as you did on the other side, but this time reverse all directions so that the two halves correspond.

THE FRONT

Follow the instructions for making the back until the front section measures 3 1/2 inches above the start of the armhole shaping. Then begin to shape one half of the neck as you did on the back, but this time work across 20 (23) stitches instead of 22 (25) stitches, and make a total of 6 decreases at the neck edge instead of 8. You will now be working on 14 (17) stitches, and the piece should measure 8 1/4 (8 3/4) inches above the start of the armhole shaping. Shape the shoulder as you did on the back. Now return to the point at which you began to shape the neck, and skip 17 (20) stitches at the center of the work. Work the other half of the front neck and shoulder edges as above, reversing the directions so that the two halves correspond.

THE SLEEVES

Chain 57 (61) stitches and turn. Work in the lacy twist pattern for 1 inch.

Shaping the sleeve cap: On the next row, slip stitch across each of the first 6 stitches. Continue across the row in the pattern stitch to within the last 6 stitches. Chain, and turn, without working these last stitches. Work the next row even in the pattern stitch. On the following row, decrease 1 stitch at the beginning and end of the row. Then work the next row even in the pattern stitch without decreasing. Continue to repeat the preceding 2 rows—decreasing every other row—for 5 1/2 (5 3/4) inches. Work the next 4 rows—still in the pattern stitch—decreasing 1 stitch at the beginning and end of every row. On the last row, slip stitch across the remaining stitches.

THE FINISHING TOUCHES

Sew the shoulder seams to join the front to the back. Then join yarn at one shoulder and, working back and forth from this point around the neck edge, make 4 rows of single crochet stitches, working on 149 (159) stitches. On each sleeve bottom, make 4 rows of single crochet stitches in the same manner, working on 37 (41) stitches. At the point that you began the neck edging, sew the short ends of the single crochet band together. Sew the sleeve and side seams. Sew in the sleeves. Block the finished work (Glossary).

GLOSSARY

BACKSTITCH: To reinforce the beginning or end of a seam by making several machine stitches backward over the seam line.

BATTING: A sheet of loosely matted fibers for use as insulation and interlining in garments, quilts, sleeping bags and the like. Batting is sold by the yard in various widths and thicknesses. Some batting comes already stitched between two layers of cloth, but most of it needs to be quilted to fabric backing.

BASTE: To make long, loose stitches for the purpose of holding together pieces of fabric temporarily or to indicate pattern markings on both sides of a piece of fabric. A row of basting is usually held at the end with a fastening stitch.

BIAS: A direction diagonal to that of the threads in woven fabric.

BLOCK: To set the final shape of finished knitting or crocheting. The work is pressed with a warm iron through a damp cloth.

CLIP: A short cut made with scissors into a seam allowance to help the seam lie flat around curves and corners.

CUTTING LINE: A long, unbroken line marked on a pattern to indicate where it must be cut.

DART: A stitched fold, tapering to a point at one or both ends, used to shape fabric around curves.

DRESSMAKER'S CARBON: Heavyweight white or colored carbon paper that is used with a tracing wheel to transfer pattern markings to fabric.

EDGE STITCH: Machine stitching on the visible side of the garment, very close to an edge, to hold a crease in place or to hold the edge flat.

EYELET: A small hole reinforced with a metal ring to hold a cord tie or provide ventilation in fabric. Also, the ring itself.

FACING: A piece of fabric that is sewed along the raw edge of an opening, such as a neckline, and then turned to the inside to give the edge a smooth finish. Facings are usually cut from the same cloth as the garment itself.

FOOT: See PRESSER FOOT

GATHERING: Bunching fabric together by pushing it along basting threads to create fullness.

GRADING: The act of trimming each seam allowance within a multilayered seam to a different width to reduce bulk.

GRAIN: In woven fabric, grain is the direction of the threads: the warp (the threads running from one cut end to the other) forms the lengthwise grain; the woof, or weft (the threads running across the lengthwise grain from one finished edge to the other), forms the crosswise grain.

GRAIN-LINE ARROW: The double-pointed arrow marked on a pattern piece to indicate how the piece should be aligned with the fabric grain.

GROMMETS: Metal rings used to reinforce eyelet holes. See also EYELET.

INTERFACING: A special firm fabric attached between two layers of garment fabric to stiffen, support or strengthen parts of the garment. A type of nonwoven interfacing can be fused to the fabric by ironing.

INTERLINING: A special fabric—such as lamb's wool or flannelette—shaped exactly like the lining and sewed together with the lining to add warmth. The term may also refer to batting. See also BATTING.

LINING: Fabric covering the inside of part or all of a garment.

MACHINE BASTING: Long, temporary stitches made by machine for marking or testing the placement of seams.

NOTCH: A V- or diamond-shaped marking made on the edge of a garment piece as an alignment guide, intended to be matched with a similar notch or group of notches on another piece.

PIVOT: A technique for machine stitching around angular corners by stopping the machine with the needle down at the apex of a corner, raising the presser foot, pivoting the fabric and lowering the presser foot before continuing to stitch.

PLACKET: A garment opening with an overlapping edge covered by a visible strip of fabric running the length of the opening. It is used with openings that are equipped with fasteners.

PRESHRINK: The process of treating fabric to shrink it to an irreducible size before cutting. Washable fabric can be preshrunk simply by washing it as directed by the manufacturer. Nonwashable fabric should be preshrunk by a drycleaner.

PRESSER FOOT: The part of a sewing machine that holds down fabric while it is being stitched. An all-purpose foot has two prongs of equal length and is used for most stitching. A rollerpresser foot has two rollers with grids to prevent bulky or sheer fabric from sticking or slipping while being stitched. A straight-stitch foot has one long and one short prong and can be used for straight stitching and for stitching fabrics of varying thicknesses. A two-pronged even-feed foot, for use on machines that do zigzag stitching, has teeth on the bottom to move one or more layers of fuzzy, slippery or heavy fabric at the same speed. A zipper foot has only one prong and is used to stitch zippers and cording.

REINFORCE: To strengthen a seam with additional stitches, or to add an extra layer of fabric to a stress area.

SEAM: The joint between two or more pieces of fabric, or the line of stitching that makes a fold in a single fabric piece, e.g., a dart.

SEAM ALLOWANCE: The extra fabric—usually 5/8 inch—that extends outside a seam line.

SEAM LINE (also called stitching line): the long broken line marked on a pattern to indicate where a seam must be stitched.

STAY STITCH: Machine stitches along the seam line of a garment piece before the seam is stitched to keep the edges from stretching.

TAILOR TACKS: Hand stitches taken through a pattern piece and fabric with large loops of thread that are clipped when the pattern and fabric layer or layers are separated, leaving the thread ends in the fabric as markings; used on cloth that cannot be easily marked or might be damaged by chalk or carbon.

TAILOR'S CHALK: Flat squares made of wax, stone or clay, used to transfer pattern markings or adjustments onto fabric.

TOPSTITCHING: A line of machine stitching on the visible side of the garment usually parallel to a seam.

TRACING WHEEL: A small revolving disk attached to a handle and used with dressmaker's carbon paper to transfer pattern markings to fabric. Tracing wheels with serrated edges can be used for most fabrics; plain edges are used for knit fabrics to prevent snagging.

UNDERSTITCHING: A line of machine stitches sewed alongside a seam attaching the seam allowance to the facing.

VELCRO FASTENER: A flexible fastener consisting of one piece of fabric covered with tiny polyester hooks or needles and a matching piece with a surface of soft, fuzzy nylon loops. The two surfaces interlock firmly on contact.

ZIGZAG STITCH: A serrated line of machine stitching.

ZIPPER FOOT: A presser foot with only one prong that is used to stitch zippers and cording.

ZIPPER SHIELD: A narrow strip of interfaced fabric sewed on the inside of a garment along the length of a zipper for additional warmth.

BASIC STITCHES

The diagrams below and on the following pages show how to make the elementary hand stitches and the knitting and crocheting stitches referred to in this volume.

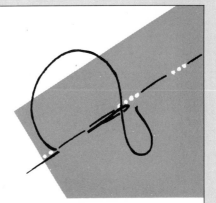

THE FASTENING STITCH

To end a row with a fastening stitch, insert the needle back 1/4 inch and bring it out at the point at which the thread last emerged. Make another stitch through these same points for extra firmness. To begin a row with a fastening stitch, leave a 4-inch loose end and make the initial stitch the same way as an ending stitch.

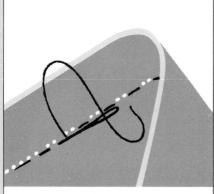

THE RUNNING STITCH

Insert the needle, with knotted thread, from the wrong side of the fabric and weave the needle in and out of the fabric several times, making 1/8-inch, evenly spaced stitches. Pull the thread through. Continue across, making several stitches at a time, and end with with a fastening stitch. When basting, make longer stitches, evenly spaced.

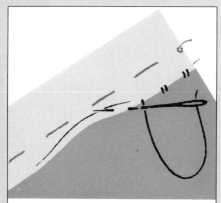

THE SLIP STITCH

Fold under the hem edge and anchor the first stitch with a knot inside the fold. Point the needle to the left. Pick up one or two threads of the garment fabric close to the hem edge, directly below the first stitch, and slide the needle horizontally through the folded edge of the hem 1/8 inch to the left of the previous stitch. Continue across in the same manner and end with a fastening stitch.

THE OVERCAST STITCH

Draw the needle, with knotted thread, through from the wrong side of the fabric 1/8 to 1/4 inch down from the top edge. With the thread to the right, insert the needle under the fabric from the wrong side 1/8 to 1/4 inch to the left of the first stitch. Continue to make evenly spaced stitches over the fabric edge and end with a fastening stitch.

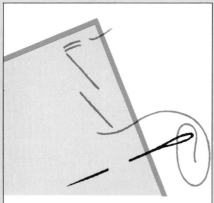

THE DIAGONAL BASTING STITCH

Anchor the basting with a fastening stitch *(above)* through all fabric layers. Keeping the thread to the right of the needle, make a 3/8-inch stitch from right to left, 1 inch directly below the fastening stitch. Continue making diagonal stitches, ending with a backstitch if the basting is to be left in, or a 4-inch-long loose end if the basting is to be removed.

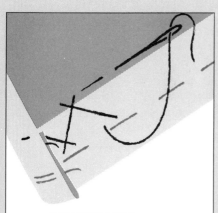

THE CATCH STITCH

Working from left to right, anchor the first stitch with a knot inside the hem 1/4 inch down from the edge. Pick up one or two threads of the garment directly above the hem; pull the thread through. Take a small stitch in the hem only (not in the garment), 1/4 inch down from the edge and 1/4 inch to the right of the previous stitch. End with a fastening stitch.

KNITTING

CASTING ON STITCHES
1. Form a slipknot in the yarn, leaving a free end long enough for the number of stitches to be cast on (allow about 1 inch per stitch).

2. Slide a needle through the slipknot and hold the needle in your right hand. Loop the yarn attached to the ball over your right index finger and loop the free end of the yarn around your left thumb.

3. Insert the tip of the needle through the loop on your left thumb and bring the yarn attached to the ball under and over the needle from left to right.

4. Draw the tip of the needle back through the loop on your thumb, then slip the loop off your thumb. Pull the short end of the yarn down to tighten the loop, which is now a stitch. Repeat Steps 2-4 for the required number of stitches.

THE KNIT STITCH
1. Insert the right needle in the front of the stitch closest to the tip of the left needle, as shown. Bring the yarn under and over the right needle.

2. Pull the right needle back through the stitch, bringing with it the loop of yarn. Slide this loop—which is now a stitch—off the left needle and onto the right. Repeat Steps 1 and 2 for each knit stitch.

THE PURL STITCH
1. Insert the right needle into the stitch closest to the tip of the left needle, as shown. Bring the yarn around and under the right needle.

2. Push the needle back through the stitch, bringing with it the loop of yarn—which is now a stitch. Transfer this new stitch to the right needle, letting it slip off the left needle as you do so. Repeat Steps 1 and 2 for each purl stitch.

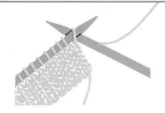

DECREASING STITCHES
1. Insert the right needle into two stitches instead of one, either from front to back as shown, for a knit stitch, or from back to front as for a purl stitch. Proceed as though you were knitting or purling one stitch at a time.

INCREASING STITCHES
1. On a knit row, insert the right needle through the back of a stitch. Knit the stitch, but do not drop it off the left needle.

2. Knit the same stitch in the ordinary way, and transfer the two stitches to the right needle.

1. On a purl row, insert the right needle from right to left through the horizontal loop at the bottom of a stitch. Make a purl stitch but do not let it slide off the left needle.

2. Now insert the right needle into the vertical loop above the horizontal one. Purl the stitch in the ordinary way, and slide both loops onto the right needle.

BINDING OFF STITCHES
1. Knit (or purl) two stitches. Then insert the left needle through the front of the second stitch from the tip of the right needle.

2. With the left needle, lift the second stitch on the right needle over the first stitch and let it drop.

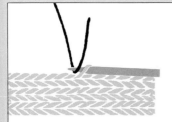
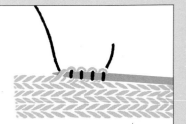

PICKING UP STITCHES AT AN EDGE

1. To pick up stitches along a finished edge, as when you intend to add ribbing, start by inserting the needle into the first stitch to be picked up. Then wrap another strand of yarn around the needle; draw the yarn through the stitch.

2. Continue in this manner along the edge, drawing the yarn through each successive stitch to be picked up.

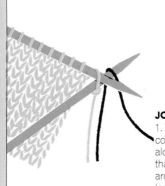
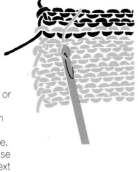

JOINING YARN

1. To introduce a new ball or color of yarn at any point along a row, wrap the yarn that you have been using around the working needle, leaving long ends. Then use the new yarn to knit the next stitch.

2. When you have knitted two or three rows with the new yarn, use a crochet hook to weave the loose ends through nearby stitches on the wrong side of the work.

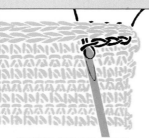
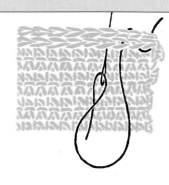
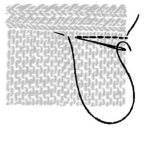

JOINING KNITTED PIECES

1. Knitted garments can be seamed by crocheting, weaving or sewing. For all three, place the edges together, wrong sides out, and align the stitches and rows. To crochet pieces together, insert a crochet hook through the first stitch on each edge, and draw a loop of new yarn through both stitches. Repeat on each pair of stitches, drawing the new loop through the loop on the hook.

2. To weave two pieces together, insert a blunt-tipped tapestry needle through the outermost stitch on each edge. Then turn the needle, and repeat. Continue weaving back and forth until the pieces are joined.

3. To sew two pieces together, insert a blunt-tipped tapestry needle through both pieces 1/4 inch below the aligned edges. Leaving a long end of yarn, insert the needle 1/4 inch to the right of the first stitch, and bring it out, from back to front, 1/4 inch to the left of the first stitch. Continue making stitches in this manner along the edges.

CROCHETING

THE CHAIN STITCH

1. Form a loose slipknot around the crochet hook, about 1 inch from the end of the yarn. Grasp the yarn attached to the ball with the tip of the hook and pull the yarn through the slipknot with the tip of the hook, as shown.

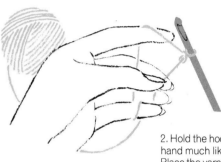

2. Hold the hook in your right hand much like a pencil. Place the yarn from the ball around the left little finger, then up and over the left index finger. Grasp the free end of the yarn between the thumb and middle finger of the left hand.

3. With your left index finger, bring the yarn from the back to the front of the hook and catch it under the tip of the hook.

4. Pull the tip of the hook through the loop in the hook, bringing the yarn with it to create the first chain stitch in the foundation chain. Repeat Steps 3 and 4 to form a chain of the desired length.

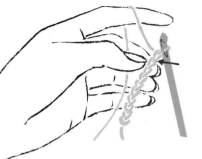

THE SINGLE CROCHET STITCH

1. To single crochet the first row after a foundation chain, insert the hook through the second chain stitch from the hook (arrow)—do not count the loop on the hook.

2. With two loops now on the hook, bring the yarn over the hook from back to front and catch it under the tip as shown. Then draw the yarn caught under the tip through the loop closest to the tip.

3. Bring the yarn over the hook again and draw it through both of the loops that were on the hook; there is now only a single loop on the hook. Insert the crochet hook into the next chain stitch and repeat Steps 1 and 2. At the end of each row, chain one stitch if the next row is to be worked in single crochet, two stitches for a double crochet pattern, and three stitches for a triple crochet pattern.

4. Turn the work to crochet back across the previous row. Insert the hook through both loops of the second stitch from the edge, as shown, and all subsequent stitches on this and all rows after the foundation chain.

THE DOUBLE CROCHET STITCH

1. To double crochet the first row of stitches after a foundation chain, chain 2 and count back to the third chain stitch from the hook *(arrow)*—do not count the loop on the hook. Swing the yarn over the hook from back to front, then insert the hook through this third chain stitch.

2. Bring the yarn over the hook again and draw it through the loop closest to the tip. Bring the yarn over the hook again and draw it through the two loops closest to the tip.

3. Bring the yarn over the tip again and draw it through the remaining two loops on the hook. At the end of each row, chain one stitch if the next row is to be worked in single crochet, two stitches for double crochet and three stitches for triple crochet.

4. Turn the work to crochet back across the previous row. Bring the yarn over the hook and insert the hook through both loops of the first stitch from the edge *(arrow)* on this and all rows after the first.

THE HALF DOUBLE CROCHET STITCH

1. To half double crochet the first row of stitches after a foundation chain, start by chaining 2. Then bring the yarn over the hook from back to front, and insert the hook through the second chain stitch from the hook *(arrow)*.

2. With 3 loops now on the hook, bring the yarn over the hook again.

3. Catch the yarn under the tip of the hook, and draw it through the loop closest to the tip.

4. Bring the yarn over the hook again, and draw it through all 3 loops remaining on the hook.

5. Repeat the stitch in each succeeding chain across the row. At the end of the row, chain 2, and turn.

6. To crochet the second row, bring the yarn over the hook, insert the hook into the first stitch and make a half double crochet stitch, following Steps 2-4. Then continue to make half double crochet stitches in each succeeding stitch across the row. At the end of the row, chain 2, and turn. Continue repeating row 2.

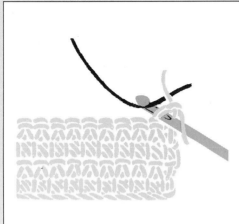

JOINING YARN

1. Join a new ball of yarn at the beginning of a row by drawing it through the first loop; leave a 1-inch-long end. Join a new color at the end of a row, working the last two loops on the hook with the new yarn.

2. When you have crocheted two or three rows, weave the loose ends of the yarn through nearby stitches with the crochet hook.

DECREASING STITCHES, SINGLE CROCHET

1. To decrease in a row of single crochet stitches, insert the hook into both loops of a stitch. Bring the yarn over the hook and draw it through the two loops closest to the tip; this leaves two loops on the hook.

2. Insert the hook through both loops of the next stitch. Bring the yarn over the hook and draw it through the two loops closest to the tip. Bring the yarn over the hook again and draw it through the three remaining loops on the hook.

DECREASING STITCHES, DOUBLE CROCHET

1. To decrease in a row of double crochet stitches, bring the yarn over the hook and insert it through both loops of a stitch. Bring the yarn over the hook again, as shown, and draw it through the two loops closest to the tip. Then bring the yarn over the hook again and insert it through both loops of the next stitch.

2. Again bring the yarn over the hook and draw it through the two loops closest to the tip, as shown; there are now five loops on the hook. Bring the yarn over the hook again and draw it through the two loops now closest to the tip. Repeat the process until there are three loops remaining on the hook. Then pull the yarn through the three remaining loops.

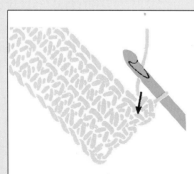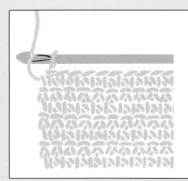

INCREASING STITCHES

To increase stitches, work one stitch—either a single, double or triple crochet, as called for in the instructions —then insert the crochet hook back into the same loop or loops (arrow) and repeat the stitch.

FASTENING OFF

Cut the yarn from the ball, leaving a 2-inch-long end. Pull this end through the loop on the hook to secure it and weave it through one or two nearby stitches.

CREDITS

Sources for illustrations in this book are shown below. Credits from left to right are separated by semicolons, from top to bottom by dashes.

Cover—Fabric by Corhan Fabrics Inc. 6,7—Arnold Maucher. 11—From *Victorian Fashions & Costumes from Harpers Bazar 1867-1898,* Dover Publications Inc. copyright 1974. 12 through 19—Photographs by William Plützer. 12,13—Golfing clothes from Saks Fifth Avenue, except man's jacket from B. Teller of Vienna Corp.; woman's warm-up suit from White Stag Manufacturing Co.; man's warm-up suit from Princeton Skate and Ski Chalet. 14,15—Tennis dress from Saks Fifth Avenue; man's tennis outfit from Head Ski and Sportswear, except sweater from Princeton Skate and Ski Chalet; bathing suit from Paragon Athletic Goods Corp.; man's jacket from White Stag Manufacturing Co.; pants from Saks Fifth Avenue. 16,17—Foul-weather gear and man's knickers outfit from Abercrombie & Fitch Co.; riding clothes from H. Kaufman and Sons Saddlery Co., Inc., except for sweater from Irish Pavilion; man's safari suit from Ralph Lauren for Polo. 18,19—Woman's ski suit from Saks Fifth Avenue; man's ski suit from Princeton Skate and Ski Chalet; skating hat and boots from Lonergan's; man's cross-country skiing outfit from Paragon Athletic Goods Corp. 20,21—Stephen Green-Armytage for SPORTS ILLUSTRATED. 24 through 29—Richard Jeffery. 30,31—John Zimmerman for SPORTS ILLUSTRATED. 34 through 37—Richard Jeffery. 38—Arnold Maucher. 39,40,41—Drawings by Carolyn Mazzello. 42—Arnold Maucher. 43 through 47—Drawings by John Sagan. 48—Arnold Maucher. 49 through 61—Drawings by John Sagan. 62—Arnold Maucher. 63 through 67—Drawings by Raymond Skibinski. 68—Raymond Skibinski except bottom right, Kay Hirsh. 69 through 73—Drawings by Raymond Skibinski. 74—Arnold Maucher. 75 through 81—Drawings by Raymond Skibinski. 82, 83—Wayne Wilson/Leviton-Atlanta for SPORTS ILLUSTRATED. 86—Underwood & Underwood—No Credit. 87—Wide World—Ken Regan from Camera 5; Al Satterwhite from Camera 5. 88,89—Arnold Maucher. Warm-up outfits by Shirley Botsford. 90 through 101—Drawings by Carolyn Mazzello. 102,103—Arnold Maucher. Tennis dress by Shirley Botsford for Ruth Rogers Enterprises. 104 through 111—Drawings by John Sagan. 112,113—Arnold Maucher. Shirts by Shirley Botsford for Ruth Rogers Enterprises. Duffel bags by Shirley Botsford. 114 through 125—Drawings by Raymond Skibinski. 126 through 129—Drawings by Angela Alleyne. 130,131—Arnold Maucher. Ski outfit by Dea Lupu. 132 through 149—Drawings by John Sagan. 150,151—Al Freni. 154,155—Tasso Vendikos. Knitting by Annette Feldman. 156,157,158—Drawings by Jean Held. 160 through 165—Tasso Vendikos. Crochet by Annette Feldman. 166 through 169—Drawings by Jean Held. 170,171—Tasso Vendikos. Dress by Dorothy Leeds. 172,173—Tasso Vendikos. Crochet by Annette Feldman. 179 through 184—Drawings by John Sagan.

ACKNOWLEDGMENTS

For their help in the preparation of this book the editors would like to thank the following individuals: *in England:* Major Alan Mansfield; *in New York:* Catherine Cox and W. Reed Hanks, Cotton Inc.; Toby Des Roches, Ski Industries of America; Don Earnest; Don Foley, Talon Division of Textron; R. Carl Freeman, The Wool Bureau, Inc.; Paul Hamilton; Craig Malsch, Darlington Fabrics; Bill Siegel, Travis Mills; Stan Stanfancies, Beaunit Corporation; Doris Taplinger, Ski Council of America; Kelly Tasker; Monika Tilley; *in Columbia, Maryland:* Alex Schuster, Head Ski and Sportswear; *in Portland, Oregon:* Harold Hirsch, White Stag Manufacturing Co.

The editors would also like to thank the following *in New York:* Abercrombie & Fitch Co.; American Fabrics and Fashion Magazine; Avila Group, Inc.; Beconta, Inc.; Bike Yards; B. Teller of Vienna Corp.; The Camel; Darlington Fabrics Corp.; E. I. Dupont de Nemours; Head Ski and Sportswear; The Irish Pavilion; H. Kaufman and Sons Saddlery Co., Inc.; Lonergan's; M & J Trimming Co.; National Looms Corp.; Paragon Athletic Goods Corp.; Pellon Corporation; Princeton Skate & Ski Chalet; Ralph Lauren for Polo Fashions Inc.; Saks Fifth Avenue; Springs Mills, Inc.; Uncle Sam Umbrella Shop; Woolrich Woolen Mills; *in Cincinnati, Ohio:* Sterns & Foster Company.